The Playwright's Art

Stage, Radio, Television, Motion Pictures

BY

ROGER M. BUSFIELD, JR.

GREENWOOD PRESS, PUBLISHERS
WESTPORT, CONNECTICUT

Contents

Preface

FOR centuries the dramatic writer has written for only one medium, the stage. In the twentieth century he is now faced with three additional dramatic media—the motion picture screen, the radio loudspeaker, and the television picture tube. Each of the four dramatic media has its own peculiar traits and limitations and a thorough knowledge of each of them is essential in order to use them to their fullest dramatic effect. There is a danger, however, of elevating the mastery of media techniques over the more important ability to handle the basic elements of the playwriting process such as plot, character, theme, dialogue, and language. After all, the task of telling a compelling story about vital people remains unchanged from one medium to another. There may be four dramatic media but there remains only one dramatic writer.

This book is directed to the young writer contemplating the dramatic form for the first time. The approach, however, is not primarily of the scholar arriving at conclusions from perusing published masterpieces of dramatic literature. It is true that much can be learned from an analysis of finished products, yet it must be admitted that such an analysis will afford the beginning writer little, if any, insight into the problems that confront the playwright from his conception of the initial idea to its culmination in a tested script. This book, therefore, is an attempt to approach dramatic writing from the playwright's point of view. Wherever possible, the views and opinions of dramatic writers who over the years have been consistently able to please their audiences have been cited.

The book begins with a general consideration of dramatic writing

as an art. An attempt is then made to isolate and differentiate the task
of the playwright from that of the novelist and other writers of nondramatic forms. This is followed by two chapters on dramatic instinct,
how it is acquired, and the methods of developing or sharpening it.
Chapter 5 discusses the playwright's audience, since the receiver of
drama should be considered before any attempt is made to provide him
with a dramatic experience. Chapters 6 through 11 deal more directly
with the essential elements of the playwriting process: finding dramatic material, thematic treatment, character creation, plot construction, dialogue, and language problems. Other aspects of dramatic
writing are treated in the subsequent chapters: actual writing procedures and practices, methods of collaboration, the processes of
dramatization and adaptation, and rewriting or revising the manuscript during the rehearsal period. The final chapter, suggested by
George Savage of UCLA, outlines some of the various devices available to the nonprofessional dramatic writer in making the transition
to writing professionally for the four dramatic media. I am deeply
indebted to Professor Savage for his suggestions in writing this
chapter.

Appendix A, "Exercises and Projects in Dramatic Writing," could
not have been written without the coöperation of many playwrights
and teachers of dramatic writing. Their suggestions and, in some cases,
their own exercises have been set forth in a list of 72 projects for
individual and group use. The author, therefore, gratefully acknowl-
edges the contributions of the following: Joseph Baldwin, University
of Mississippi; Herbert Blau, San Francisco State College; James
Clark, Brooklyn College; E. P. Conkle, University of Texas; Marian
Gallaway, University of Alabama; John Gassner, Yale University;
Russell Graves, Lycoming College; Robert L. Hilliard, Adelphi College; Thomas R. Long, Michigan State University; George McCalmon,
Cornell University; Gene McKinney, Baylor University; Ronald
Mitchell, University of Wisconsin; Richard Moody, Indiana Uni-
versity; Thomas M. Patterson, University of North Carolina; William

R. Reardon, State University of Iowa; Charles C. Ritter, Stetson University; George Savage, UCLA; Pauline K. Schmookler, Minneapolis, Minnesota; Samuel Selden, University of North Carolina; Webster Smalley, University of Illinois; Warren S. Smith, Pennsylvania State University; Angus Springer, Southwestern University; and Fairfax P. Walkup, University of Arizona.

Speaking personally now, I want to acknowledge the splendid coöperation and encouragement of my colleagues in the Department of Speech and College of Communication Arts at Michigan State University. I must also acknowledge that the shaping of this book has been directly influenced by the needs of the students of dramatic writing in my classes over the past 11 years, first at Southwestern University in Georgetown, Texas, then at Florida State University in Tallahassee, Florida, and for the past four years at Michigan State University. I find their imprint and the answers I have given to their many questions, and they have been many, varied and frequently unexpected, in every chapter. It is my hope that the following pages will in some way reduce the number of hazards and pitfalls awaiting the writer who elects the dramatic form as his mode of expression.

ROGER M. BUSFIELD, JR.

May, 1957
East Lansing, Michigan

The Art of Dramatic Writing

MAN, from the moment he became a social being and began to live and work with other men in a tribe, displayed both an artistic sensitiveness and an insatiable appetite for that which is dramatic.

To understand the rudiments of early playmaking and its direct relationship with the function of the modern playwright, it is first necessary to visualize the activities of the tribe back in that period of time before written history. It is safe to assume that survival was even more of a preoccupation of life then than it is now. To this task all efforts of the tribe were directed.

Visualize, if you will, the return to the tribe of the hunters. They carry the carcass of their kill. Great joy sweeps through the village in anticipation of the feast and celebration that follows a successful hunt. The race against famine which every man begins at birth has been extended for another day. The village seethes with activity. A fire is built and the flesh of the game is carefully prepared and cooked on an open spit. Meanwhile, the animal's skin is being scraped clean by others to condition it for use as clothing or in the construction of shelter. Other members of the tribe hang portions of the meat on racks to be smoked and then stored against those days the hunters return home empty-handed. That evening the feast is devoured and a happy, peaceful group rests near the campfire. Logs are added and the shadows recede as the flames radiate their warmth and light. It is the theatre hour and the actors are ready to perform.

The drama is at the same time spontaneous and purposeful. One of the hunters throws the animal skin about his shoulders and, getting down on all fours, begins to *imitate* the actions of the beast, pawing at the ground, sniffing the air for the scent of his strange enemy—man. The other hunters, spears in hand and at the ready, circle downwind, silently stalking their game. Noiselessly they crawl forward a few yards at a time. Suddenly, a rock is dislodged with a clatter! Instantly all hunters blend into the ground as the animal-actor raises his head, cocks an ear, and slowly surveys the landscape. The suspense is shattering.

At last the beast appears convinced it is safe and the hunters move in quickly on four sides, blocking all avenues of escape. As the frightened animal whirls about in enraged defiance, a hunter darts in quickly, spear held low, and thrusts it at the animal's soft underside. Bellowing with pain the beast slashes out at its tormentor who falls heavily to the ground clutching his torn side. Another hunter rushes in, another, and another until finally a desperation lunge by the remaining hunter drops the animal to the earth. Immediately the hunters pounce on the injured prey, stabbing its vulnerable points repeatedly until it lies still. Exhausted from the fight the hunters slip wearily to their knees. A mighty cheer goes up from the campfire audience. Shedding his skin-costume, the "dead" animal returns to "life" and the hunters acknowledge their tribe's shouts of approval. The drama is done—the play making is over.

But what was happening to that primitive audience as it witnessed the reënactment or imitation of the hunt? As a group they were thrilled by the excitement of the action, vicariously sharing the experience of the hunters as they went about their quest of securing food for the tribe.

Identification was strong. As the hunters stalked their game the audience was tense. When the rock was noisily dislodged hearts skipped a beat. When the animal remained still the audience relaxed momentarily but only to become aroused again as the hunters rushed forward to do battle with the beast. The excitement built rapidly to a peak of high intensity climaxed by the final spear thrust and the death of the animal. The elders sitting near the campfire, too old for the hunt, clucked nostalgically as they relived younger days. The standing young men, not yet old enough for the hunt, carefully observed every movement of the hunters—noting how they circled stealthily downwind, how they stalked their prey, and the mistakes they made. As man learns from the cradle by *imitation,* the young men unknowingly were *instructed* by their dramatic experience.

The women of the tribe gasped as the hunter-actor was slashed and wounded by the beast. This was real. This was an experience their men had faced and their boys would face and they needed to know. Knowing seemed to make acceptance of their daily roles understandable. That night the women would hold their men close, each thankful the wounded hunter was not hers. But they would also realize it could have been and might still be. Life and its significance had been made very real for that audience and they felt better because of it. This was dramatic art—crude but genuine—and it had gratified the artistic senses of its viewers. The basic dramatic experience of that tribal audience was universal. It differs slightly, if at all, from the emotional and intellectual experience of the contemporary theatre audience.

THE CONTAINED SPACE FOR DRAMA

For several thousand years the dramatic storyteller, the playwright, has had to limit himself to a contained space for the presentation of his dramas. This space, or playing area, has had many forms through the centuries, but a singular aspect always remained unchanged. The contained spaces were all arranged so that an audience of people, gathered together as a group, not as individuals, could observe the action being portrayed or imitated. This blending together of play, acting area, and audience civilization has called *theatre.*

There was the threshing circle of Homeric Greece and the sunken orchestra or dancing floor of Athens backed by a superstructure or *skene* and fronted by a sweeping tier of seats embedded in a sloping hill beneath the Acropolis. The Roman playwright wrote for a platform stage overwhelmed from above by the rich and ornate opulence of an architectural *frons scaenae*. Wherever civilized men have gathered there has been theatre—whether it be the market place of the Middle Ages, the innyard of Elizabethan England, the royal gardens of France, or the courts of noblemen in many lands. In the centuries following the flowering of the Renaissance some playwrights found their plays being shoved rudely indoors away from the sun and on a raised stage with an encroaching proscenium arch. Yet, in each instance, the dramatic storyteller has always written for an audience observing a contained space.

With each change of the contained space the writer changed his techniques, and in many instances his techniques produced the change. Somehow the essential quality of telling a story dramatically in terms of action and language endured. This quality remains unchanged today. Only the techniques and media differ.

FOUR MEDIA—ONE WRITER

With the dawn of the twentieth century and the inventions of Edison and Marconi an age of electronics was ushered in and the theatre began a new period of transition. The dramatic writer no longer had the single medium of the stage through which to tell his stories but three more—the motion picture screen, the radio loudspeaker and, most recently, the television picture tube.

First came the motion picture, and the spatial barrier of two thousand years crumbled. The searching lens was able to seek out the subtlest emotion and magnify it upon a large screen. The actor's art of facial expression and the use of the hesitant pause reached a new high. The audience still remained together and reacted as a group; but the circular response between live performers and audience disappeared, and the playwright had to change his techniques again.

Next came the radio medium, and the theatre of the imaginative mind was born. The group audience of twenty centuries was at last dissolved into individuals whose minds became the playwright's stage, and sound, voice, and music its provocative stimulus. The dramatic storyteller discovered new techniques to relate the action and characters of his plays to the perceptiveness of the human ear.

But science was not finished with the playwright. By marrying the visual elements of the motion picture screen to the capabilities of electronics to transcend space, the twentieth century has provided the playwright with still another medium, television; and the living rooms of the world have become his new auditorium.

The playwright still satisfies the dramatic need of mankind. The physical limitations of each of the contained spaces or media has demanded that new techniques be created and mastered in order to relate a story dramatically to its fullest effect. Regardless of the medium, the modern playwright remains a maker of plays or dramas. The very spelling of the word *playwright* still indicates that a play is actually *wrought* rather than written.

A disturbing trend is becoming evident in the field of dramatic writing. Unlike the actor who is still referred to as an actor regardless of the medium through which he plies his art, the playwright is becoming categorized in terms of the medium for which he labors. Terms like *scenarist* and *motion picture writing, scriptwriter* and *radio writing,* and *television playwright* and *television playwriting* have come into existence to label the writer and to describe his media function. The media mania has attempted to elevate the mastery of media techniques over the ability to tell a story dramatically. There may be four media today; but there still remains one dramatic writer who is faced with the task of focusing attention upon the really essential elements of plot, character, dialogue, and theme.

The multiplication of the dramatic medium by four certainly has increased the demand for more creative artists than the current supply of playwrights affords. But in the haste to satisfy the need there is the danger of imbuing the aspiring writer with concepts of unique camera angles and attention-arresting sound effects to the detriment of telling a meaningful story skillfully. One need look no further than some of the contrived plots superficially rendered on television to realize there is some truth to this claim. Before a writer concerns himself with compressing a story into the time and structural pattern of television he must first have a story worth telling and characters worth writing about. The emphasis must not be in terms of closeups, dissolves, and segues, but on dramatic action and characterization, if there is to be a theatre worth having, worth attending, no matter what its medium—the stage, the loudspeaker, or the screen.

ART AS COMMUNICATION

A work of art is not an accident. Whether it is a painting, a statue, a musical composition, or a play, it has something to say—to communicate. Though undoubtedly produced in a burst of inspired artistic creativity, there is an intent behind it. Whether this intent is to express a feeling, an attitude, or a point of view is immaterial. That it has something to communicate makes it a work of art.

An artist may look into the face of a woman and see there more than meets the casual eye. What he sees, what he feels, i.e., what he experiences, he will seek to express. The form may be one of many, but what he wants to say will be communicated, even if it is only to a sensitive few. For a work of art without its viewer, its receiver of the experience, is no work of art at all.

Drama, like all modes of communication, reflects the customs, morals, and lifeways of a given society; and the dramatic artist is a participant in that life he seek to interpret. As John Howard Lawson has said of the artist, "His creative activity is both personal and social; his portrayal of the world around him is an extension of his own life, projecting social meanings, values, aspirations, hammered and shaped white-hot on the forge of living experience." [1]

---

[1] John Howard Lawson, *Theory and Technique of Playwriting and Screenwriting,* G. P. Putnam's Sons, 1949, p. ix.

The form of a work of art may and does change as the culture of a society changes. It changes with the times, yet its function of uniting the creative activity of the artist to the society he represents remains unchanged. As new media are discovered and developed, the forms change again, yet they still remain the key to the content of a work of art. The form of a sonnet is rigid, inflexible. In spite of this the poet-artist manages to express a meaning, a content.

Since art is communication, the artist finds himself in a peculiar position. He must communicate within the bondage of the modern communication media or be deprived of self-expression and therefore no longer exist as an artist. As the poet is able to communicate through the bondage of the sonnet so must the dramatist be able to communicate through the limitations of the stage, the loudspeaker, and the screen.

Form cannot be divorced from content, for what is content without form? How can the audience, viewer or receiver, understand the content unless it has been translated into a communicative form such as language or color or sound or shape or texture? What is the content of a novel once the written word of the book has been destroyed? To those who have read it, perceived it through its form, it is everything; to those who will never read it, it is nothing.

Dramatic technique has moved away from the esoteric to the practical, thus causing the theatre to enjoy its prestige as one of the more popular arts. The abstract movements in music and painting have succeeded in satisfying only the few, while the theatre as an art has shied away from those forms that obstruct communication to the many. The art of the playwright is dramatic communication.

THE FUNCTION OF THE ARTIST-WRITER

Many successful playwrights characterize their work as art and themselves as artists, though they probably would be the first to admit that much of what they produce fails to reach an artistic level.

The end product of the playwright's artistic process, the play, and theatre, the experience the audience has when it is coupled to the play, is the subject of this book. It is the purpose of the present discussion to determine the relationship of the artist-playwright to his work.

If one delves into the personal writings of playwrights he will encounter an apparent reluctance on the part of these artists to discuss dramatic writing as an art. This is understandable, for there is often something embarrassing in the published statements of artists and writers. They should be allowed to say what they have to say in their work and let it go at that. The artist who brings a message of any importance to his generation will find it difficult to reduce that message to a bald statement, for, as Maxwell Anderson believes, "the things an artist has to communicate can be said only in the symbols of his art." However, when artists do write of their art what they say may be very illuminating.

The artist's role is an individual matter, an intimate relationship between the artist and his concept and its expression through the symbols of his art. In the dramatist's realm the symbols are dialogue and action. A work of art is so much a product of the individual that if two artists agreed to write the same story as a play, the finished products would bear little resemblance to each other.

Anderson sees a work of art as a "hieroglyph" and the artist's function as "to set forth his vision of the world in a series of picture writings which convey meanings beyond the scope of direct statement. There is reason for believing that there is no other way of communicating new concepts save the artist's way, no other save the artist's way of illuminating new pathways in the mind." [2]

The feeling of being a communicator, as in the sense of an electric conductor, between the concept or vision and the audience to whom the artist directs his message, has been expressed by other successful dramatists. The artist gives a message to the world, claimed A. A. Milne, "expressing the truth as he sees it." A work of art, asserts Elmer

[2] Maxwell Anderson, "Whatever Hope We Have," *Off Broadway,* William Sloane Associates, 1947, p. 30.

Rice, "is merely the artist's attempt to represent reality by the use of symbols. He succeeds exactly to the degree in which the selection and arrangement of his symbols makes his meaning intelligible." It is Rice's contention that "it is his control of his material which makes an artist." [3]

John Galsworthy recognized the communicative function of the artist but felt that art, to remain art, cannot be molded into a pattern of conformity. According to Galsworthy, "The essence of art is the power of communication between heart and heart—Yes! But since no one shall say to human nature, 'Be of this or that pattern,' or to the waves of human understanding, 'Thus far and no farther,' so no man shall say these things to art." [4]

WARNING! TRAVEL AT YOUR OWN RISK

Each year many new writers are attracted to dramatic writing by dreams of quick wealth and the excitement and glamour associated with visions of opening nights, box-office hits, and fantastic sums paid for motion picture rights. The truth is that playwriting is a lonely art and only the very talented and frequently only the very lucky ever become financial successes. Most good writers struggle for years, gambling for a big box office and critical hit, only to settle for moderate acclaim and a small but steady income from their efforts.

To explain why so many people try playwriting one must first realize that to the uninitiated the apparent simplicity of dramatic dialogue leads them to believe the task is easy. After all, they reason, a play is just people talking and anyone can write down talk.

This "it must be easy" group soon discovers that just the opposite is true. Writing is hard work demanding many solitary hours of grinding labor. To some there is nothing more depressing, more hellish. Moss Hart even found the task so difficult that he once drew

---

[3] Elmer Rice, "Preface," *Two Plays,* Coward-McCann, 1935, p. vi.
[4] John Galsworthy, "Art and the War," *A Sheaf,* Charles Scribner's Sons, 1916, p. 273.

upon history to compare it to the Spanish Inquisition and the bloodiest portions of the First World War. Science tells us that one of the most painful human experiences is the birth process. Playwright Channing Pollock made a literal analogy when he said, "Becoming an author is not very different from becoming a mother. There must be conception, a period of gestation, labor and labor pains, with eventual delivery, and every author must have remarked the similarity of symptoms throughout both processes.[5]

When appraised of the increasing numbers trying to be writers, Somerset Maugham issued a strong warning: "All those millions of people are quite right to want to be authors. The job is entertaining and the rewards can be great. They are wrong, of course, about writing being romantic, and they should never forget that it is damned hard work." [6]

THEATRE—THE COLLABORATION OF ARTISTS

Due to the electronic age's creation of additional dramatic media there is some confusion regarding dramatic terminology. When something new comes along, such as radio or television, a descriptive vocabulary is also created. Unfortunately, the "new" terms may be very "old" words, but since they describe different functions or processes they find themselves in conflict with their earlier meanings. An attempt is also made, often by the users of the new vocabulary, to categorize or redefine the terminology of the original source from which the term is derived or borrowed.

A key example of word confusion is the term *theatre,* since some people today mistakenly use it as a synonym for the *stage.* This confusion is understandable. For many centuries the acting space was an elevated stage fronted by an auditorium and since it was there that theatre transpired, the building containing the stage and its auditorium was called *a* theatre.

---

[5] Channing Pollock, *Harvest of My Years,* The Bobbs-Merrill Company, 1943, p. 253.

[6] Harry Gilroy, "How to Write—By Maugham," *New York Times Magazine,* January 23, 1949, p. 10.

But theatre is *not* a building. It is *not* the *medium* through which the play meets its audience. It is rather the meeting itself between a play and an audience through performance. If the author's manuscript or play has been skillfully and artistically interpreted by actors under the guidance of a sensitive director, then the audience witnessing the performance may have a dramatic experience. If they do, then *theatre* has occurred.

Theatre is the name of one of the arts, and yet confusion still exists as to its meaning. Fortunately, music has yet to be divided upon the carving block into radio music, motion picture music, and television music. Music has remained music while theatre tends to lose its identity when the stage as a medium is replaced by the loudspeaker or the screen or the picture tube. Theatre is still, however, the occurrence when a play is performed for an audience.

The analogy of theatre to music as an art can be applied further. The composer writes a score; the playwright writes a play. This in itself is an art. Both the score and the play may be read, but the score does not become music until it is played, and the play does not become theatre until it is performed. The score is turned over to musicians and a conductor; the play is turned over to actors and a director. These artists become the living link or interpreters between the score or play and the audience. The analogy is appropriate. Have not the arts of music and theatre joined forces to give us operas like *La Traviata* (based on the play *Camille*) and musical plays like *Oklahoma?*

Theatre art, therefore, is an art employing many artists at many levels of artistry, all actively collaborating to create a dramatic experience for an audience. Not the least of these is the playwright, without whose art the others could not exist. The audience is in a sense a collaborator, too, for without its presence and participation, theatre cannot exist.

NO FORMULAS FOR SUCCESSFUL PLAYWRITING

Living in a society beset with a "do-it-yourself" craze, many would-be American dramatists quite naturally look for a sure-fire formula or blueprint for successful dramatic writing. A playwright may discover some of the tested ingredients that make a play palatable to an audience, but he will have to learn for himself how to concoct his own broth with its own distinctive flavor. A recipe will not make a good cook, nor will a formula make a successful playwright.

There are basic ground rules or laws of playwriting that every playwright should know. They are for the most part rules that are constantly changing and therefore not "ironclad" or binding. In the learning stage of any art adherence to rules is essential. This is as true of the art of the dramatist as it is of the art of the musician, the painter, or the sculptor. "As with drawing, and with the laws of harmony," John van Druten has said, "it is essential first to know what the rules are, to be able to submit to them, and deliberately to set out to refute them." [7]

Rules of playwriting as they exist at any given time may be broken. They often are, but as Eugene O'Neill once said, "The only ones who can successfully break the rules are the people who know them." Rachel Crothers echoed O'Neill's sentiments and enlarged upon them when she declared, "The laws of playwriting are loose and fluid. They may always be broken, changing always, adaptable to the material in hand, so illusive they may seem to contradict themselves or not be there at all." [8]

Those who feel that a knowledge of formulated principles will impair the writer's spontaneity need have no fear. Not only will knowing the ground rules not do this—it will help them discriminate between ideas and mere notions.

There are two kinds of general rules governing the dramatist. There are those created by the limitations and peculiar characteristics of a certain medium, and they may very well vary from one medium to another. These rules are of primary importance in adapting the play

---

[7] John van Druten, *Playwright at Work,* Harper & Brothers, 1953, p. 70.
[8] Rachel Crothers, "The Construction of a Play," *The Art of Playwriting,* University of Pennsylvania Press, 1928, p. 129.

to the particular medium so that it may achieve its fullest dramatic effect. However, the media rules have only an indirect bearing on the more basic laws, those essential elements of the dramatic writing process such as constructing the story into a plot, creating believable and worthy characters, treating theme, writing dialogue, and handling language problems. These are the essential elements common to the drama of all media.

This book is an attempt to acquaint the dramatic writer with the principles of the essential elements of the playwriting process from the inception of the initial idea through its ultimate performance before an audience. There may be four dramatic media in the twentieth century but there is only one dramatic writer. To his development this book is dedicated.

The Play and Fiction

IS it easier or more difficult to write a play than a novel? Each form requires an entirely different kind of ability, and the ability to write well in other fields does not necessarily imply ability to write well or even tolerably for the various dramatic media. Playwriting and novel writing, for instance, are by their distinctive natures basically incompatible and success as a novelist certainly does not guarantee success as a playwright. There are notable exceptions, of course, such as John Galsworthy, J. M. Barrie, A. A. Milne, J. B. Priestley, and Somerset Maugham; but, generally speaking, a talent for fiction writing excludes a talent for dramatic writing.

Many of the world's greatest writers, Milton, Cervantes, Byron, Shelley, Dr. Johnson, Thackeray, and Henry James, to mention but a few, failed when they tried to write plays. Today there are many eminent literary men and women who find it impossible to write plays, and a lengthy list could be compiled of successful novelists who failed when they tried to write for the theatre. There are also many playwrights who have found it impossible to write a good novel.

DRAMATIC WRITING—A TIME ART

Underlying all differences between fiction writing and dramatic writing is one basic distinction: fundamentally, dramatic writing is a time art whereas fiction writing is not.

The author of a play, in unfolding his plot and developing his characters, is under a strict time restriction which does not hamper the fiction writer in writing his novels and short stories. The average long play in the theatre may run approximately two and one-half hours and on television for 60 to 90 minutes. After the rise of the opening curtain there is no opportunity for the audience to turn back a scene and see it again if the relationships have not been clearly established.

The novelist has no such time limitations. He may develop his characters and discuss motivating forces. The playwright has little freedom. He must be precise. Each line, each piece of action must reveal everything. There is no time for comment. Once the action starts it must run its uninterrupted course, and if the playwright has not been able to concentrate everything into immediately comprehensible situations and lines of dialogue he will fail his audience.

The reader of the novel is actually in complete control of the time factor. How many readers set a nightly goal for themselves by first looking ahead to see where a chapter or unit ends and then, placing their fingers at that point, read to it? How many readers upon picking up a novel after having set it aside for a few hours or even a few days thumb through the previously read pages to reëstablish the story line or to reacquaint themselves with the characters and what they were doing when the book was laid aside? What member of a play's audience can set aside a play in performance? How often have you seen the child leave the television set for dinner only to become upset later because he is unable to see what was being performed when he left?

The distinction between the play and the novel is actually one of tense. Augustus Thomas explained it when he said, "The difference between the novel and the play is the difference between *was* and *is*. Something has happened for the writer of the novel and for his people. He describes it as it was; and them as they were. In the play something is happening." [1]

---

[1] Augustus Thomas, "Preface," *In Mizzoura*, Samuel French, 1916, p. 10.

Since in a play something is *happening,* the writer must keep the action of his drama flowing from the rise of the curtain to its fall, with no pause for comment or explanation. Almost everything which makes a novel interesting, such as vivid description, minor incidents, character studies, and stream-of-consciousness technique, will make a play talky and undramatic. This is why so few novels can be successfully transferred to the stage or motion picture screen without some modification. However, the problems of adapting the novel to the various dramatic media are more fully treated in Chapter 14.

In a play each character must explain himself, and in as few words as possible, whereas in a novel the writer may devote an entire chapter to each character and still hold the reader's interest. In a play every superfluous word, every inconsequential bit of "business" threatens to retard the action. "From the moment the curtain rises," David Belasco once said, "the flight of the dramatist should be straight as an arrow toward the denouement of the play." The reader of the novel, once he becomes the viewer of a play, a member of its audience, reacts differently than he does in the privacy of his library. This difference and its influence in the shaping of a play is more fully explained in Chapter 5.

THE NOVELIST'S FREEDOM

The novelist practicing his non-time art enjoys a freedom denied a playwright. A. A. Milne crystallized the advantages held by the novelist in creating characters when he said: "The advantage which a novelist has over a dramatist is that he is always there to explain his characters. He can occupy twenty pages in analysis of his heroine's thoughts as she wonders whether to wear the pink or the heliotrope. On the stage you merely see her in pink. If the hero is to commit a murder, his soul will have been laid bare before you in a couple of chapters." [2]

An idea or point of view that can be developed in the leisured pages of a book often can die of malnutrition in the brief confines of a play.

[2] A. A. Milne, "Introduction," *Four Plays,* G. P. Putnam's Sons, 1932, p. xiii.

The art of the playwright is more difficult than is the novelist's, for the play is a tight, unbending form in which to write.

The novelist has greater freedom in the creation and sustaining of mood, for that which may be described for the reader through narrative description must be *shown* in the play as it is staged. Still another advantage fiction holds over the play is its ability to create beauty through long and eloquent descriptive passages. There is a part of the artist that hungers for beauty. Playwriting will seldom satisfy that hunger, whereas the creation of beauty often gets the upper hand in novels. It is possible that many novelists when turning to playwriting attempt to carry over the creation of beauty from the fiction realm, which may produce a maximum of nicely rounded sentences and a minimum of drama.

Perhaps the major difficulty encountered by the fiction-writer-turned-playwright is his use of dialogue. So accustomed to detail, the novelist, for example, invariably attempts to incorporate what he would normally say in prose narrative into his passages of dialogue.

A prominent Broadway producer once received a play from a famous woman novelist. It was her first play and the producer opened it with great expectations, since the novelist had a wide reputation in delineating certain types of characters. The producer found the play's heroine unfolding her own character in the dialogue, the masterly handling of which the producer had always admired in the author's novels. But the other characters were flat, lacking dimensionality, for without the "literary" explanations and reflections at which the novelist was so adept the characters in the play failed to come to life. The novelist had found it impossible to make her dialogue and the attendant action carry the story alone.

Owen Davis, reflecting upon his long career as a dramatist, observed that many of his novelist friends who attempted playwriting were far better writers than any of the dramatists he knew, but most of them failed, declared Davis, for "their words won't play, no one can act their scenes." [3]

[3] Owen Davis, *I'd Like to Do It Again*, Farrar & Rinehart, 1931, p. 99.

THE PLAY AS LITERATURE

Plays are written primarily to be acted, not read. Good plays also may be read as good literature, and for this reason the publishing of successful Broadway and television plays is an accepted practice. But the reason for their being is performance, not the library lamp, for it is inherent in the nature of the dramatic art that the written word shall be translated into speech and action.

Many directors and actors have known plays that read well but have not acted well. They have also encountered the script that reads like an impossibility, yet when produced, plays beautifully. There are, of course, many plays that read as well as they play. These are the ones most often found in the play anthologies studied in English and American literature classes.

There are usually three versions of a play. There is that raw manuscript turned over to the director and his actors. After the play has been produced the many changes occasioned by the process of getting it successfully mounted are then incorporated into an acting version published by play brokers and sold to off-Broadway groups. Directions to the actor are to be found in this version. Then there is the published version of the play for popular sale in bookstores. Often this version has been tailored for the reader with certain changes, usually detailed and descriptive additions, so that the reader may visualize as fully as possible the scene the playwright had before him as he wrote his action and dialogue.

Bernard Shaw and J. M. Barrie both realized that the printed form of their plays would be inadequate unless changed somewhat. These two Englishmen made a practice of writing long prefaces and incorporating within the published play detailed description of the action and characters. This was primarily for the benefit of the reader. In their original manuscript form these plays were not so encumbered. Although the publication of contemporary plays from Broadway and television is becoming more popular with the reading public, this does not mean that the plays are being written for the study. They were never being written more deliberately, more carefully, for performance. Ironically, most plays that are to endure for posterity must succeed not only on the stage but also in the library. The truth of this is evident by the fact that the great plays of the ancient Greek and Roman periods, the Elizabethan age, and such remote epochs as the Hindu period of Kalidasa, have all been preserved for the present generation by way of written reproduction. History tells us that one of the most popular, exciting forms of theatre was the *commedia dell' arte* of the late sixteenth century. Since the style of the theatre was dependent upon the spontaneous endeavor of the performers as they portrayed their stock characterizations, there were no play scripts. There were scenarios giving scene-by-scene descriptions of the action and these have been preserved, but they are without detail or dialogue. Fortunately, diaries of the playgoers have left us vivid descriptions of the scope and influence of the Commedia, but beyond that we must hypothesize and reconstruct.

Since the wealth of the world's dramatic literature has been perpetuated by libraries, so to speak, does it necessarily follow that a play must be literature to survive? Apparently not, for although a good play may be good literature, a good play will endure whether it contains elements of good literature or not.

A genuine play is a very distinct and special form of writing regardless of the medium for which it is designed. There are many compositions extant, in the form of colloquies and dialogues, containing elements of literature such as poetry, rhetoric, and eloquence, which are nevertheless not acceptable as theatre fare. Plato's *Dialogues* and Shelley's *The Cenci* are excellent examples of this type of literature. On the other side of the ledger are many excellent plays which are insignificant as literature.

It is neither the intention nor the wish of professional playwrights to be literary in their plays, but it is certainly difficult for them to disabuse their minds of the notion that a play must be literature. This difficulty is understandable in light of the many dramatic literature courses carried in English department curricula. If a play turns out to be literature, in addition to being a good play, so much the better, but in producing plays we are not trying *primarily* to produce literature.

The province of literature is entirely outside the province of theatre. Literature is for the individual. But is the province of the play limited to the stage or the motion picture or television screen? Libraries have perpetuated the dramatic literature of all ages and the plays that have lasted are valuable to us as both literature *and* theatre. The beginning playwright would do well to acquaint himself with the masterpieces of this depository, for only in this way may he understand his link to the dramatic tradition of the past and comprehend his function as a dramatist of the present.

Clyde Fitch, a popular playwright in the early years of the twentieth century, recognized the true perspective of viewing dramatic literature when he wrote, "Many more dramatists write plays that have value as dramatic literature, than do literary men write plays that are good drama." [4]

Plays are written to be performed before an audience, not to be read by the individual in his study. Often plays that read badly are played beautifully. The test of whether a good play is also good literature is whether it reads as well as it acts, which is the only valid test of *dramatic* literature.

[4] Clyde Fitch, "The Play and the Public," *Plays by Clyde Fitch,* IV, Little, Brown & Company, 1921, p. xxiv.

Dramatic Instinct and the Creative Process

PERHAPS the vaguest and most nebulous concepts in the whole mystery of dramaturgy are those of dramatic instinct and the creative process. The concepts are nebulous because they concern the functionings of the human mind, how it operates and what triggers it into a burst of artistic creativity. To analyze the thought process of an artist is a presumptuous task for any writer. To define just what one is trying to label is an extremely difficult, if not impossible, task.

Dramatic history reveals that though some dramatists have been small in intelligence or learning those who have left their imprint upon mankind were usually great in perceptiveness. They possessed a fondness for human illusion and were sentimental in the finest sense. Though some of their plays reveal their author's insight to have been narrow, their sympathy and understanding was often broad. The great masters, Sophocles to Shakespeare to O'Neill, had an uncanny ability of placing their fingers on the pulse of mankind and consequently the lives of their audiences.

THE MENTALITY OF THE PLAYWRIGHT

It is impossible, of course, to measure the intelligence of an artist and then to correlate it with his work. How does one measure the intelligence factor? What tests could be devised to predict with any certainty the future success of the creative artist? Education is certainly not a legitimate yardstick. If it were, the phenomenon of Shakespeare would be impossible to explain. O'Neill was ousted from Princeton and then went on to become America's foremost dramatist.

Playwrights of the recent past have indicated that some interesting problems exist in the relationship of a playwright's mentality to his work. Owen Davis, for instance, held the view that it is impossible for a dramatist to write below his own mental level. Whenever he heard a man talk about "writing down" to an audience or "giving them what they want," Davis never hesitated to counter that no man "ever successfully wrote a play below his own mental level."

A. A. Milne, on the other hand, keenly felt the problem of writing above one's mental level. Specifically, he thought the most difficult character to delineate upon a stage is the figure of a "great man" of history or literature. The genius, according to Milne, is an impossible stage character to create if the playwright's mental level is not up to the task, for it is obvious that a character in a play can never be wiser or wittier than the author of the play.

Playwriting certainly requires as much intellectuality as any other line of endeavor, but it is the skillful writer's ability to keep his stamp of intelligence hidden that makes a good play. Avery Hopwood, who went on from the University of Michigan to become one of the foremost dramatists of his day, pointed to men of obviously superior intelligence like Lamb and Kipling, who were far from successful in their playwriting ventures, and said, "A man must have some sort of knack for the writing of a play."

The arguments recounted in the previous chapter to show that many successful and profound novelists often fail at dramaturgy serve to illustrate that brilliance of mind is no guarantee of an ability to write a drama. Intelligence is without a doubt an essential ingredient for creativity but something else is needed to write plays. Dramatic history has proved this and, as Rachel Crothers once said in a lecture at the University of Pennsylvania, "Whether one can write a play or not is not at all a question of intelligence or experience, but of that indefinable thing, the dramatic instinct."[1]

DRAMATIC INSTINCT—WHAT IT IS AND HOW IT IS ACQUIRED

Among the arts there exists an argument as to whether a human being, through training and practice, may become a success, or whether that human being must first be endowed from birth with an artistic talent which lies dormant until it bursts full-blown upon the artistic scene. Playwriting, as an art, does not escape this ageless and yet unresolved argument.

A story told by Channing Pollock offers an interesting point of departure on the question of whether a playwright is born or made. "The German comic weekly *Fliegende Blätter* once printed a cartoon of a tramp looking at a gaudily dressed girl and exclaiming, 'Lucky sex, born with a trade.' " Pollock then commented, "Nobody was ever born with a trade, but one may be born with an aptitude and a determination to learn, as people are born with a *tendency* to tuberculosis." [2] Pollock chose the terms "aptitude" and "tendency," which would indicate a belief in a latent talent for the writing of plays. However, Pollock, in his book, *The Footlights Fore and Aft,* makes a distinction between the poet and the dramatist: "Poets may be born or made, according to the field they occupy, but playwrights must be born *and* made." [3]

In the chapter comparing the playwriting process to the novel-writing method it was pointed out that many novelists have attempted to write plays, but these efforts, for the most part, have failed. The basic reason emerging from the illustrations offered was that novelists often lack dramatic instinct. Instead, most successful novelists possess a keen narrative talent or faculty for description, which is certainly

---

[1] Rachel Crothers, "The Construction of a Play," *The Art of Playwriting,* University of Pennsylvania Press, 1928, p. 122.

[2] Channing Pollock, *Harvest of My Years,* The Bobbs-Merrill Company, 1943, p. 314.

[3] Channing Pollock, *The Footlights Fore and Aft,* Richard G. Badger, 1911, p. 93.

not the same as the ability to express action, which a play must do. To write dramatic dialogue requires a special talent—this conclusion is inescapable.

Whether or not Pollock's cited view is valid is immaterial. The argument is not essentially founded on a necessity for the talent to exist from birth. The view, however, is analogous to the religious argument concerning "divine birth," which makes a plea that it is necessary to believe a certain act occurred before the existence of a subsequent belief can take place. The important thing is that many playwrights sincerely believe that it is necessary to possess *dramatic instinct* before one can successfully follow the playwriting trade.

There are dramatists besides Pollock who have declared that dramatic instinct, regardless of the training necessary to cause its blossoming, is an instinct acquired at birth. Owen Davis, for example, referred to being "born with the trick of creating dramatic narrative," and Charles Klein acknowledged that a playwright is "born to his craft and builds dramas instinctively, as a beaver builds dams." Edward Knoblock echoed even more closely Pollock's view, saying that "in a sense the playwright is . . . born not made," the qualification being that even with the definite gift from the start the dramatist "must work hard and long to acquire perfection."

In a newspaper interview Somerset Maugham went on record as believing it essential for a playwright to be "born with it" and then commented, as did Crothers, that intelligence is not a chief factor. "The most important thing—the *sine qua non* of a dramatist, in fact," said Maugham, "is the knack of writing it, and by knack I mean deliberately to imply that one is, as the average person explains the situation, 'born with it.'" This knack, according to Maugham, cannot be acquired and cannot be taught, "one either has it or hasn't it, and I sometimes think that because the knack of writing a good play is so rare the rewards of the successful dramatist are so great. All the intelligence and industry in the world will avail one nothing without the knack." [4]

[4] *New York Press*, December 21, 1913.

Even the literary giant George Bernard Shaw has said that "nature" must have done "ninety-nine per cent of the work," and John van Druten, from the contemporary school, has explained that a man is willing to take on the arduous labor, both physical and mental, involved in writing a play because he is "born a writer."

Other successful playwrights have stated that a playwright must have dramatic instinct, and that without it he cannot possibly write a play. Other terms have been introduced to clarify this meaning, such as "creative imagination" and "dramatic sense," but in the final analysis these playwrights found it impossible to define the quality they could only vaguely describe but attest they believe must exist in order to write drama. Some of these playwrights are J. M. Barrie, David Belasco, George Broadhurst, Edna Ferber, Harriet Ford, John Galsworthy, Eckert Goodman, Clare Kummer, Hartley Manners, Roi Cooper Megrue, Eugene O'Neill, and Robert E. Sherwood.

Pollock's statement likening dramatic instinct to hereditary tendency or aptitude provides perhaps the best basis for understanding just what these famous playwrights meant when they referred to the necessity of having the knack of writing from birth. In reducing Pollock's analogy to its fundamental concept it is important to realize that a person born with the tendency toward tuberculosis will *not* necessarily develop the disease. In like manner, there is no assurance that a man possessing dramatic instinct will become a playwright. But, as it is entirely possible for a person with an hereditary record of tuberculosis, under certain conditions of environmental exposure, more easily to develop the disease, so it is that the man born with dramatic instinct and given the proper circumstances will more easily become a successful playwright.

Perhaps a comment by the late Owen Davis more aptly characterizes the belief that dramatic instinct exists: "It's probable that the hedge sparrow has quite as much technique as the meadowlark, but only the song bird can sing." [5]

Courses in playwriting, especially at the undergraduate level, are more easily justified if the aforementioned belief in dramatic instinct

[5] Owen Davis, *I'd Like to Do It Again*, Farrar & Rinehart, 1931, p. 148.

is accepted. College is a period of self-discovery, in which the student is given the proper opportunity and environment to develop and blossom. Who knows? The college course in playwriting may equip many hedge sparrows with the technique of the craft; but then again the course may well be the beginning of an Arthur Miller, as it was in Kenneth Rowe's class at Michigan, or a Eugene O'Neill as it was in George Pierce Baker's English 47 workshop at Harvard, or a Tennessee Williams as happened in Marian Gallaway's course at Iowa.

OBJECTIVITY AND THE CREATIVE PROCESS

If it is granted that such a thing as dramatic instinct does exist, then inevitably the question arises as to whether or not the creative process is a conscious, subconscious, or unconscious activity.

The play one writes is such an intimate matter that it is almost impossible to look at it with a critical mind. To ask a playwright to reveal the conception of his own play is like asking why one's child squints or why the cook spoils the dinner. It is an embarrassing moment when the playwright is interrogated about his play. Why? Is it possible to analyze the creative process employed in the writing of plays? No, said J. Hartley Manners, "No one can analyze the artistic instinct that separates good art from poor art." Manners felt that a fine play, well acted, is one of the "miracles" of the theatre.

Too much objectivity can be of definite harm to the creative impulse. Furthermore, too much analysis, too much careful studying of effects, is apt to be harmful to the creative impulse, which is the one thing the young writer ought to cherish much more than any of his acquired technical ability. "For if one has the creative impulse," Crothers has said, "all other things shall be added unto him." Conscious technique in any art is very painful. Sculpturing offers an interesting illustration. The sculptor knows that under his clay are trusses to hold up the figure. If he forgot to put them in, his beautiful work would become a shapeless mass on the floor. But as an artist he doesn't let the trusses show nor does the viewer have any idea they are present. Art owes much of its effectiveness to the skill with which its objective aspects are concealed.

John Galsworthy once issued a warning to those who would inquire into the functionings of an artist's mind. "There is something destructive in a cut-and-dried examination of the creative process," cautioned Galsworthy; "that bird is shy enough at all times, and might cease suddenly to lay any eggs if it were subjected to too much scrutiny." [6] On one occasion Galsworthy characterized the nature of the imaginative artist as "sensitive, impressionable; impatient of anything superimposed." But it was when the English playwright implied that the scholar, employing his scientific method of investigation, was not capable of becoming a creative writer of any achievement, that he came closest to analyzing the attributes of the creative artist. "Precise scholars are rarely imaginative writers of any force, they know too much and too little," said Galsworthy. "The vividly imaginative seldom have relish for the exact study of anything except—life. Feeling for the colour and rhythm of words may be helped by reading poetry and fine prose, but it is due more to inborn sensibility and a musical ear." [7]

In line with the above, John van Druten feels that "self-forgetfulness is of great importance." The reason suggested by van Druten is that the objective awareness of self as a creator or a writer "gets in the way of true expression." The danger of a writer remembering himself, his past, his reputation, the things that friends and critics have said, increases with each play he writes. The author of *I Remember Mama, Bell, Book and Candle,* and *I Am a Camera* feels that the sense of oneself stands like a great block in the way of surrender to the work itself and "the great need is a total submergence of that self's involvement, a submission to the idea and to what is called inspiration." [8]

[6] H. V. Marrot, *The Life and Letters of John Galsworthy,* Charles Scribner's Sons, 1936, p. 720.
[7] John Galsworthy, *Castles in Spain,* Charles Scribner's Sons, 1927, p. 207.
[8] John van Druten, *Playwright at Work,* Harper & Brothers, 1953, p. 202.

PLAYWRITING AND THE SUBCONSCIOUS

Too much objectivity is harmful to the creative process. In playwriting, conscious and subconscious techniques are utilized alternately, though the writer is sometimes startled when he discovers in retrospect that he has been working subconsciously.

The subconscious appears to operate in three distinct ways in the development of a play. There are playwrights who evolve a story subconsciously and others who solve plot problems while they sleep or work at other activities. Another contribution of the subconscious is in the development of a character. Some playwrights are firm in their belief that they develop a character to a point where the character becomes a subconscious reality operating in a logical and interesting pattern. In the chapter dealing with character, this function of the subconscious is probed more fully. Lastly, some playwrights believe they get lost in the work of actually transcribing the dialogue of the play and when reviewing the day's work consciously they are surprised at what they have written. Some people employ the term "inspiration" to describe this manifestation of the subconscious.

Owen Davis made a fine distinction between inspiration and imagination. "I believe that some men and women upon some fortunate occasion write from an emotional prompting deeper and finer than their conscious mind could inspire," said Davis, though, "I do not confuse the mental pictures of an imaginative mind with so exalted a word." [9]

Davis said that there are and always have been two sorts of writers, the writer who tells what he sees, or has read, or thought, or been told, and the writer whose mind is a sort of "old-fashioned kaleidoscope that forms little mental pictures quite without conscious effort." It is with the second type of writer that most playwrights classify their profession. Davis made a further distinction between the two writers, saying "one writer uses trained observation, and the other has the gift of spontaneous creation."

[9] Davis, *op. cit.*, pp. 156–157.

Clifford Odets has made the same distinction between the two types of writers as did Davis. "In the first case," says Odets, "the writer sits down to 'fabricate,' without personal affiliation or inner relatedness to the material; he is reporting an objective event, manufacturing a yarn, performing a technical operation or what you will, but fabricating he is." Of the second type of writer, Odets says that "with equal technical grasp of his medium he begins always with the premise of expressing a personal state of being. Fabrication, do not misunderstand me, may exist on a very high level of observation, technique and competence; but it is only the second kind of writing in my opinion which merits the use of those dread words 'creative' and 'art.' " Odets felt that with the fabricating writer, "objective taste and the conscious mind are everything; but with the creative writer the conscious mind is only a guide and moderator." [10]

Davis in his autobiography related that on several occasions he had seen the story line of an entire play laid out before him in one flash at a time when he, to the best of his knowledge, was not thinking of any such thing at all. "I can, on a bet," said Davis, "at any time close my eyes and shake my head and look up and tell a story that, so far as I can discover, I have never for a moment thought of before."

J. M. Barrie confessed that he often got lost in the play he was writing, occasionally becoming sadly disillusioned when it was finished and he read it over in "cold blood." Davis attempted to analyze this process, saying, "What really happens is that in the course of the weeks you go about with this junk shifting about in your head, the subconscious part of your mind does most of your work for you, and when you start to write it out you will be amazed to read what your hand has written." [11]

Edna Ferber, too, confessed to having the odd sensation of writing a line, a paragraph, a page about something of which she had no actual knowledge or experience. This woman dramatist-novelist saw the writer in a peculiar light. "The writer himself is only a test tube,"

10 *New York Times*, April 22, 1951.
11 Davis, *op. cit.*, p. 156.

according to Ferber, "a retort and a lamp through which the chemicals are mixed and from which they emerge, transformed. That he himself should be the substance and the subject of the experiment has seemed to me akin to the case of the strange insect that eats itself for nourishment." [12]

The artist, therefore, takes life as he finds it, observes, connotes, and stores it, then out of the storehouse creates according to his own temperament. The distinction which labels each writer's work as his own the literary world calls "style." This distinctive essence, or style, is something which the writer cannot consciously work to achieve. As John Galsworthy has said, "A man may have many moods, he has but one spirit; and this spirit he communicates in some subtle, unconscious way to all his work. The real artist does not anticipate and certainly cannot regulate the impulse that shall move his brain and heart and hand. What exactly starts him off, even he cannot tell." [13] "The whole business of writing is a totally mysterious thing," writes John van Druten, "springing from one knows not what source."

The conclusion is inescapable that a majority of the work entailed in writing a play is conducted subconsciously. Davis was so convinced of its value that he even employed a method to encourage the use of his subconscious. While working on a play he made it a rule to go over the story fully in his mind before going to sleep. It was his feeling that upon awakening points suddenly become clear that were clouded the night before. "I find that the part of my mind that remained active while I slept has been helping me pay the rent," concluded Davis.

Van Druten reasons that the best things one writes seem to arrive as total surprises to the author who is apt to stop and say, "Now, how did I know that?" According to van Druten the whole impulse comes from some uncomprehended spring of one's being, some other level of consciousness, "some compulsion that one does not understand." As

[12] Edna Ferber, *A Peculiar Treasure*, Garden City Publishing Company, 1940, p. 4.
[13] John Galsworthy, "Some Platitudes Concerning Drama," *The Inn of Tranquility*, Charles Scribner's Sons, 1912, p. 197.

to the level of consciousness from which the playwright creates, he declares, "It is from the subconscious that one creates."

Maugham, upon being asked if he felt the subconscious played a vital role in creative writing, revealed an interesting interrelationship between the conscious and subconscious processes while he was at work on a play. "Yes," said Maugham, "I have had the experience, as many writers have, of reading over what I have written and wondering, 'How the dickens did I ever write that?' I claim that the best of writing is done by the subconscious . . . so long as the original writing is under way, I try to keep the subconscious flowing. When the story is done, I go back, my intelligence takes over, and I write and rewrite." [14]

Alternate production from subconscious bursts of inspired creativity and conscious deliberation over what has been written would appear to be the most sensible pattern for a playwright to follow. The use of subconscious and conscious reflection in plot construction and character development has been clearly indicated. However, it is time to turn to what has been implied—that dialogue is often written in inspirational flashes, since it is in dialogue that the play is actually transcribed onto paper.

What a character will say in a given situation under given circumstances appears to flash into being. In the chapter concerning character it is concluded that the ease with which a playwright finds the appropriate line depends upon the degree of successful character conception, which is more a matter of careful, whether conscious or subconscious, character development.

George M. Cohan liked to refer to the act of putting words into a character's mouth as something that is in "the author's blood, not in his dictionary." Davis preferred to link the writing of dialogue to his concept of dramatic instinct and the use of the subconscious. "One may learn a lot about what not to write, may learn much of literary style and taste and many of the tricks of construction," declared Davis, "but

[14] Harry Gilroy, "How to Write—By Maugham," *New York Times Magazine,* January 23, 1949, p. 10.

I doubt if anyone without the instinctive feel of the born dramatist can learn how to time a speech or pitch a climax and without this all the rest is useless." [15]

This chapter has explored the vague concepts of dramatic instinct and the creative process. It has discovered that a definite relationship exists between the conscious and subconscious levels of creativity. The human mind, as it is constituted, usually creates in the pattern of alternate bursts of subjective creativity followed by objective retrospection. In summary, the following revelation from John Galsworthy's "Creation of Character in Literature" will perhaps better establish the role of each factor discussed:

The vitality and freedom of character creation derives, as a rule, from the subconscious mind instinctively supplying the conscious mind with the material it requires. In attempting an illustration of the process you must forgive my being personal for a moment. I sink into my morning chair, a blotter on my knee, the last words or deed of some character in ink before my eyes, a pen in my hand, a pipe in my mouth, and nothing in my head. I sit. I don't intend; I don't expect; I don't even hope. I read over the last pages. Gradually my mind seems to leave the chair, and be where my character is acting or speaking, leg raised, waiting to come down, lips opened ready to say something. Suddenly my pen jots down a movement or remark, another, another, and goes on doing this, haltingly, perhaps for an hour or two. When the result is read through it surprises one by seeming to come out of what went before, and by ministering to some sort of possible future. Those pages, adding tissue to character, have been supplied from the store-cupboard of the subconscious, in response to the appeal of one's conscious directive sense, and in service to the saving grace of one's theme, using that word in its widest sense. The creation of character, however, untrammelled and unconscious, thus has ever the guidance of what, perhaps, may best be called "the homing instinct." [16]

---

[15] Davis, *op. cit.*, p. 99.
[16] John Galsworthy, "Creation of Character in Literature," *Candelabra*, Charles Scribner's Sons, 1933, pp. 305–306.

POSTSCRIPT

Since the possession of dramatic instinct is of such importance to the successful playwright, it is only natural that the aspiring playwright ask himself, "Do I have it? Can I learn to write good dramas?"

There is no aptitude test that will predict the dramatic potential of a writer. He can only discover his instinctive capacity by pushing it to its limit. Those writers who feel compelled to express themselves dramatically may possibly possess dramatic instinct. It is certain they will never know unless they try to write plays.

Since the attempt to discover one's capacity to write plays is a period of self-discovery, is it not logical that a course in dramatic writing can in some measure provide the writer with the challenge necessary to test the strength of his inherent inclination? By subjecting himself to the discipline and guidance required to explore fully the essential elements of the playwriting process, the aspiring dramatist may soon discover for himself the answers to the questions, "Do I have it? Can I learn to write good dramas?"

Developing the Playwriting Ability

PLAYWRIGHTS are born *and* made. Since nothing can change a writer's birth, what can be done about developing his ability to write plays? How much or how little should be his acquaintance with the storehouse of dramatic literature? How wide or how limited should be his knowledge of the various media for which he will some day write? What pursuits or activities will sharpen and channel his dramatic instinct toward the successful shaping of dramas?

VALUES OBTAINED FROM THE STUDY OF PLAYS

A thorough knowledge of what one proposes to create should supersede any serious attempts at creation. An automotive engineer would hardly attempt to design a new model automobile without a basic knowledge of the models that led up to and make his concept possible. Nor is it feasible for a playwright to attempt to write plays if he is not acquainted with at least a portion of the wealth of dramatic literature which has accumulated over the past two thousand and more years.

Before probing the values obtained from examining plays, let us review two specific methods of acquiring dramatic writing skill as employed by two successful contemporary American playwrights. At the core of each method is the study of plays.

Channing Pollock, in his autobiography, *Harvest of My Years*, set forth a method he recommended in lectures on playwriting at numerous universities. Pollock would read acknowledged masterpieces and and then give himself time to forget everything but a bare outline of the plot. Then he would write a scenario of the story as he would have written it. Finally, he would compare his work with the original, observing carefully whether any characters were superfluous or any scenes out of order. "In all," commented Pollock, "I made about two hundred of these scenarios—a course in dramaturgy that filled nearly seven thousand pages."

George Broadhurst taught himself dramatic structure with a method, similar to Pollock's, based on a comparison of his own version of a play with a successful drama. The essential difference was that in Broadhurst's method only a portion of a play in production would be observed; then the playwright would attempt to pick up the story line and develop the drama to its logical conclusion. Broadhurst claimed that this method aided him in compensating for his deficient knowledge of play construction. In setting forth his plan, he said, "Having abjured the reading of all advance notices and criticism by which I might learn the story, I would go opening night of each play, sit in the gallery, see the first act only, then go home and work out for myself what I thought should be the development of the plot. When this was finished I would go back to the theatre, see the dramatist's completed work and compare it with what I had done." [1]

Both the Pollock and the Broadhurst methods could, with some alteration, be utilized as exercises for the student playwright. Care, however, would have to be taken not to create the impression that the student should imitate the dramaturgical technique of the original author.

A certain amount of craftsmanship may be acquired through the reading of plays. Many successful playwrights once held positions as play-readers for Broadway producers. These positions afforded them

[1] George Broadhurst, "Some Others and Myself," *Saturday Evening Post,* November 6, 1926, p. 165.

unusual opportunities to examine a great number of untried plays, many possessing every fault a script could possibly have.

Plays of certain masters of the past should be on the required reading list of every student playwright. Henrik Ibsen is of especial value in learning plot construction and providing the student with an insight into the modern treatment of contemporary themes. Playwrights of such diversified natures and temperaments as George M. Cohan, Clifford Odets, and Somerset Maugham attribute much value to a study of Ibsen. Maugham even once translated Ibsen's play, *Ghosts,* in order to acquire a knowledge of technique. William Shakespeare, of course, was a master technician, and his handling of "stage time" provides an excellent model for the beginning playwright. Some authors have found such playwrights as Pinero and Strindberg especially helpful. John van Druten feels that the would-be dramatist should read almost any play and that something will be learned from each. Elmer Rice once said that as a beginner he read all the plays he could get his hands on and went to see all the plays he could, adding, "Don't you think that's the only way to learn to write plays?"

Seeing plays is perhaps more important than reading them—especially for the beginning writer. The typewritten or printed manuscript is an incomplete play, lacking life until it is produced. The reader has the burden of visualizing in his mind's eye the finished product and he is apt to put the emphasis in the wrong place. This is not to say that one should see plays to the exclusion of reading them. Values may be obtained from both pursuits. Just remember that on a stage, under production conditions, it is much easier to see what is important and what is not, and particularly what is and is not dramatic.

Primarily, a playwright can obtain an understanding of plot construction and some idea of stage time in reading and seeing plays. Observing plays makes one realize the value of economy in structure and plot. In some bad plays an act will waste ten or fifteen minutes before an audience will discover its connection with the previous act.

VALUES OBTAINED FROM ACTING OR WORKING IN THE THEATRE

The values obtained from working within the environment of the theatre are readily apparent. The playwright produces a work meant to be performed on a stage and witnessed by an audience, therefore, it is only logical to conclude that, like any other craftsman, he should have a good working knowledge of the medium for which he labors.

The particular values obtained from acting or working in the theatre disclose a relationship between the playwright's understanding of the theatre and his development of an ability to write stage-worthy and successful plays.

The theatre worker best known to the general public is of course the actor. The actor is the direct link between the stage and the audience, and it is usually to him that the applause is directed. It may be significant that many successful American playwrights such as George Abbott, David Belasco, George M. Cohan, Noel Coward, Frank Craven, Rachel Crothers, George Kelly, Clifford Odets, Eugene O'Neill, and Winchell Smith were actors before turning to playwriting. A study of comments made by some of these actors-turned-playwrights will reveal that they attribute to their acting experience the knowledge of how to write plays worth producing and plays that can be acted. After all, Pinero, a master of construction, was an actor and who will ever surpass the plays of William Shakespeare, the actor?

There is little likelihood that anyone who has acted himself will ever write "unactable" lines of dialogue, words that refuse to marry on an actor's tongue, which is the revealing characteristic of the beginning playwright. "There is a certain limit beyond which it is not safe to go in speeches on the stage," wrote J. Hartley Manners. "The actor knows what that limit is by acquired instinct—and a playwright must know it, too, if he wishes to be effective." [2]

However, there is a danger in the student playwright's associating

2 *New York Press,* December 7, 1913.

entirely within the environs of the theatre. Too great an intimacy with the theatre sometimes leads one to employ hackneyed stage tricks. It is far better for the prospective playwright to cultivate friends outside the theatre as well and to develop his own personality along healthy and realistic lines. "Study, observation, friends, and travel especially will help," says Maugham, adding, "It is the personality that counts." Though Maugham holds certain reservations against intimate contact with theatre people, he believes that the only place for a playwright to learn his craft is in the theatre, that attendance at rehearsals of plays, for example, is to be especially encouraged. In observing a director at work, the dramatist sees what situations carry and the sort of dialogue that is effective. Charles Klein also urged student playwrights to attend rehearsals of plays in production, saying, "It is marvelous how a play will stand incessant surgical operations—cutting, eliminating, and stitching of loose ends together!" The operation, however, may be extremely painful when it is the playwright's own play which is under the scalpel, nevertheless, the student will learn something about dramaturgy from the operation.

David Belasco once posed the question that if the acquisition of facility in dramatic composition requires a thorough knowledge of the "cash register code," i.e., what has box office appeal, why, then, are there not schools where the secrets may be learned? There are—the theatres. Belasco shared the common belief that dramatists should first be seasoned theatre workers.

The drama is an art of expression wherein many conventions and complex mechanisms must be duly seen to before the vision, or idea, of the artist becomes intelligible. To become familiar with these conventions and these mechanisms it is necessary to work in the theatre itself for a while. Augustus Thomas revealed a thorough understanding of the theatre and its conventions when he said, "I speak the language of the theatre. I am of the theatre. I have done everything in the theatre except work the lights. I have worked as an usher from the orchestra to the balconies. I have sold and taken tickets. I have shifted scenery. I have written plays, produced plays, and even acted in plays." [3]

Play-readers and agents in New York are deluged each year with a tremendous number of scripts. It has been estimated that most of the yearly crop is bad or absolutely hopeless. In almost each instance the weakness or triteness of the script could be attributed to the writer's lack of theatre experience, and, in consequence, their attempts are as the earth was reported to have been in the beginning, without form and void.

JOURNALISM AS A TRAINING GROUND FOR PLAYWRIGHTS

A survey of the most successful Broadway playwrights of the twentieth century reveals an interesting point: many of them received their early training as newspapermen.

Such famous American dramatists as Maxwell Anderson, S. N. Behrman, George Broadhurst, Marc Connelly, Edna Ferber, James Forbes, Jules Goodman, Ben Hecht, Lillian Hellman, Avery Hopwood, George S. Kaufman, Charles MacArthur, Willard Mack, Roi Cooper Megrue, Max Marcin, Eugene O'Neill, Channing Pollock, Robert E. Sherwood, and Augustus Thomas were active journalists at one time in their careers.

The same is true of English playwrights. James M. Barrie, A. A. Milne, and George Bernard Shaw, for example, once wrote columns for London dailies.

It may seem difficult to pinpoint how journalistic experience prepares the dramatist for his task. However, a study of statements made by some of these ex-newspapermen reveals five distinct values which they felt contributed to their success as playwrights.

First, in learning news values as a reporter the future dramatist is sharpening his understanding of the relative value of scenes. Augustus

---

[3] W. A. Davenport, "Augustus Thomas—From 'Mizzoura,'" *World's Work*, May, 1923, p. 81.

Thomas, who worked on newspapers in St. Louis, Kansas City, and New York before turning to the theater to write such hits as *The Witching Hour, Arizona,* and *The Copperhead,* claimed that "the climactic situation for a play would be almost always a first-page story in a newspaper office."

Max Marcin held that any "honest-to-God newspaperman, with the true newspaper instinct, should be able to write a good play." He claimed that writing a newspaper story is more or less like writing a play: "You select the dramatic thing first, and then it is a process of elimination." Others felt that playwrights who were former newspapermen were trained to see the story and put it foremost with a punch.

Second, a reporter develops an ear for dialogue and learns to write expressive language appropriate to character through his interviewing experiences. Edna Ferber, author of *Stage Door* and many other plays in collaboration with former newsman George S. Kaufman, has stressed this value gained from her early years as a reporter.

Willard Mack also admitted that the knowledge he gained from interviewing gave him his "entering wedge" into playwriting. In an interview Mack said: "I had worked on a newspaper as a police reporter. That's where I learned how crooks think. I had been on the stage a while when I found fault with a play. I found most fault with the language. 'People don't talk like that,' I told the producer. 'I suppose you think you know how they do talk.' I rewrote the dialogue. After that I began writing plays and to date have written sixty-two." [4]

Mack's statement suggests a third value gained from reporting— the ability to draw characters from life. The reporter in his daily work meets people from every walk of life and every economic level. Few professions enable a man to mingle with members of the upper economic classes one hour and a bum in a Skid Row soup line the next. The newspaperman can—and does—because he has a peculiar "social immunity." People of all classes accept him and open up to him where

[4] Ada Patterson, "Gaieties and Gravities," *Theatre Magazine,* June, 1928, p. 34.

they usually become reticent around strangers. Marcin pinpointed this value when he said, "A newspaperman learns much of life during his daily work . . . he knows how people react under great stress, which is dramatic material."

Fourth, reporting provides the playwright with a knowledge of the situations out of which plays are made. "Like many playwrights," Marcin stated, "I began as a newspaperman. The experience which I gained in reporting was invaluable in my later work. It gave me a vast fund of the rude, raw material out of which plays are fashioned." [5]

Fifth, working in a newspaper office under the pressure of deadlines demands of the reporter an intense concentration. He must be able to exclude all distracting elements while he writes. After describing the bedlam of newspaper work, Thomas, in his autobiography, then relates his acquired sense of concentration to the task of the playwright: "More than once since then at a dress rehearsal and its attendant hubbub I have been thankful for much of that control as was then acquired, which has helped me to sit at a music-stand in the orchestra pit and patch up some limping scene." [6]

W. Somerset Maugham, novelist and playwright, but never a journalist, summarized the relationship of playwriting to journalism in his book, *The Summing Up,* when he said, "The playwright and the journalist need very similar gifts, a quick eye for a good story and a telling point, animation and a vivid way of writing."

THE VALUE OF TEXTBOOKS AND TREATISES ON THE DRAMA

It may be presumptuous for a book concerned with the playwriting process to estimate the values to be obtained from such books and other treatises on the drama. The truth of the matter is that no textbook can provide a do-it-yourself formula for writing plays. However,

[5] Max Marcin, "How I Sold My Plays," *Theatre Magazine,* November, 1916, p. 268.

[6] Augustus Thomas, *The Print of My Remembrance,* Charles Scribner's Sons, 1922, p. 202.

a good textbook, when used in combination with other, more practical pursuits, can be of value to the student playwright.

This is neither to condemn textbooks nor to justify them, but whatever values are to be obtained from any book treating an art or a craft are directly proportional to the ability of the individual artist to fit them into a total picture of dramatic instinct, practical application and experience, and textbook knowledge.

Much controversy still surrounds the earliest known treatise on dramatic composition, Aristotle's *Poetics.* For centuries critics have interpreted and misinterpreted the Greek philosopher's observations. Some have attempted to canonize his dictums into unbreakable laws of the drama. Others have set up opposing theories reflecting the dramatic temperament of their times.

In the *Poetics,* Aristotle defined tragedy as "an imitation of an action that is serious, complete, and of a certain magnitude; in language embellished with each kind of artistic ornament, the several kinds being found in separate parts of the play; in the form of action, not of narrative; through pity and fear effecting the proper purgation of these emotions." Aristotle also described laws of composition necessitating a beginning, middle, and end in a drama, an observance of which has come to be known as a "well-made play."

The *Poetics* also lists the six parts of a drama and purports to rank them in their order of importance. First is *plot,* which has also been translated as "fable," "story," and "action." Next comes *character* followed by *thought* or, according to one translation, "sentiments." Fourth, said Aristotle, is "diction" or what is referred to today as *dialogue,* and fifth is *rhythm,* also translated as "melody" or "music." Last in importance is "spectacle" or *scenic effects.*

Aristotle also set forth the law of unity of action which has remained valid down through the centuries. In the rediscovery of Greek culture in the Renaissance two other unities were attributed to Aristotle, the unity of time and the unity of place. Actually, Aristotle treated these two elements only slightly and in no way claimed they were to dominate drama in structuring plays. Unfortunately, the critics after the fourteenth century not only called "the three Unities" Aristotle's but attempted to force playwrights to observe them strictly in writing their plays.

Aristotle was not assuming the role of the prophet, an expert handing down a set of principles which should reign for eternity. There is no argument that some of his observations are still as valid today as they were two thousand years ago. This is probably because human nature has changed very little over the centuries rather than because the theatre has remained static. To place Aristotle and his reflections in proper perspective for the beginning playwright, it should be stated unequivocally that Aristotle was the theatre critic of his day. Greek civilization was in the Age of Pericles and the Arts had reached a zenith. The theatre was a public ritual in which the masses took an active interest. This was also the age of Aeschylus, Euripides, and Sophocles. Aristotle observed the plays and their effect upon an audience. He then reported what he saw and endeavored to explain the audience's response and his own. Sophocles undoubtedly was Aristotle's favorite playwright and, consequently, his plays became the models upon which many of Aristotle's theories were based.

Brooks Atkinson, of the *New York Times,* and the other influential contemporary critics in a sense attempt to do the same thing for the American theatre as Aristotle did for his. A legion of critics keep their fingers on the dramatic pulse of the audience and fairly accurately predict what will or will not please them. If it will please, they can supply some vague ideas on why it will. However, if, in their opinion, the play is weak and without dramatic merit, they can supply their readers with many concrete reasons why they should not attend its performance.

If beginning playwrights will treat such writings as personalized observations reflecting a spirit of the times, much value may be obtained from reading criticism and analyses of the theatre, both past and present. However, if the playwright attempts to formulate or derive a standardized approach to the theatre from published critical works he allows these sources to lose whatever value they may possess.

Books on playwriting and the art of the theatre, though valuable, can never replace practical knowledge. They can provide a short cut to that knowledge, however. Attendance at plays, both in rehearsal and at performance, and working actively in the theatre cannot be replaced by vicarious participation through the pages of a book. A proof of this contention was offered by Elmer Rice when he said, "I read William Archer's book and Brander Matthews. I even tackled Freytag. They're all good, sound writers, and when you finish with them you say enthusiastically: 'So, that's how they do it. I'll do it myself.' But by the time you've rustled out your paper and pencil you've forgotten what it is you were told to do." [7]

THE VALUE OF COLLEGE AND UNIVERSITY THEATRE PROGRAMS

The prospective playwright will find many of the nation's colleges and universities in an excellent position to prepare him for his profession. These educational centers *cannot* make him a playwright but they can offer him many *opportunities* to obtain the values already mentioned and possibly add several more.

Higher education has become a big business and is now in the unique position of being able to offer professional preparation where the profession itself is unable to do so. This is especially true of the theatre and the other dramatic media. No longer is it possible for the young writer to serve an apprenticeship in the professional theatre and through the process of osmosis absorb the values of being a participant and an observer.

What are the values of college and university training? How can they help develop the playwright's ability?

First, the humanities and liberal arts programs can introduce him to the realm of dramatic literature. In addition, most English departments have courses that will expose the student to the richness of the World

[7] *New York Times,* August 30, 1914.

Theater. From the ancient Greek tragedies and comedies through the plays of Shakespeare and Marlowe to those of Ibsen, Strindberg, O'Neill, Anderson, Williams, and Miller, he can become acquainted with those scripts that when produced excited their audiences and quickened their pulses.

The many active university theatre programs can offer the student playwright a working knowledge of the stage, the broadcasting studios (radio and TV), and in some universities he can even work in a motion picture studio. In many cases these facilities are as excellently equipped as their commercial counterparts. Most of the new theatre construction has been on the nation's campuses rather than in the metropolitan centers. In many instances these theatres are far ahead of their times, incorporating elements as yet unseen in a New York theatre. It is because the educational theatres are not operated for profit that they can offer the student playwright so many opportunities to develop.

Even the smaller colleges have theatre groups that can introduce the student to the mysteries of production before a live audience. For the most part these organizations offer a balanced diet of classics, the latest Broadway offerings, and experimental pieces that will probably never see a commercial performance.

The university theatres have recognized their obligation to the new playwright and the number offering original plays in their season's bill increases each year. In addition, many of these organizations operate studio theatres dedicated to the development of the student actor, director, and playwright. It is in these theatres that most of the original writing on a campus receives a production. Here is the laboratory where the playwright can observe for himself what happens to his plays when they are married to an audience. Nothing can replace the value of a production to a playwright; nothing can help him develop more rapidly, more fully than seeing his plays in performance.

The number of universities operating radio stations is already large and the number operating television stations is on the increase. These facilities offer additional laboratory resources to the student playwright.

There are close to seventy colleges and universities offering courses in dramatic writing. These courses acquaint the student with the basic dramaturgical practices of the day. They differ from most courses in that the orientation is toward the individual student and his creative inclination rather than being a class conducted along the customary competitive and comparative methods.

It is the wise teacher of playwriting who provides an atmosphere conducive to creativity, instead of setting forth didactic principles or rules to fetter the aspiring writer. From the class and the teacher the student playwright can expect forthright criticism. The collective critical effort of creative individuals can help to hasten the development of the dramatic writer.

Playwrights are born *and* made. But the *making* is up to the individual. The pursuits are there if he chooses to follow them. In learning there is no point of completion. As David Belasco once said, "It is the irony of fate that we live only long enough to learn how—and then die before we can make use of the knowledge." If the masters of the theatre had waited until they felt they had learned how to write great plays they never would have written them. If one is inclined to write, then he must write, for only as he writes can his playwriting ability grow and prosper.

The Playwright and His Audience

The spectator as well as the actor is an active participant in a performance.

—STANISLAVSKY

A PLAY as a piece of theatre remains incomplete as long as it is in its manuscript form. A produced play is not the work of a single artist, but a collaborative effort requiring the talents of many artists for its successful execution, and is therefore a fusion of many elements. The most important of these are the script itself, the actors under the leadership of a creative director, and, finally, the most active and unpredictable element of them all—the audience.

THE SPECTATOR AS A PARTICIPANT

The basis of all spectatorship is a combination of appreciation and participation. We may praise the skill of a certain athlete as he performs, but we are more apt to identify with him and to share his experience vicariously. For what other reason do most of us go to an athletic event if not to participate? How many extra points have we kicked, touchdowns made, and opponents knocked out?

Audience identification usually takes one of several forms and may vary at any one event. For example, a Detroit sports fan goes to a baseball game between the Tigers and the Yankees. Why does he go?

Probably because he is a Tiger supporter and he is going to see the perennial world champions from New York get beaten by *his* team. Now once the game starts and the pressures mount the fan may transfer his identification from the group to the individual players. For instance, the Tigers are behind 3–0, it is the last of the ninth inning, the bases are loaded, two men are out and Tiger outfielder Al Kaline is at the plate. The count is three-two and the last pitch is on its way. The fan's arms strain muscularly for he, figuratively speaking, is holding that bat with Kaline as he mutters, "C'mon, Al—a homer in the left field bleachers and we win 4–3." The ball comes to the plate. Al Kaline swings. The fan's muscles, having momentarily adjusted to the muscular tonality of Kaline, strain and, in a fashion, he too swings at that ball. A strike! Kaline is out and the Yankees win. The fan's muscles slump, he relaxes, the tension is over.

During that baseball game the Tiger fan played every position. He was the pitcher fanning the mighty Mickey Mantle, he was the shortstop starting a double play, and he was the last Tiger batter in the crucial ninth. He was identifying with the nine-man Tiger baseball team and his participation is more properly called *empathy*. In many respects the game was similar to a drama. The Tiger supporters naturally polarized around their team as they struggled toward their objective—victory over the Yankees. The Tigers, as a group, became the protagonists, while the Yankees were cast in the role of villains. If the game had been played in New York the roles would have been reversed.

But what about the spectator who is not an active supporter of either an individual participant or a team? For instance, why will a sports fan tune into a televised boxing match between two fighters he knows nothing about? Perhaps he is initially attracted by the prospect of physical conflict. But as the match begins it is very much like the unfolding of a stage play. In the opening round the spectator remains impersonal as the two apparently evenly matched fighters explore each other's defenses and test their patterns of attack. In this round there is probably little identification as the spectator sizes up the two participants, admiring their skill.

Perhaps between rounds he learns from the announcer that one fighter is from the Bronx. Being a New Yorker himself, the fan's interest is then directed toward the boy in white trunks, the Bronx gladiator. During the next round, however, it is the boy in black trunks who absorbs the most punishment. Black Trunks is now established as the underdog, the one who must come from behind to win. One fighter's apparent superiority has created an obstacle for the other to overcome. The fan's interest—and his identification—shifts toward Black Trunks.

For several rounds the fan's interest and identification with Black Trunks intensifies. Muscularly, his tonality adjusts to that of the fighter as he bobs and weaves, ducks and counterpunches. He may even attempt to *project* control over the fighter as he boxes. White Trunks is carrying his left low and the fan shouts to his man to throw a right and the muscles in his own arm adjust to throw the punch he desires. But, instead, Black Trunks brings up a left which hits White Trunks below the belt—an obvious foul. Suddenly, the fan's support for Black Trunks evaporates and his interest shifts back to White Trunks, who now becomes the hero who must dispatch the foul villain!

From these two examples from the world of sport it can be seen that audience identification requires the existence of certain factors. First, there must be an individual or group worthy of identification and, second, there must be an objective worth attaining. In other words, we must care about what happens and we must have some genuine concern for the person or persons to whom it happens.

Though a play is not complete until it has been presented to its audience, the playwright begins his dramatic-writing process with a consideration of the audience by creating a protagonist around which the audience will polarize and by providing him with an objective the audience will care if he attains. That is why the playwright must first have a basic understanding of audience identification and the role it plays in successful play making.

THE PLAY AND ITS AUDIENCE

"A play should be a successful blood-transfusion between the actors and the audience," says Marc Connelly. "Without the proper union between the two, there can be no chance of success. The more easily the audience takes the new blood into their veins, the more skillful the writer." [1] In a very true sense, then, the playwright and the audience are collaborators.

How does the partnership of writer and audience take place? As the English playwright, A. A. Milne, used to say, every play is a bluff and yet the success of the bluff depends entirely on the willingness of the audience to coöperate. Though what an audience is asked to witness did not happen so or could not happen so, they are willingly bluffed, at least for a few hours, that things did happen so.

The manner of the bluff, of course, depends upon the attitude of the contemporary audience toward the drama, the intelligence of the people, and the conventions of the period. Audiences of today, as yesterday, recognize that in the theatre there must be a willing suspension of disbelief, for without that suspension there can be no theatre experience.

The author puts up a bluff and the actors carry it out, yet the fate of the playwright is very much in the hands of the audience. If the audience won't be carried away, it just won't be carried away. A good playwright, therefore, is a good student of audiences and he either knows or learns what will register with it and what will not. In this respect he is very much like the public speaker who analyzes his audience before composing his speech. It is a certainty that before a playwright can really succeed he must get over the footlights and collaborate with his audience.

Unlike his fellow artists—the poet, the painter, the sculptor or the novelist—the dramatist may enjoy or endure, at first hand, the im-

[1] B. F. Wilson, "A Satirist Turns to Fantasy," *Theatre Magazine,* May, 1926, p. 30.

mediate response of the audience to his work. As Elmer Rice has said, the playwright has the prerogative to sit incognito in the theatre where his play is being performed and know far better than his fellow artists "the taste of honey and the taste of gall."

A major reason why all aspiring dramatic writers should write first for public performance is the *presence* of an audience. The stage is one of the dramatic media where the playwright can observe his play meeting the audience. If he is to write for the motion pictures, television, or radio he is forced to allow for the reaction of an unseen audience. However, if he has sharpened his skills on a live audience he will find it much easier to compensate for their absence.

In witnessing his play in performance the playwright will observe his lines meeting across the footlights, actor to audience, and this will reveal the play's appeal or lack of it; the effect of the play may then be measured. The action of the play is reciprocal. Each of the three constituents—words, actor, and audience—is susceptible. The actor receives from the audience and takes on an added and measurable quantity. "The audience is not the least important actor in the play," claims Somerset Maugham, "and if it will not do its allotted share the play falls to pieces. The dramatist then is in the position of a tennis player who is left on the court with nobody to play with." [2] A play that does not appeal to an audience may have merits, but it is no more a play than a mule is a horse. The emotion of the audience, its interests, its laughter, its tears, are all part of the action of the play.

THE POWER OF THE PUBLIC

A play must have public approval in order to survive. It is the audience that says in the last analysis whether a play is a success or not. George M. Cohan coined two expressions to describe the audience's role, saying that it was the only "Loud Speaker" to which he listened and the "Big Critic" that counts, since it is the one that pays to come

[2] Somerset Maugham, *The Summing Up*, Doubleday, Doran & Co., Inc., 1939, p. 127.

in. In referring to the public's method of demonstrating approval, George Broadhurst wrote: "Three things point to the success of your play—laughter, applause and tears. If the playwright has one, he has a chance for success; if he has two, he has a certain success; if he has the three, he has that tremendous masterpiece we are all looking for." [3]

Since the public is the ultimate judge, the playwright must to some extent consider the audience. The theatre belongs first to the public and liens are held successively by the dramatist, the producer, and the actor. No better proof of the control exerted over the drama by its public can be found than in the fact that the best advertising a good play has is its audience. Newspaper advertisements and reviews may help a little, but it is the man who has seen the play and advises his friends to see it who helps most.

THE NATURE OF THE AUDIENCE

The American audience is more intelligent and more receptive to progressive ideas than most writers think. In the past quarter of a century our playwrights have discovered that their audiences have grown in knowledge and that the writer is no longer limited to but a few common subjects. This is indeed fortunate, for the playwright alone can soar no higher than the mean level, the average intelligence of a nondescript and miscellaneous public.

The theatre audience is composed of heterogeneous elements homogenized into a group, welding together many types and levels of intelligence, and the unifying or homogenizing force is the appeal to basic emotions. The audience is not a thoughtless mob, though as a group it is subject to "mob appeal," which is much different from saying that as a group they are without intelligence. Over fifty years ago Clyde Fitch recognized the complex nature of the audience and commented, "It is only by an appeal to the emotions common with all human nature that this naturally unwieldly body is molded into one great sounding board."

[3] George Broadhurst, "Plays—the Greatest of All Gambles," *Green Book Magazine*, March, 1916, p. 533.

The playwright is faced with the extreme difficulty of appealing not to one leisurely reader in the library, but to an audience of eight hundred on the other side of the footlights. In order to do this effectively, it is mandatory that he learn as much as he can about the audience and its component elements.

For example, there are apparently two publics, though the membership of both may be the same. There is the public that delights in the subtle and the public that revels in the obvious. "On one side are those whose brain is reached through their ears first," said John Galsworthy, and "on the other side, those whose brain is reached through their eyes first." Does this mean that there is one public that is highbrow and the other lowbrow? No, it merely means that there are two different kinds of intellect, one more attracted by action, the other more given to speculation. The first may find a *Desperate Hours* or a *Dead End* more to their liking whereas the second will find a *Man and Superman* and even a *Waiting for Godot* more satisfying.

Some playwrights probably feel their audiences are always changing in regard to their tastes and are actually fickle in their likes and dislikes. However, so long as a playwright keeps within the bounds of decency he can do almost anything that strikes his fancy. The playwright must remember however that public taste changes from year to year, and that there is a psychological moment for every play. Call the public fickle, but few people of their own free will subsist on the same diet year in and year out. Several seasons ago the preference was for more serious plays. The 1956–1957 season was keynoted as a season of comedy and a slight return to romanticism, despite the arrival of Eugene O'Neill's tragic Pulitzer Prize winning *Long Day's Journey Into Night* and Tennessee Williams' *Orpheus Descending*. During the 1955–1956 season an excellent play, *Time Limit,* failed to win support because it concerned itself with what happens to an American prisoner of war who is subjected to brainwashing. The public had already been saturated with the arguments in the newspapers and were apparently tired of the subject when it became the basis of a play.

The theatre, since the beginning of civilization, has changed in form and kind—from classicism to romanticism, back to classicism and then to realism, and again back to romanticism and then to symbolism, constructivism, expressionism, and even a new *ism*—existentialism. The theatre continually changes in form and kind—but so has the public, and it may be taken for granted that the demand has had something to do with the supply.

Any actor knows that audiences are notoriously inconsistent and that one audience will seldom react the same way as another audience nor at the same points in the same play. Some evenings the audience appears unusually cold; other times it can scarcely restrain itself. At a comedy the audience is usually triggered into laughter by an alert sensitive few. Two or three persons in a particularly amiable mood will have a wonderful influence on their neighbors, and once they start laughing it has the effect of arousing the rest of the audience. Centuries ago playwrights and producers discovered this secret and introduced paid claques or members of the audience planted to stimulate laughter or applause. Since they were used primarily as a triggering agent their presence can't be considered too unethical. Even a claque cannot save a bad play. Experience will also prove to the playwright that whatever amuses one audience is likely to amuse another. The difference between them is rather in degree than in kind.

The audience dislikes being deceived. Young playwrights sometimes think that to dupe the audience is clever, whereas, as a matter of fact, it is simply unwise from a theatrical point of view. The modern audience is neither easily deceived nor easily convinced. Clyde Fitch in his penetrating essay, "The Play and the Public," claimed that the theatre audience does *not* react as a child who delightedly starts to play "let's pretend." It was his opinion that the twentieth century audience actually keeps out of the game at first and watches others "pretend," never crossing the footlights itself but from its own vantage ground criticizing even with its own emotions. It says to the play, "Convince us if you can!" and "We dare you to move us!" Fitch claimed that "it is only when we start out boldly and take their dare honestly, by first convincing ourselves, that we win success." By being honest our chances of winning audience identification with our protagonist is heightened, and once this process begins it is only a short distance to winning the audience's willing suspension of disbelief. Honesty, not deception, is the key.

The audiences of all playwrights are basically loyal to the play and its author when they have been pleased with his previous offerings. However, the audience expects, and has the right to expect, that the writers who provide their theatrical entertainment shall be dissatisfied with their achievements and constantly strive to greater effort and progress.

OBSERVING THE AUDIENCE

Playwrights should observe an audience closely and learn from that observation how to write plays that will get favorable reaction, which situations and characters have the most audience appeal, and, most important, the role the audience plays in revising or rewriting a play during its early stages of development on the road or prior to the New York opening. The rewriting aspects of dramatic writing are treated in Chapter 15.

The willingness to learn from the public is perhaps the most valuable attitude the young dramatist could possess in approaching his profession. Thus only can he learn to estimate unerringly the relative value of "method" employed to make action convincing and compelling behind the footlights and later in front of the cameras with the audience, of necessity, absent.

An audience is the most fascinating of studies. So many things are true about it and one doesn't know why. For example, when an audience laughs it rocks back and forth in the seats, but when it is saddened, it moves from one side to another. Stand in the rear of any theatre and watch the audience, observe how it adjusts to the muscular tonality of that which it observes, see it respond empathically, vicariously to that which stimulates them. When you wanted them to laugh, did they? When you wanted them to cry, did they stifle a sob? You can tell. Just plant yourself at the back of the house and watch. This is another reason why colleges and universities produce a new playwright's work —to provide him with an opportunity to learn from his greatest critic, the audience.

In April, 1957, Tufts University afforded playwright Bernard Reines such an opportunity when they produced his new play, *The Midnight Cry.* The manuscript had already been given a "Rehearsed Reading" under the auspices of the New Dramatists Committee in New York. According to Reines this reading proved an important help toward revising the play into form for the Tufts production. But it was the campus performance that marked a new phase in the evolution of the play towards its final form. Reines wrote: "For this is the first time I shall be able to observe the impress of the various elements of the play on an audience, and so be able to draw important conclusions as to the final shaping of the drama. After talent and discipline, no one thing is as important to the growth of a playwright as production—for only through productions of his plays is he able to learn from his ultimate judge and teacher—the audience." [4]

THE PLAYWRIGHT'S OBLIGATION TO THE AUDIENCE

As long as the curtain stays up, the audience must remain interested. The playwright may use his own discretion in the method that he adopts, but that one result he must always obtain. Public approval of a play is very rarely concerned with its underlying idea or theme. What it insists upon is that the idea be told interestingly and that they be asked to identify with a protagonist, either an individual or a group, that they can care what happens to.

The writer must not only be the creator of drama, but also, imaginatively, one of its audience. As Channing Pollock wrote, in looking

[4] Bernard Reines, "Case History of a Play," *Prologue,* April, 1957, p. 4.

back over his long career in the theatre, "No scene that moved me as I wrote it failed to move an audience, and no scene that failed to move me was ever successful in the theater."

The playwright should possess a deep sense of responsibility to his audience. With their assistance he is everything, without them he is nothing.

Finding Dramatic Material

A MAJOR problem confronting beginning playwrights is the finding
of dramatic material from which they can fashion plots, develop characters, and write dialogue. Every teacher of playwriting encounters the
average student who claims that he knows nothing worth basing a play
upon and that since he is so young in years and experience he has had
little opportunity to develop a dramatic sense.

Chapter 3 discussed the relationship of dramatic instinct and the
creative process. This chapter is mostly concerned with the specifics of
discovering dramatic material, noting the controversy between writers
who advocate writing from experience and those who attribute to the
powers of imagination the largest burden in supply material.

WHAT IS DRAMATIC MATERIAL?

There is little wonder that confusion exists in the mind of the young
playwright as he attempts to find his way through the morass of
theories regarding the dramatic and the undramatic. The various
philosophies and approaches are duly recorded and may be examined
at great length, yet because of their disagreements it is doubtful that
the beginning or untrained playwright will be able to derive or isolate
an overall point of view that will serve as a reliable guide. The difficulty stems from confusing definitions of *the drama* with definitions of

what is *dramatic*. The drama is the formalized structure for stage presentation of what is dramatic, and has been defined in different manners with varying degrees of emphasis upon its component elements from Aristotle to the present.

Confusion in modern theory stems from the arguments surrounding Ferdinand Brunetière's "Law of the Drama," written in 1894, in which the French critic declared: "The theater in general is nothing but the place for the development of the human will, attacking the obstacles opposed to it by destiny, fortune or circumstances." It is readily seen that Brunetière was primarily concerned with the drama as a whole and not the material from which it is fashioned. He became more specific in his declaration that "drama is a representation of the will of man in conflict with the mysterious powers or natural forces which limit and belittle us; it is one of us thrown living upon the stage, there to struggle against fatality, against social law, against one of his fellow mortals, against himself, if need be, against the interests, the prejudices, the folly, the malevolence of those who surround him." [1]

William Archer, the English critic, took issue with Brunetière's conflict theory, holding instead that the essence of drama is crisis. "What, then," asked Archer, "is the essence of drama, if conflict be not it? What is the common quality of themes, scenes, and incidents, which we recognize as specifically dramatic?" Archer replied to his rhetorical question in saying that the essence of drama is crisis. "A play is a more or less rapidly developing crisis in destiny or circumstances, and a dramatic scene is a crisis within a crisis, clearly furthering the ultimate event. The drama may be called the art of crises, as fiction is the art of gradual developments." [2] Here, too, Archer was mostly concerned with the dramatic form rather than qualities that make material dramatic.

However, Archer nailed down the term "dramatic" as "any repre-

---

[1] Henry Arthur Jones, "Introduction to Brunetière's *Law of the Drama,*" in Barrett H. Clark's *European Theories of the Drama,* Crown Publishers, 1947, p. 461.

[2] William Archer, "Dramatic and Undramatic," in Barrett H. Clark's *European Theories of the Drama,* Crown Publishers, 1947, p. 479.

sentation of imaginary personages which is capable of interesting an average audience assembled in a theater." Again, the beginning playwright is at a loss as how to find this "dramatic material" capable of "interesting" an audience.

George Pierce Baker on the other hand concerned himself with the problem of distinguishing between the drama and the dramatic. In his discussion of the dramatic Baker took the stand that it meant material creative of emotional response. To Baker a play existed to create emotional response in an audience: "The response may be to the emotions of the people in the play or the emotions of the author as he watches these people." Baker logically concluded that all material which arouses or may be made to arouse emotion is not fitted for use in the theatre when it first comes to the hand of the dramatist. Dramatic material, said Baker, must be made theatric before it can go before an audience and become drama. Baker's definition of dramatic material as that which has the capability of arousing emotion is the one endorsed by the present writer.

The most concise explanation of what is and what is not dramatic can best be obtained by analyzing a basic and classical situation. The witnessing of two anonymous warriors locked in mortal combat may be in itself an exciting spectacle capable of arresting attention and arousing a certain amount of emotional reaction. The actual physical conflict of such a spectacle accounts for the interest of the spectator; however, it is of dubious dramatic merit unless the audience has an emotional response. The cited example of two men in combat is certainly capable of becoming truly dramatic if the audience is acquainted with certain emotion-provoking facts. If the two warriors are father and son and this fact is known to the audience but unknown to the two combatants, an element of the dramatic has been introduced that could never exist in merely watching two men struggle. Immediately the audience is interested in why this situation exists, what the outcome will be, and whether or not the fighters will recognize one another before one is slain or the other wounded. In other words, the audience now cares what happens to these two combatants, their emotions have been aroused.

What is dramatic is seldom known to be dramatic as it exists unless endowed with certain qualities. It is the task of the playwright to take his raw material, recognize its potentialities, and breathe the necessary life into it so that it may stand on a stage before an audience and evoke a response.

The ability to find the raw dramatic material presupposes that the playwright has a storehouse of knowledge of people and their behavior, a keen observation of his surroundings, and a vivid imagination. After all, the playwright writes about people and their experiences for an audience of people who have had their own experiences. The playwright's task is to wed the experiences of his characters to those of his audience, linking them together through the universal qualities that exist for both.

THE EXTREME WINGS AND THE MIDDLE

There are writers who advocate that a writer utilize his imagination to describe actions and places unknown to him, and there are writers who claim that a dramatist should write only about what he knows personally. The extremes are actually just theoretical, for both groups recognize that there exists a common meeting ground between actual and imagined experience. Some playwrights even feel actual experience is not a necessary prerequisite in molding dramatic material. In addition, the faculty of observation plays an important part in the processes of both groups. An attempt will be made in this chapter to indicate various explanations as to what causes an idea suddenly to grow into a full-blown play.

WRITE ABOUT WHAT YOU KNOW

There is little disagreement among teachers of playwriting that beginning playwrights should write about the things they know best.

It is only sensible that man departs from the known to the unknown and that before he can skillfully depart he must first be weaned on that which is familiar rather than that which is unfamiliar.

John Galsworthy placed the problem on a higher plane, saying that "art is not art unless it is made from what the artist himself has felt and seen, and not what he has been told he ought to feel and see." The British dramatist advocated that a writer draw directly from life for his material, saying, "It is from the stuff of his own life that the creative writer molds out for the world something fine, in the form that best suits him, following his own temperament."

Galsworthy's *The Pigeon* is an excellent example of the playwright's adherence to his theory. In this play "riff-raff" are thrown into direct contact with a more acceptable member of society. Galsworthy, in a newspaper interview, explained his first-hand knowledge, saying, "Having lived in the middle of just such incidents as I used in *The Pigeon,* however, and having seen the impingement of just such derelicts upon the more stable members of society, I keenly feel the reality of the fantastic conditions they create." [3]

TRIVIAL INCIDENTS MAY PROVIDE THE SPRINGBOARD

A trivial incident in a writer's surroundings may be the springboard for a drama if the writer can recognize the incident when he sees or hears it. The problem, however, is not whether the writer is or is not consciously aware of the dramatic potentialities of an incident but whether or not his mind is sensitive, as is the film of a camera, so that when exposed to the trivial but potentially dramatic incident it will record the event for future use.

What is a trivial incident? It is an observed occurrence that in itself is unrelated to its background or situational context but is arresting enough to make an impression when it occurs. It may be a small physical movement, a chance meeting on a street corner, a snatch of

[3] *New York Dramatic Mirror,* April 3, 1912.

overheard conversation on the subway, an unusual face in a crowd, or a casual remark. It may be any of these and more, but its occurrence must happen and it may be an event that will either trigger or be triggered into a full-blown play.

Many playwrights never deal with anything they have not experienced or with people and places they do not know first hand. Several playwrights have admitted that as apprentices to the craft they located their stories in exotic settings conjured up by sheer imagination. But later, with maturity and a growing awareness of the dramatic potentialities of what they knew first hand they, as Channing Pollock put it, "learned to find them in the flat across the way, or, at the farthest, around the corner."

ABILITY TO DIALOGUE REALISTICALLY RELATED TO WHAT YOU KNOW

John van Druten, in his autobiographical analysis of his own growth as a dramatist, *Playwright at Work,* reflects on his early efforts as examples of not having learned to write about what he knew. Van Druten feels that when he began to write about the things he knew best his dialogue became much better and more believable. "I went on trying to write plays," comments van Druten, "and as I wrote about the things I knew, the dialogue became better. My ear was getting trained. When I wrote about the things that I did not know, and when I tried to make jokes, it stayed bad." [4] The problems of writing dialogue will be explored in Chapter 10, and it is only necessary here to indicate that the problem is considerably lessened when the dramatist remains on familiar ground, writing about people he knows well. Owen Davis, asked to crystallize the result of his own experiences into a single sentence, appropriately said, "Dream out a story about the sort of persons you know the most about and tell it as simply as you can."

[4] John van Druten, *Playwright at Work,* Harper & Brothers, 1953, p. 19.

HUMAN LIFE ITSELF IS A DRAMA

Life, itself, with its many manifold experiences, is a drama of a sort. Human experience is filled with crises both major and minor, events that can be pyramided toward a climax to state a point of view. The incidents are there awaiting the selectivity and arrangement of the playwright, the skilled dramatist need only know the people he creates or draws upon.

"Every moment of human life is drama," declared Samuel Shipman, a prominent American playwright of thirty years ago; "moments accumulate into three or four important events in a lifetime. The intermissions we call years, the events may be the four acts of a play. The curtain is not always anticipated, as in the theatre, but it concludes a drama. Some human lives are in three acts, some in one act; but they are all moving, gripping, stirring dramas, of one kind or another." [5]

As a rule the public is not interested in a man who has written from books and second-hand sources. To write from life requires that some time should be spent in living it. This does not mean that the beginning playwright must take a recess from his writing hours to "live," but does imply that before an author can become successful he must attune himself to the reactions of the human emotions as they encounter the obstacles of life and extract those universal qualities or traits of human nature that would apply to people in any situation, circumstance, or setting.

OBSERVING LIFE

It is only logical that playwrights should possess a keen sense of observation as an essential prerequisite for creative writing. The ability to observe the real without confusing it with the stereotype is to many the most difficult task of the playwriting process.

An excellent example of the ability to distinguish the genuine from

[5] Samuel Shipman, "All Life Is Melodrama," *Theatre Magazine*, April, 1919, p. 198.

the false is demonstrated in certain experiences of the student actor. An outstanding eastern teacher of acting once took a summer teaching job in a southwestern university. The students flocked to take a course from this acting coach who received fabulous fees from New York professionals. One event of particular significance to the beginning playwright occurred that summer. The teacher, a woman, asked a girl student to walk across the stage as a prostitute. With a few minutes preparation the girl announced that she was ready. She made her entrance and the class was treated to an exhibition of the gum-chewing, hip-swinging, come-up-and-see-me-sometime stereotype. The teacher stopped the girl and asked, "Have you ever seen a prostitute?"

The girl blushed, dropped her head, and said "No, but isn't that how street walkers act?"

The teacher retorted, "You should find out. You have 24 hours." The girl blushed even more deeply, causing the teacher to inquire as to her age.

"Eighteen," came a mumbled reply.

"All right, then," countered the teacher, "meet me at my apartment at nine o'clock tonight."

That evening the girl met the teacher and accompanied her to an all-night bar and cafe. They ordered coffee and sat chatting in a booth for about 30 minutes. Suddenly the teacher leaned over and asked the girl how many prostitutes she had seen in the place. The girl looked about her confusedly and said she hadn't seen any. The teacher commented that there had been five pick-ups since they started their coffee.

"But—," stammered the girl, "the women look just like anyone else?"

"Precisely," replied the teacher. "But now look closely at the woman near the bar. What do you see?"

"I see a woman—about 35 or 40. No. Her hands and neck look younger. Her dress is inexpensive but neat. It looks like she's trying to make up her mind to speak to the man at the end of the bar."

"Good—so far. Now I would say that the woman is actually closer to 25 than 35 or 40 and that she is not plying her trade from choice but necessity. Forwardness is still difficult for her."

"Look," reported the student actress, "she's talking to the man now. I wish I knew what she was saying?"

"Never mind. The words are without importance."

"They're leaving now—together."

"Then she has been successful," commented the acting coach.

"She doesn't look like what I thought a prostitute looked like. She's attractive and not overdressed or over made-up at all. She could pass for a housewife or a department store clerk."

"But there is a difference, isn't there? Now in class tomorrow I want you to repeat the assignment I gave you this morning. Try to capture the difference."

The next morning the girl performed again. This time she gave a sensitive portrayal of a woman driven to sell her body in order to live. The created character was basically repelled by what she had to do but some strong drive kept her at her task. This was her only means of livelihood and she appeared most business-like in its execution. Beneath the surface, however, emerged a feeling that this prostitute was trapped with no chance of escape and that the fee she would collect would be most gratefully received.

The student actress had received an important lesson in observing life, in looking beneath the surface to discover the real, the genuine. The playwright could well place himself in the position of the acting student as he watches life parade past him.

A quick and keen sense of observation can provide the playwright with a wealth of dramatic material. The late Frank Craven, an actor and playwright, declared that he used a system learned as a schoolboy to exercise his powers of observation in supplying himself with a storehouse of dramatic material. With some adjustments for individual personality this system could well be employed by the beginning playwright: "At school one of the exercises I used to shine in was when a lot of us were marshaled past a window containing a number of things and afterward required to write what we saw. I have kept the exercise up. If I see a man coming down the street who attracts my attention, I study him and see what it is that has made me look at him." [6]

There may be a similarity between the faculty of observation as described here and the power of concentration. In any event, Craven's exercise as it would apply to the playwright is to sharpen his ability to focus his attention upon his surroundings, examine it in minute detail, then commit the findings to memory for future use.

Elmer Rice, a New York born and educated playwright, sees his home town as a city of raw material for the drama. The playwright need only observe, asserts Rice, and he will have at his fingertips the essentials of a play. In an article in the old *Theatre Magazine,* Rice declared, "I think that this unique and amazing city, the arena of six million souls and the focus of many millions more, is an almost undeveloped mine of dramatic material. It is impossible, if one keeps one's eyes and ears open, to move about the streets of the big city for a single day without seeing and hearing a thousand things—sordid, pathetic, vulgar, comic, entertaining, astonishing, tragic, trivial—which reveal character in action (which I believe is somebody's definition of drama)." [7]

The Craven exercise emphasizes that dramatic material may be found anywhere, whereas the Rice explanation is probably more to the liking of the beginning playwright who instinctively seeks the unusual and the glamorous and associates the term dramatic material with that which is to be found only in the metropolitan areas. It will be the wise student who realizes, however, that the Craven exercise will supply the same results when applied in Podunk, U.S.A., as in Chicago, New York, or San Francisco.

The playwright of necessity has to be a close observer of human

---

[6] *New York Press,* March 15, 1914.

[7] Elmer Rice, "New York: Raw Material for the Drama," *Theatre Magazine,* March, 1929, pp. 26, 82.

affairs if he wants to appeal to a large public. People like to see familiar incidents and characteristics transferred to the stage. The dramatist should take as his task to echo everyday hopes and fears, and the more universal these are, the more deeply rooted, the more nearly an author will approach the accomplishment of his mission. Many of the exercises in the appendix of this book, collected from some of the leading teachers of dramatic writing in the United States, are concerned with sharpening the observation faculties of the playwright, making him increasingly aware of the wealth of dramatic material about him that is his for the taking.

IMAGINATION IN PLAYWRITING

The power of observation by itself is akin to photography, but when operating in conjunction with the power of imagination it can become a tool for a higher art than is possible with a camera. Clyde Fitch, in his essay, "The Play and the Public," declared that "observation will press the button and imagination will do the rest." Fitch gave voice to what is probably the primary use of imagination in the playwriting process, the combination of the observation with the imagination.

Imagination enables the playwright to project incidents, places, and characters with which he is not familiar from observed or reflected experience. Some writers believe that the imagination is actually more important than writing about what one knows. However, it is the ability to use the imagination to depart from the known to the unknown that heralds the maturity of a writer.

It is obvious that a "stamp of authenticity" of period and setting may be acquired through research, but the behavior or emotional reaction of people, whether in the past, present, or future, is basically the same—only the language and terminology differ. Some commentators contend that Shakespeare must have studied law, been a doctor, a courtier, in order to make his people speak as they did. It is certainly possible to imagine certain experiences the author wishes to portray without having actually lived them. "If experience were absolutely essential," Edward Knoblock, author of *Kismet,* declared, "then every writer of thrillers must of necessity have been a burglar, a detective, a victim and a murderer—which is an absurdity on the face of it." [8]

Edna Ferber is one playwright-novelist who feels she can project herself by imagination to the scene of her writing. "I can project myself into any age, environment, condition, situation, character or emotion that interests me deeply," says Miss Ferber. "I need never have experienced it or seen it or, to my knowledge, heard or read about it. I never have been on the Mississippi or in the deep South. I wrote *Show Boat.*" [9]

Before the beginning playwright becomes convinced by Miss Ferber's testimonial that all one need do is sit back and allow the mind to transport him through time and space to the realm of the unfamiliar, it should be recognized that there is a universality of human nature that *must* be behind the imagination. People in all ages and all countries behave in very much the same way emotionally, self-preservation in one form or another being the fundamental purpose of all actions in life. A knowledge of human nature, therefore, can feed and stir and drive an author to create that which will evoke an emotional response. A lengthy list of motive-appeals or drives that are universal to human nature can easily be compiled by an author. For instance, some of the more basic and universal drives are love, hate, jealousy, hunger, thirst, reputation, honor, greed, avarice, wealth, property, and patriotism. The dramatic writer's knowledge of each motive and drive may be derived entirely from his own limited experience, but by projecting himself through the faculty of imagination he can transport these qualities to situations that are unfamiliar to him or to his audience. For example, is it necessary for a young writer to have been a defeated candidate for the United States Senate to understand the bitterness at having not been elected? Is it not possible for the writer to draw upon his own experience, to reach back to an occasion of extreme personal disap-

---

[8] Edward Knoblock, *Round the Room,* Chapman & Hall, Ltd., 1939, p. 109.

[9] Edna Ferber, *A Peculiar Treasure,* Garden City Publishing Company, 1940, p. 277.

pointment, and to project this experience imaginatively to describe
realistically a political candidate's reaction to defeat? Disappointment
is an experience all of us have felt to some degree.

Archibald Henderson once asked George Bernard Shaw what it is
that creates a play. Shaw answered, "Imagination. If I could tell you
more than that, my dear Henderson, I should be famous, not as a playwright, but as the greatest psychologist that ever lived." [10]

Like so many phases of the creative process, the use of imagination
defies objective treatment. One either possesses and uses it, or he possesses it and can learn to use it, or he does not possess it at all. However,
it would be wise for all aspiring dramatic writers to make themselves
students of human nature, for imagination without the knowledge of
human behavior or emotional response is of no use at all.

SOURCE OF IDEAS

Since the origin of an idea for a play is usually so complex and
subjective in nature, it is difficult to be specific regarding sources that
may give rise to full-blown plays. Some playwrights feel that generally
it is a process of suggestion and germination and probably, entirely
unknown to the dramatist, a seed is sown which eventually fructifies.
In a few cases the writer may be able to trace the suggestion to its
source in some definite scene or action, but this is the exception rather
than the rule.

"A play starts in my mind from any one of a number of different
points," claimed George Broadhurst. "I may write it all from any one
of a number of different points. I may write it all from the climax. A
character may appeal to me as sufficiently entertaining to be presented
on the stage. Sometimes an incident on the street starts a train of
thought that results in a piece for the theatre." [11] In this statement
Broadhurst touched upon two primary sources which may give rise to a

[10] George Bernard Shaw and Archibald Henderson, "Is Shaw a Dramatist?"
Forum, November, 1926, p. 260.
[11] George Broadhurst, "Some Others and Myself," Saturday Evening Post, November 20, 1926, p. 117.

play—an interesting character and an incident which may catch the attention. Other playwrights have attributed many of their plays to interesting characters they have observed.

In Chapter 3, certain contemporary dramatists were cited as receiving an idea for a play in "an inspirational flash." Whether this is true or not is of little importance, for in most of the cases discussed the playwrights agreed that an idea emerges from the subconscious turmoil of material being rotated in the mind. Moss Hart, for example, puts it this way: "One feels dry, empty, utterly without impulse or idea . . . then suddenly, sitting in the tub, eating breakfast—there it is, the germ idea, the nucleus, the jumping-off place." Now compare Hart's explanation with that offered by van Druten as to where that idea that one wants to write, that one needs to write, comes from. "How did it first strike you?" asks van Druten. "That is a question that is hard, sometimes impossible to answer. It did not come from looking for it. No amount of search is going to give you that play idea, or any idea truly worth writing. It happens to you, and you may well not always recognize it when it happens. But the moment of conception has occurred. Somewhere, in the creative cells of your being, the germinative process has started. Often, afterward, you look back to see what started it. Sometimes you can remember, sometimes you cannot." [12]

Suggestion, to some playwrights, plays an important role in the evolution of a play. Stimulating conversation is also an especially fertile source for play ideas. To listen to the talk of people, barring of course politics and religion, since these topics seldom suggest plays that beginning playwrights should touch, one is able to get a true mental stimulus. Ideas that later develop into a play come to some playwrights while listening to people talk. Mental sparks caused by the conjunction of two clever minds, a chance word, but one fully charged with drama, plays an important part in the evolution of a piece for the theatre.

[12] van Druten, *op. cit.*, p. 40.

KEEPING A NOTEBOOK

Whether it be on a scrap of paper, the back of an envelope, in a manila filing folder, or on a sheaf of paper, it is always wise to record ideas for plays and characters. It is not always possible to write down that snatch of dialogue or passing dramatic incident when it occurs, but, nevertheless, every effort should be made to record it while it is still a recent and vivid memory. The mental note soon blurs and with passing time becomes increasingly difficult to recall if the opportunity to use it arises.

Many, if not most, of our successful dramatists keep writer's notebooks. An interviewer, for example, once asked Avery Hopwood if a fat notebook reposing on his desk was part of his system. "Part?" he ejaculated, "It's practically the whole of it! It's my all-in-all, my Webster, my Baedeker, my family Bible. Into it goes every idea or notion that happens to seep into my poor old head. All my plays have come out of it." [13]

Somerset Maugham began as a young writer to fill notebooks with ideas for stories and plays, scraps of dialogue and his own reflections on what his reading and experiences suggested to him. During his long career Maugham compiled fifteen thick volumes of such notebooks. Finally, in 1949, his publisher persuaded the novelist-playwright to edit, but not rewrite, this bulk into a single volume that could be made available to the writing student as a model and a guide for keeping a notebook. Maugham complied with the request and, subsequently, *A Writer's Notebook,* covering a period from 1892 through 1944, was released to the public.

Another contemporary playwright is so adamant about the value of keeping a notebook that he once declared, "I had sooner go without my trousers than without my notebook." This writer's notebooks were crowded with descriptions of people and places, bits of dialogue and commentaries on minor incidents.

[13] John van Doren, "How to Write a Play," *Theatre Magazine,* October, 1921, p. 212.

Channing Pollock, author of *The Fool, The Enemy,* and many other successful plays, had a unique method of collecting ideas on specific themes that could well be considered by some beginning playwrights. He assigned a filing folder to each theme and this folder became a catchall for all subsequent information and material relating to that theme. "When I get a theme for a story or play or lecture, and what not," he relates in his autobiography, "I summarize it on the label of a folder. It becomes a sort of sticky flypaper. There are more than three thousand of these folders in my files; some of them have been there many years." [14]

Maugham's fifteen volumes of notes and Pollock's three thousand folders are testimony to the prodigious labor that goes into recording ideas and materials. Writing, however, is not an easy profession and whoever plans to follow it must accept its tedious as well as its rewarding moments. Not the least of these is the conscientious development of a method of recording and classifying dramatic material as it is encountered.

[14] Channing Pollock, *Harvest of My Years,* The Bobbs-Merrill Company, 1943, p. 163.

Theme and Purpose

> To act with a purpose is what raises man above the brutes, to
> invent with a purpose, to imitate with a purpose, is that which
> distinguishes genius from the petty artists who only invent to
> invent, imitate to imitate.
>
> —LESSING, *Hamburgische Dramaturgie* (1769)

A PLAY, like any other work of art, should have the overall purpose
of entertaining its audience. *To entertain,* unfortunately, is often associated with the term to *amuse.* Many people consider the two terms
synonomous. But to understand what it means to say that the primary
purpose of a play is to entertain, it is first necessary to broaden one's
understanding of the term.

To entertain is an all-embracing expression that includes amusement
but goes beyond it. Many people are honestly entertained by a debate
on foreign policy, or a lecture on horticulture, or a discussion of meta-
physics. A parliamentary body *entertains* a motion when it considers it.
Semantically, the term *to entertain* has many meanings, but when
applied to a work of art it is basically concerned with the reaction of
the viewer. In this case, to entertain should be thought of as a gratification of the senses—in other words *to please.*

The senses, however, are not gratified by emotions alone. Oftentimes
the gratification is on an intellectual plane. This is to say that to entertain is the ability to please an audience emotionally and/or intellec-

tually. If one accepts this broader definition of the term it is possible to understand that the primary purpose of the drama is to entertain.

THE AUDIENCE DEMANDS ENTERTAINMENT

The public, the people who frequent theatres and motion picture palaces, who turn to television channels, do so for a purpose. The dramatic media are to many people places where one may escape from a burdened existence. The various media, therefore, take as one of their primary missions the giving of relief and pleasure, which may be accomplished both by laughter and tears.

According to David Belasco, a play gives relief and pleasure through dramatic action and dialogue "of what stirs, burns and works within" and reveals "to duller eyes and colder hearts the lonely, sympathetic and endearing elements of human nature." Therefore the audience is primarily responsible for the overall purpose of the play being to entertain rather than to enlighten. The drama has been a great popular form of entertainment and relaxation because of the demands of the public, but it should be carefully noted that the truly great plays, such as *Oedipus Rex, Hamlet,* and *Death of a Salesman,* appeal to both the *mind* and the *heart.*

EVERY PLAY IS WRITTEN TO PLEASE EMOTIONALLY AND/OR INTELLECTUALLY

To quicken the pulses in one way or another is to many dramatists the chief purpose of dramatic art. Every play is written to please—emotionally and/or intellectually. The first duty of a dramatist is to be entertaining, and while many faults can be forgiven a play the fault of being dull is unpardonable.

Drama at its best combines the appeal to the intellect with an appeal to the emotions. Successful playwrights instinctively strive to strike a happy medium between emotional and intellectual appeal. It is the province of the dramatic media *to entertain.* There are some who will insist that the drama should *instruct* its audience. Such plays, perhaps, have their place, although most of them are best examined under the library lamp. However, if in addition to appealing to the emotions and intellect, a play *also* instructs, such instruction is usually acceptable and often very effective.[1] But the plays which do appeal, not to a minority section of the public but to most sections of it, must first of all be entertaining.

The living theatre, therefore, is for all the people, not for any especially enlightened few. The common desire for entertainment, and the means by which it is gratified, certainly have altered only super-ficially during the last fifty years—perhaps in the twenty-odd centuries before that.

GRATIFICATION OF THE SENSES

That which provokes laughter among men is cherished as an imme-diate means of gratifying the senses, since that which causes man to look at himself and smile is an instantly observable occurrence. It is understandable why so many choose to attend or view the various forms of the comic muse, such as comedy or farce, as the chief means of gratifying or pleasing their senses.

But in the realm of serious drama, from classical to modern tragedy, the gratification of the senses also has been of primary concern. Eugene O'Neill, who wrote almost entirely in the realm of the serious, conceived his overall task to be similar to that of the Greek dramatists, to show man's struggle to conquer life and give it meaning. By showing that struggle, O'Neill believed he was showing that man loves life. He was once called upon to defend himself against the charge that he wrote of only the sordid, seamy side of life, of poor and sinful wretches, all apparently contrary to the conceived purpose of the drama to enter-tain or please. "As for this type of play having a depressing effect, or accentuating the futility of human endeavor, I do not agree with any such opinion," asserted O'Neill. "We should feel exalted to think that

---

[1] The young men, not old enough for the hunt, were being effectively in-structed while being entertained by the primitive drama recounted in Chapter 1.

there is something—some vital, unquenchable flame in man which makes him triumph over his miseries—over life itself. Dying, he is still victorious. The realization of this should exalt, not depress." [2] Does an audience feel depressed at Antigone's defeat at the hands of the tyrant Creon, or Hamlet's death at the end of his duel, or Willy Loman's suicide with an automobile?

EVERY PLAY SHOULD HAVE A THEME

Though contemporary dramatists—indeed, almost all of the great dramatists of the past and present—conceived the drama to be a form of entertainment, they have been equally insistent that a play should have a theme, a central thought or underlying idea, which serves as the unifying agent.

The importance of the theme, the unifying agent, to the success of a play was stated thus by playwright Charles Klein: "The important thing is the idea, not the lines, but what is between the lines, the theme of the playwright. It is what binds the play together, what gives it that most important thing in all art—unity of impression." [3]

Playwrights are essentially in agreement with Mr. Klein. Rachel Crothers, for instance, says, "I have convictions. I believe every playwright has or no play could be written." John Galsworthy suggested that a drama must be so shaped as to have a spire of meaning. It is necessary for a play to have something to say, otherwise it is a work of incoherent platitude or indecent appeal that contradicts the purpose of the drama.

The late Robert E. Sherwood, author of such moving plays as *Abe Lincoln in Illinois* and *There Shall Be No Night,* saw a universality of message in describing what the great plays of the past and present have had to say: "What Sophocles and Shakespeare said—which all of the great dramatists, tragic and comic, have said—is that man is frail, man

---

[2] Carol Bird, "Eugene O'Neill—The Inner Man," *Theatre Magazine,* June, 1924, p. 9.
[3] *New York Press,* March 1, 1914.

is vain, man is mortal—but that he is still capable of reaching, as did Prometheus, into the highest heaven and snatching the very fire from the hand of God." [4]

THE THEMATIC APPROACH IS SUBJECTIVE

Every work of art expresses a point of view. As the artist approaches his material, which may be the same material for other artists, he brings to it his own approach. He attempts to express something. The material is shaped and fashioned, whether it be paints, clay, or words, to state a point of view. It is this point of view, this underlying concept, that lends unity and coherence to the whole. Without this unifying ingredient there would be no purpose, no meaning to the work of art.

How one playwright fashions or tells a story will differ drastically from the approach another dramatist may adopt in telling the same story. What determines the difference? The playwright brings to his telling of a story the reflection of his own ideas, his own outlook on things and events. This shaping of the material along certain lines is in all likelihood an unconscious process.

A writer's outlook on his material is in part a result of his heritage and the influence of the civilization or society within which he exists. Modern society is a moral society and as a product of this society it is inescapable that the writer reflects the basic tenets of that society. It all began when men became civilized and learned to live together. In this sense, the playwright imparts a message to his play, his work of art, though he may be unconscious that he is doing so when he approaches his material.

MOST THEMES ARE SERIOUS

There is naturally a distinction between the major purpose of a play from the audience's point of view and the function of the theme from the playwright's standpoint. Drama is an art, and as such its use is

[4] Robert E. Sherwood, "The Vanishing American Playwright," *Saturday Review of Literature,* February 1, 1941, p. 41.

undeniably to stir the emotions—but because a play is capable of stirring emotions is not alone sufficient justification for its presentation. "The emotions may be constructive in their effect, or destructive," said Augustus Thomas, "the urge may be toward or away from the animal in man. It is essential that the emotions to which the play appeals shall be those whose urge is the benefit of our present civilization as we understand it." [5]

No matter how one approaches a work of dramatic literature it usually can be reduced to a statement of theme that is calculated to move men to acts of good rather than evil. This is as true of comedies as it is of serious dramas. Three examples should suffice to establish the universality of serious themes among comedies.

In 1845 Anna Cora Mowatt made American history when she became this country's first successful woman dramatist, with a comedy entitled *Fashion*. Not only was it well received here but it became the first American-authored play to achieve fame in Europe. *Fashion* may still be successfully revived today and often is. The reason for the comedy's continued success is probably due to the timeliness of its serious theme. Though poking fun at people who live by fashion rather than being themselves, *Fashion* paints a vivid picture of how ridiculous people appear when they try to be something they aren't. Since many people of the mid-twentieth century strongly resemble their 1845 "fashion plate" counterparts, the play still drives home its serious message, and modern audiences are as convulsed with laughter by the ludicrous scenes as were those over a hundred years ago.

A play of more recent vintage, *Solid Gold Cadillac,* became the laugh sensation of Broadway and the Civic Theatre circuit and afterward on the nation's motion picture screens by showing what could happen when a middle-aged actress, "between engagements," drops in at the annual stockholders meeting of a large corporation in which she holds the magnificent sum of ten shares, and starts asking embarrassing

[5] Augustus Thomas, "A Playwright's Views," *Review of Reviews,* April, 1927, p. 402.

questions of the management. Before the lady, Mrs. Laura Partridge, is through the entire board of directors has been toppled and control of the corporation rests in the hands of the millions of small shareholders who have given Mrs. Partridge their proxies. The play adroitly pokes fun at big business and in doing so drives home the theme that even the smallest stockholders should take an active interest in how the large corporations they own are run. There is an amusingly presented but serious secondary theme in *Solid Gold Cadillac* which reveals the Congressional red tape that drives out of government this nation's talented leaders of industry and business who have accepted presidential appointments.

The last example to illustrate the contention that comedies, regardless of the farcical antics presented, usually have themes of a serious nature is drawn from one of television's most popular situation comedy series, *I Love Lucy*. In one episode, Lucy's husband, Ricky, had an opportunity to take a screen test for the role of Don Juan in a motion picture based on the romantic hero's escapades. Lucy was overjoyed at her husband's good fortune and promptly set about to help Ricky learn his lines. On the day of the screen test a problem arose. The actress who was to appear opposite Ricky was ill. Ricky had to complete the test on that particular day so that the film could be sent immediately to Hollywood for consideration. There was not time to train another actress. There was only one other person who knew the lines—Lucy. She was thrilled at the chance to appear before the cameras—too thrilled as a matter of fact. For most of the play the audience was amused by the sight of Lucy stepping between her husband and the camera as she tried to take the spotlight away from Ricky. Of course in the end Ricky won the role of Don Juan, but not before Lucy and the audience became aware of the play's serious theme—that we often hurt those we love most when we selfishly think of ourselves.

It is true that there must be room in the dramatic media for plays with strong themes, such as stated by *Death of a Salesman,* for the task of the true dramatist is to translate the best thoughts into action, to reduce them to terms understood by the average man, to dramatize them, and to make them interesting to him.

SUBJECT-THEME CONFUSION

When a theatregoer is asked what a play's theme is, he often will reply, "Well, it's *about*—" and then proceeds to tell what the play's subject is, believing he is answering the question. What a play is about is its subject or topic, but the point of view, the stand it takes or wants the audience to take, is its theme.

Damaged Goods by Eugene Brieux offers an example of the subject-theme confusion that may arise. The play is about venereal disease and its effect. While the subject is the same as Ibsen's *Ghosts,* Brieux is more interested in its physical ravages and how they can be prevented, whereas Ibsen was mostly concerned with the moral aspects of venereal disease.

When first produced in the United States, *Damaged Goods* caused quite a furor, not because of its theme, which was calculated to benefit society, but because its subject, venereal disease, was then surrounded by secrecy and ignorance. In the play a young man learns on the eve of his wedding that he has syphilis. Disregarding the advice of a reputable doctor, the man marries after six months treatment by a "quack." A child is born and it inherits the syphilis. The man goes back to the physician and is told he may not even keep a nurse for the child since she and her offspring may be contaminated. The wife learns the secret and wants a divorce. Her father wants to shoot the scoundrel. The doctor intervenes, pleads for tolerance, and holds out hope for a cure.

The play is charged with action and conflict, not sermons. The action demonstrates to an audience a point of view which may be phrased as the play's theme: Strip venereal disease of its secrecy and by adopting compulsory premarital physical examinations eliminate the ravages of the disease being passed on from one generation to the next.

STATEMENT OF THEME SHOULD BE IMPLICIT

A play should definitely have an ethical purpose but not one thrust sermonlike upon an audience. The moment a play assumes an attitude of *educational* seriousness, then it is obviously conspiring to utilize the stage as a teacher's platform, and this oversteps its artistic limitations. The man who writes a popular hit does not attempt to sermonize, for the playwright's and the missionary's calling are distinct and should not be permitted to overlap; an audience does not come to the theatre to hear a lecture.

Entire plays have been spoiled by being smothered in the theme. If a play's theme is so stated that the play becomes a sermon or a long preachment of a point of view or sheer propaganda, then its overall purpose becomes subservient to its central idea, or theme. In this respect a playwright should strive to remain outside of his play and avoid filling it with pet theories of life. The shadow of the author must never fall across the play *explicitly,* but instead be embodied within the action *implicitly.*

Remember the motion pictures produced during World War II? They have begun to haunt us on television's late shows, especially those dedicated to proving how just the cause of the Allies was. To establish the premise that the enemy was morally depraved and basically evil and therefore a worthy foe for our honorable boys in khaki, the motion pictures availed themselves of several explicit devices. Remember the number of closeups of the grinning Japanese aviator as he pressed the trigger when he had a helpless parachuting American aviator in his sights. The scene was sheer propaganda designed to anger the populace against the enemy.

The portrayal of an act as either heroic or lunatic depends upon the point of view of the audience. If an American pilot crashed his stricken plane with its cargo of bombs onto the deck of an enemy carrier, he was heroic. However, if the enemy pilot did the same thing, he was a lunatic, a suicide pilot probably hopped up with narcotics. Other such explicit scenes, usually divorced from the story line of the war drama, were dished up for the American public. There were scenes showing drunken German soldiers forcing themselves upon the helpless women of a conquered country, and closeups of enemy officers giving the order to torture a captured American soldier. Today the scenes are no longer timely. The adhering quality of the device, like that of the pasted-on label, has lost its holding effect. There should be a lesson in this for the writer who desires to impart a point of view calculated to move men to good acts rather than evil.

A play dealing with the problem of integrating Southern schools was delivered to a teacher of playwriting at a midwestern university. The teacher was moved by the first act as it related the story of two young schoolgirls, one a Negro and the other white, who were thrown together to share a double desk. The pair were also backdoor neighbors, which added to the conflict. The first act developed nicely. The protagonist was clearly evident and at the act's conclusion the reader turned with interest to the second act—only to be bitterly disappointed. This act was set in a schoolroom. The schoolteacher, a man who had had his house burned down for favoring integration of the races in the public school system, was presiding over a PTA meeting attended by both white and Negro mothers. The action of the play came to a standstill while the author had his new set of characters restate all of the standard arguments concerning the race problem. Act Three brought the story line back in focus, but it was too late. The explicitness of the play's message as expressed in the second act was too heavy a burden for the play to regain momentum. The play had died when the school teacher opened the meeting with, "We all face a problem. Let us discuss it openly so that we may understand each other's point of view." The playwright had decided it would be easier to *tell* us his theme rather than *show* us dramatically, as he had started out to do with his compelling first act.

"Any subject which requires long dissertation to make itself clear to the audience has no place on the stage," Belasco once said. A play must be presented through action and dialogue; if the theme of the drama cannot be put across the footlights through the medium of human action and the natural and inevitable dialogue growing out of such action, then the author should seek other than the dramatic form to expound his theories and ideas. A play loses its franchise over an audience the moment it discusses the framework of the almost perfect Utopia.

IMPLICIT STATEMENT SHOWS RATHER THAN TELLS

J. M. Barrie once wrote a letter to fellow-Englishman John Galsworthy thanking him for sending a copy of his play, *Loyalties,* and telling him that probably the drama's most striking quality was that, "You are telling your audience all the time that there is here a matter for them to think about, without ever addressing a covert word to them. That is certainly the most difficult part of playwriting, and probably its chief art." [6] What Barrie praised in Galsworthy's play "as the most difficult part of playwriting" was to Galsworthy an unconscious process, for as Galsworthy said, "It may happen that when my work is finished, it actually demonstrates or refutes something. So much the better if it does, at least from the point of view of those who wish the problem to be presented as I presented it. Personally, I am totally indifferent to the conclusion to be drawn from my premises." [7] What Galsworthy meant is that if a conviction, albeit an unconscious one, can be clothed in a dramatic story it can make an entertaining play.

Implicit statement of theme is actually the showing of things rather than dogmatically stating a philosophy. What the dramatic media can do by telling a story that *shows* things instead of preaching them is almost endless. A famous American playwright of the early twentieth century, Clyde Fitch, compiled a list that is still valid today. He wrote: "As a matter of fact, a list of what the theatre can do would be

[6] H. V. Marrot, *The Life and Letters of John Galsworthy,* Charles Scribner's Sons, 1936, pp. 514–515.

[7] Andre Triven, "An Interview with the Author of *The Pigeon,*" *Theatre Magazine,* May, 1912, p. 160.

almost endless. It can breed patriotism! It can inculcate the love of truth! It can show the disaster inevitable which follows the breaking of the law: moral and civic. It can train the mind to choose the victory of doing the right thing at any sacrifice! It can teach the ethics of life, little and big, by *example,* which is better for the careless multitude than by precept." [8]

There need be no fear that the implicit statement of a play's central idea cannot be reconciled to an overall purpose of entertainment. After all, the audience has the right to require respect and consideration in its dramatic fare. The average audience possesses a good disposition and it does not really mind being taught something so long as the message or lesson does not hit them with the force of a club. As Fitch concluded in his essay, "Don't let it know what it is taking till the lesson is down, remembering always that the theatre in our day is principally to entertain."

The young dramatist is like most young men; he is impressionable and eager to defend the rights of the oppressed and to pick up the banner of justice and wave it. Most youths go through a period of almost total liberalness in mind and spirit. In this state there is a natural tendency to go right to the heart of a message and to state it boldly, like a medieval knight throwing down the gauntlet in prelude to combat.

To succeed as a popular playwright the young dramatist must neither give up his ideas nor alter the gist of his message. He will, however, have to learn to express his ideas entertainingly. Playwright J. Hartley Manners cited one of his own plays to illustrate the edict that a dramatic writer should never preach but utilize the stage to show conditions. "For instance," said Manners, "in 'The House Next Door,' I made no attempt to have Jacobson extol the virtues of the Jews, when he might very plausibly and humanly have done so after many insults had been heaped on him by his Gentile neighbors. I made him act out his character by putting it to a visible test. He showed gentle-

---

[8] Clyde Fitch, "The Play and the Public," *Plays of Clyde Fitch,* Little, Brown & Company, 1921, p. xix.

ness and tact; he didn't preach it. And not merely did he show these qualities on the stage, but he often showed them in actual dramatic conflict with the other protagonists of the play." [9]

One of the major questions that goes unanswered by teachers of playwriting is: Why do young dramatists never seem to learn the simple principle of having a moral or intellectual thesis acted and not talked about in a play? Think of the power and eloquence of Galsworthy's *Justice,* gained for the most part by the almost elementary expedient of showing both sides without comment. As Somerset Maugham declared, "It is in the actual conflict of actual ideas as they exist side by side, however old or however new they may happen to be." The task, then, of the true dramatist is to translate the best thought into action, to reduce it to terms understood by the average man, to dramatize it for him, and make it interesting.

It is indeed possible for a playwright to teach a moral, but to find a wide public he must first be entertaining. He must realize that the public will not pay its money to be preached to unless it enjoys the methods by which the sermon is delivered. The logical answer to give the young playwright is to be as serious as he pleases in his theme, but never to show it in the play. However, he should also take cognizance of the fact that many of the great masters claimed that they never wrote with a premeditated purpose, but rather, being moral beings, the product of a civilized society, they could not avoid taking a moral stand.

O'Neill said, "I do not write with a premeditated purpose. I write of life as I see it. As it exists for many of us. If people leave the theatre after one of my plays with a feeling of compassion for those less fortunate than they I am satisfied. I have not written in vain." [10]

One cannot deny the need for important and vital themes in American drama. It is hoped that as new writers emerge they will acquire the skill necessary to cover and conceal a high purpose while communicating it through a story devised to be presented to an audience.

9 *New York Press,* December 7, 1913.
10 Bird, *op. cit.,* p. 9.

Character Creation

The dramatist who hangs his characters to his plot instead of hanging his plot to his characters is guilty of cardinal sin.
—JOHN GALSWORTHY

THOUGH plot is probably of more importance to the audience than character, the characters of a play are usually of greater interest to the dramatist. A plot is often contrived and its construction is frequently more mechanical than creative. Since the playwright is essentially an artist, it is only natural that he should be more concerned with the elements of the playwriting process that afford him the widest opportunity for creativity. As indicated in previous chapters, plays evolve from characters in action and in conflict with one another, and an audience will instinctively polarize around a character or a group of characters striving to attain a worthy goal. This chapter is concerned with the process of creating characters from which drama may spring.

Once the idea for the play is germinated, many playwrights begin the dramatic-writing process with the development of characters. Rachel Crothers, for instance, said that in her experience "the idea comes first, the characters second and the story last of all."

Plays of all periods which have achieved real fame are usually associated preëminently with character creation. Whether it be an Oedipus, a Hamlet, a Hedda Gabler, an Anna Christie, or a Willy

Loman, the vitality of the character creation is the key to such permanence as may attach to the play. Characterization is the life of comedy, tragedy, and serious drama, for it is characters and not ideas that give them power. This perhaps explains why farce and melodrama, emphasizing actions and situations more than characters, seldom survive the generation in which they are written.

CHARACTERIZATION IS A MYSTERIOUS PROCESS

The characterization process defies analysis, for as John Galsworthy has said, "the whole question of character creation is mysterious, perhaps more mysterious to one who creates character than to those who smile or sniff under the creation." He continued: "The process has no dosier, is devoid of documentation, and resists precise definition." [1]

The clue to the problem lies in Galsworthy's use of the limiting adjective, "precise." Perhaps, by describing the two definite limitations faced by the playwright who attempts to create character, an indirect approach to the mysteries of character creation can be formulated.

The first handicap to creating dimensional and believable characters is the limitation of time. The evolution of a character for the dramatic media is made difficult because it must take place in a much shorter length of time than would be possible in real life or in a novel. When a dramatic writer tries to embody a complete character, one that compels audience interest, he is faced with the necessity of compressing all character-revealing traits into a short period of time.

The second drawback to the dramatist's creative freedom is the physical limitation set by the various dramatic media, especially that imposed by the stage. Regardless of the medium, however, it is certainly possible to ignore this limitation of space, though this may drive the cost-conscious producer to distraction. When one is trying to imagine a new being with the attributes and qualities of a real person, it is most frustrating to remember that his characters can only

---

[1] John Galsworthy, "Creation of Character in Literature," in *Candelabra,* Charles Scribner's Sons, 1933, p. 291.

do this or that owing to the limitations of a time and space which cannot be enlarged.

One of the few sets of rules which must be observed during the dramatic-writing process are those governing the physical limitations of a medium. Almost inevitably the dramatist does think of these limitations while writing. To think of them is called "obeying the rules of your medium," and demonstrates that a thorough knowledge of them is a prerequisite to writing an effective play.

CHARACTERS SHOULD BE FULLY CONCEIVED BEFORE WRITING BEGINS

It is essential to fully conceive and develop each character prior to actually writing the play. Some playwrights find it helpful to write complete histories, beginning with the character's actions since early childhood and coming up to the moment of his entrance in the play's action. This enables him to have an overall picture that can later be crystallized or heightened into a believable dramatic character. Often the writing of such profiles will in themselves suggest possible situations that will reveal character traits and may even possibly lead to full-blown plays. This is the reason so many teachers of playwriting have their beginning students concentrate on the writing of profiles of unique or unusual persons.

In the next chapter, on plot construction, the writing of the scenario will be more fully treated. It is appropriate here, however, to indicate that some playwrights in writing a scenario include the action a character would perform while off-stage so that the forward development and growth of the character in relation to the other characters and to the plot will be clearly formulated in their minds.

Rachel Crothers, who claimed that simultaneously with the inception of the idea for a play an imaginative picture of the characters appeared in her mind, said in an interview that it was absolutely necessary for the playwright to visualize his characters strongly and sympathetically before writing a single line. A certain danger exists in not developing a character fully before writing the dialogue. If they are not rich characters and have to be built up later, then they give just as much trouble, if not more, than the story itself. Every dramatist should not only know the story of each character as he or she appears in the play, but he should know their antecedents, their background and history.

Many theorists on dramaturgy believe that a play arises from the conflict of characters. "It is the clash of these characters upon each other," one playwright claims, "that produces drama." But before any real clash can take place between any two characters, or a conflict arise within a character, it is necessary first to fully conceive and develop the personalities of all characters. Unless the playwright knows the strengths and weaknesses of his people, then it is unlikely that he can have any genuine conflict that will give rise to the action of the play.

"The perfect dramatist," wrote Galsworthy in discussing the achievement of character creation, "rounds up his characters and facts within the ring-fence of a dominant idea which fulfills the craving of his spirit." Galsworthy's next step was then to take his characters and knit them together with his idea.

The playwright, poised with pen in hand, must see the characters clearly in his mind. He does not consciously make a character logical, or characteristic; he imagines him, creates him, becomes for the moment the character, and then turns him loose.

Shaw, in a conversation with his official biographer, Archibald Henderson, said, "My procedure is to imagine characters and let them rip, as you suggest, but I must warn you that the real process is very obscure." He then explained that the end result, the created character, always shows that there has been something behind the creation all the time, though it defies analysis or definition.[2]

Willard Mack, writing in 1927, provided perhaps the most all-embracing summation of the detail with which a character must be conceived in the mind of the playwright: "When writing a play of today you must visualize people as they are, their mode of living, their home, associates, conversation, aims and ambitions; in fact, the most minute detail must be carefully considered and measured before the finished product is presented to the public." [3]

CHARACTERS SHOULD MOLD THE ACTION

Fully conceived characters can give rise to the plot or action. The dramatist first elaborates an idea, then supplies the characters to better illustrate or convey that idea. As Edward Sheldon once said, "The idea demands certain types of characters," which in turn require "a certain kind of story." Rachel Crothers, who followed the same process of idea-to-character-to-story, said that "given a certain character, she must live out her destiny. What she does is the logical outcome of her character."

Writers who elect to let the story be developed by the characters usually follow the method of first creating a group of characters that interest them and then letting them live together for a while. They make their own story, since it is the clash of characters upon each other that produces drama. It is in this sense that plays will write themselves if the characters are sufficiently clear in the author's mind and are allowed to take the story in their own hands.

In explaining what is meant by "allowing" the characters to develop the plot, A. A. Milne said, "If a character be truly imagined, he will behave characteristically, almost in spite of the author; in which case, his character rather than his action may need further explanation." [4]

Owen Davis, who explored the process of plot growing out of character, prefaced his remarks with the remark that: "The plot of a play, at least the plot of a good play, should arise from the natural

---

[3] Willard Mack, "The New Realism of the Stage," *Theatre Magazine*, April, 1927, p. 21.
[4] A. A. Milne, "Introduction," *Four Plays*, G. P. Putnam's Sons, 1932, p. xiv.

actions of the character whom the author elects." Davis would dream out a complete character, surrounding him with rather vague and shadowy secondary characters. "My plot," explained Davis, "grows out of some development in the personality of these people themselves." To illustrate his process, he explained how he developed a play for a well-known character actor. The first picture that came into his mind was that of a rugged, self-made man of middle age, in a good position in society, and of certain peculiarities of disposition. As the figure grew more vivid, Davis built his family around him—wife, daughter, son, and the young people who were in love with his daughter and son. As Davis maintained this key character in different surroundings of emotional stress—happiness, sadness, etc.—the story began to crystallize itself more through its effect upon the character than through any carefully arranged system of Davis'.

If a dramatist elects the Davis method of evolving a plot then he should endeavor to see that the action shall develop naturally from the impulses which lie in the hearts and minds of the characters as they have been conceived. To quote Galsworthy once more: "The dramatist who hangs his characters to his plot instead of hanging his plot to his characters is guilty of cardinal sin."

Clearly defined and established characters will say only what is appropriate to their character. "If you know your people well," Lillian Hellman once said, "they say what they have to say for you almost of their own accord, when it comes to writing them down." In other words, by taking care of character the dialogue, like action, will take care of itself.

More will be said about this matter of dialogue in Chapter 10.

CHARACTER CREATION AND THE FORMS OF DRAMA

The four common forms of drama—tragedy or serious drama, comedy, melodrama, and farce—can be differentiated by their degree of character emphasis.

In tragedy, the action springs from the impetus of the tragic hero as he strives to attain the goal he can never reach. From his incessant drive against the obstacles he must surmount, and only from this drive, emerges the true power of the tragedy. In a melodrama the emphasis is not upon the character, but instead upon the actions and situations with which he is confronted. Tragedy is a drama of character; melodrama, however, is a drama of situations.

The same division can be drawn between comedy and farce. The humor of a true comedy stems primarily from a character as he faces certain situations. The pleasure or laughter derived from a farce is more likely to come from the emphasis upon the comic situations encountered. In a comedy, a stiff-backed conservative father may be found trying to explain the facts of life to his already knowing offspring. The humor is largely derived from the father's embarrassment, which is an outgrowth of his character. In a farce, the emphasis may be placed upon one character hitting another in the face with a lemon chiffon pie. In a comedy the characters are of most importance; in a farce the pie-throwing act receives the greater emphasis.

CHARACTER PROBLEMS

An insight into the process of character creation may perhaps be afforded by examining some of the specific problems encountered by the practicing playwright. Many writers will never be faced with these problems, or, if they are, will find little difficulty surmounting them. The following examples are cited, however, to illustrate the most common problems likely to arise in the creation of characters for the dramatic media.

Total Personality

The most common problem in character creation, other than obvious stereotyping, is probably in the creation of dimensional characters. Dimensionality suggests many-sidedness, yet writers often produce characters with only a one sided personality.

Many consider personality to be the *sum* total of a man's relationship with his constantly changing environment, yet in a new playwright's script the characters will sometimes be made to react in the same manner to different characters and to different situations. But people are not like that at all. The director knows that when he stops rehearsal to ask an actor what his attitude is toward each person on stage with him and then requires him to reflect those attitudes. If the playwright has created a one-dimensional character, the actor will find it difficult, if not impossible, to reflect any differences as he meets people in different situations and utters the dialogue given him by the dramatist.

We have all met people who are one-dimensional. There is a sameness about them no matter where you meet them. But the fully dimensional person cannot help but reveal his varying attitudes or responses. Why else are we apprehensive when we know that two of our friends with opposing personalities or viewpoints are going to be seated at the same table at the weekly bridge party?

People react differently and an individual you may know well may be an entirely different person to someone else. If you don't believe this, observe carefully the next time you attend a mixed group affair where some people know others but not everyone present and those they do know were previously encountered in entirely different situations. How is a person going to respond to being introduced about the room to the other guests? How cordial will he be to his wife's former suitor? What will be his reaction to meeting his employer whom he has only known in an office situation? Will it be the same as toward his associate with whom he plays golf every Saturday? Or toward a client from whom he hopes to land a large account for the firm? The answer is he will react differently toward each person, even though the social occasion demands a spirit of cordiality and to some extent a uniformity of manners.

The premodern playwrights were not faced with the problem of revealing a character's true feelings only through action and dialogue. The *aside,* directed toward the audience, yet apparently unheard by the other characters on stage, often revealed a character's true feelings.

For example, there is little doubt as to the real character of Count Jolimaitre when we first meet him in *Fashion*. His hostess, the fashion-struct Mrs. Tiffany, says: "I blush to confess that I have never traveled, —while you, Count, I presume are at home in all the courts of Europe." The Count replies: *"Courts?* Eh? Oh, yes, Madam, very true. I believe I am pretty well known in some of the courts of Europe." The Count then turns to the audience and gives the aside: *"Police* courts."

In presentational plays it was not unusual for a character to appear alone on stage and in a solo speech or soliloquy reveal his innermost thoughts and desires. With our present-day emphasis on representational drama, the dramatist writing for stage presentation must be content to reveal such thoughts in the course of the play's natural action. The films still find it possible to reveal a character's feelings by allowing him to speak "voice over" as the action occurs. The narrative first person approach has not been very successful when applied to the stage. Eugene O'Neill experimented with asides in modern plays when he wrote *Strange Interlude,* in which the action of the play would freeze while the character spoke his private thoughts. But by and large, unless the modern playwright is writing presentational drama, he will have to be satisfied to incorporate true feelings within natural actions and dialogue.

Just as our attitudes toward people sometimes change, characters in a play may change their attitudes toward each other as the plot progresses. It is up to the playwright to capture such changes as well as to reveal present relationships between a set of characters.

Making Characters Likeable

In the chapter on the playwright's audience the tendency of an audience to polarize around a protagonist was discussed. It was stated there that the audience must care what happens to the central character and want him to attain his goal. Identification with a character is almost impossible, however, if you are unable basically to like the person offered as the play's protagonist.

Yet dramatic literature is filled with countless examples of central figures who, if taken at face value, would not be thought likeable or worthy of identification. A few of these would be Doc, the alcoholic in *Come Back, Little Sheba*; Anna, the former prostitute in *Anna Christie*; Johnny, the young drug addict in *A Hatful of Rain*; and Willy Loman, the small man with big illusions in *Death of a Salesman*.

How does a writer make such figures acceptable to an audience as protagonists worthy of identification? William Inge solved the problem in *Come Back, Little Sheba*. Doc, the alcoholic, is earnestly trying to break the addiction and is even working with Alcoholics Anonymous to save skid row derelicts. He is also very much in love with his wife, Lola, and when we first meet him he is fixing breakfast for her.

Life has not been kind to Doc and Lola, yet we like them and in a way admire their courage to face each day. In a scene where Lola is looking at the past and reflecting on what life would have been if things had happened differently, Doc reveals his philosophy:

DOC: No . . . no, Baby. We should never feel bad about what's past. What's in the past can't be helped. You . . . you've got to forget it and live for the present. If you can't forget the past, you stay in it and never get out. I might be a big M.D. today, instead of a chiropractor; we might have a nice house, and comforts, and friends. But we don't have any of those things. So what! We gotta keep on living don't we? I can't stop just 'cause I made a few mistakes. I gotta keep goin' . . . somehow.

Doc has had bad luck, but much of it was as a result of his own weakness and inability to cope with life. Doc is like many people; he knows what he should do, but doing it is not so easy. Though Doc is weak he gives what strength he has to Lola. It is not difficult to care what happens to them.

A little humorous emphasis is often enough to transform a wicked person into a funny one, or one possessing redeeming factors, as found in the character of Long John Silver in *Treasure Island*, for example. In characterizing criminal types, crooks can be made sympathetic by making them clever. Was there ever a more attractive character than that of Raffles, the international diamond and jewel thief, even though the motion picture code decreed that he must get his "come-uppance" before the film ended, lest the audience come to believe that crime does pay?

Romantic treatment can sometimes elevate the criminal to an endearing level. In John Gay's *The Beggar's Opera*, the hero, Macheath, is the leader of a band of highwaymen. Macheath is a handsome cutthroat, attracted by and attractive to the ladies. The romantic charm of this character was such that Bertholdt Brecht and Kurt Weill retold his escapades in *The Threepenny Opera*, an epic treatment of the Gay play.

There is perhaps a deep instinct in most of us to be pleased when anyone who has committed only crimes against property "gets away with the goods." How else can you account for our acceptance of such characters as Robin Hood, overlooking, of course, the fact that his antagonists, Prince John and the Sheriff of Nottingham, have baser, more selfish motives than he? The Robin Hood character has become a standardized protagonist type in modern dramaturgy. Witness the immortality Pepe Le Moko has achieved in the various Hollywood versions of the activities of this Robin Hood of the Casbah of Casablanca.

There is a danger of making the protagonist too good. "Perfect" people sometimes alienate our affections with their unselfish "do-goodness" as much as do the most despicable and unsympathetic villains. Characters who are too good usually offend us, for we like our heroes to have some of the human failings we all possess, especially if we are to identify with them. This is a genuine problem in dramatic writing, made more so by the absence of examples from dramatic literature. Since most problems of characterization are solved before production and subsequent publication, little can be learned from the better-known plays that have been anthologized. The plays that have failed in performance rarely are preserved for inspection by the beginning dramatist. However, an example of the problem of having a protagonist that was "too good" occurred recently in a master's thesis production at Michigan State University. The central figure was a woman in her forties. For years she had been the head of the household and her brothers and sisters depended upon her. She unselfishly tended to their needs, even after they had married and had families of their own. The character was so good that she turned the other cheek every time she was hurt by her family and when she has an opportunity to find happiness through marriage, almost loses it by trying to "help" the man she loves solve a problem he wants to forget. The author tried to make the woman's goodness her flaw, but the audience cared so little for the "perfect" woman that they didn't care whether she attained her goal of happiness or not.

Most of us can understand a weakness more readily than we can a strength. For the past two thousand years dramatists have capitalized on this basic reaction by audiences. Even the noblest of the Greek tragic heroes possessed a tragic flaw and it was this chink in their armor that caused their ultimate downfall.

The sympathy of the audience that must be won by the dramatist for his central figures enters into what some playwrights consider an infallible method for writing a successful play: First, you make your audience like your central character. Second, you make them *want* your central character to attain a certain object. Third, you put in the way of your protagonist an apparently insurmountable obstacle to this attainment, and, fourth, you have him surmount it. From this approach it is only normal for one to observe how plot grows out of character.

Basing Characters upon Real Life Models

One of the topics of Chapter 6, "Finding Dramatic Material," was the discovery of ideas for plays in the study of interesting and dramatically unusual persons either observed or known by the dramatist. Many problems of character creation are alleviated when the writer bases his characters upon real life models. Not that he should photographically reproduce a real person! Instead he should draw from that person the qualities he desires and combine them with others he wants his stage character to possess. Using real life models provides a point of departure that at least solves the playwright's task of getting started, which, after all, is probably his chief hurdle.

Eugene O'Neill once wrote that he liked to write from first-hand experience about people he knew personally. In answer to a query as to why he wrote so many plays about sailors, O'Neill replied, "If I write often of seamen it is because I know and like them so well. I was once one of them. Life on the sea is ideal. The ship for a home. Sailors for friends . . . I like the man of the sea. He is free of social hypocrisy." [5]

Somerset Maugham was critical of playwrights who created "their characters in stock sizes from images in their own fancy." His advice to playwrights was that their characters would be more believable if they based them on real life models whom they knew first hand. He added: "I have always worked from the living model." Maugham's advice is sound, especially for the beginning dramatist.

Real People Versus "Warm Bodies"

Characters in a play may be divided roughly into two general groups. First, there are the "real people" essential to the play's action and without whose presence there could be no play. Second, there are those "warm bodies" who perform only a perfunctory or incidental service to the play, yet whose existence as real people is of little interest to the audience.

John van Druten chose the term "dummies" to describe this "warm body" group of characters: "The main thing is to know from the start which characters are people, and which are dummies, in the way that the doorman and the hat-check girl may be dummies to you in real life, and to establish and stick to that distinction." [6]

The playwright should establish early whether the bellhop that takes a character to his room, opens the closets, turns back the bed

[5] Carol Bird, "Eugene O'Neill—The Inner Man," *Theatre Magazine,* June, 1924, p. 60.

[6] John van Druten, *Playwright at Work,* Harper & Brothers, 1953, p. 96.

sheets, takes his tip, and leaves the room is merely performing his professional service to the play's action or whether he is to be a real person with a life of his own and therefore of interest to the audience. The practice of making such characters "real people" when they are not is usually fatal, for this makes them a part of the plot and consequently of interest to the audience. In that case to neglect them after they have performed their perfunctory service is misleading. As van Druten says: "If they are to be dummies, let them be dummies as they would be in real life, right from the beginning."

An example of what confusion can be created by thus building up a dummy was seen in a television play by J. P. Miller, *The Rabbit Trap*. As it was originally produced a "warm body" was made a real person, one who remained vividly in the audience's mind long after he was summarily dismissed from the plot. In the drama, a young account executive has slipped away with his wife and son to a long-promised vacation in the north woods. They intentionally left no word of their destination at the office, since they were at long last going to have time to themselves. The father helps the young son construct a rabbit trap and they bait it and leave it set for the night. That evening an "old man" appears at the door. His only function in the play is to bring a message from the village (they had forgotten about postmarks and sent a picture post card to the office). The father must return immediately to New York. Much time was consumed by the "old man" who at once became an engaging character, a real person. Surely he would be seen again before the drama concluded! Well, the father takes his protesting family back to New York. When they get there the boy remembers that the rabbit trap is set and there will be no one at the cabin to free the trapped animal. Most of the script is devoted to badgering the father, who finds himself under attack from all sides— his boss, his wife, and his son. Finally the pressure reaches a peak and in a mad rush the family returns to the cabin. Many members of the audience were probably saying to themselves, "I bet that wonderful old man came along and freed the rabbit." Well, he didn't, or at least we never found out if he did, for when the family got back to the cabin there was no rabbit and the "old man" whom we became interested in at the opening of the play remained in the limbo to which playwright Miller consigned him after he performed his incidental function.

Where to draw the line between making a character a real person or a warm body is a difficult question. The incidental character must be real enough to be believable as he performs his plot function, yet he must remain sufficiently in the background so as not to arouse our interest, since it will of necessity remain unsatisfied.

The Number of Characters in a Play

Many beginning dramatists will ask, "How many characters should I have in a play?" as if there were a prescribed number. This type of writer also probably expects a sure-fire formula for writing a success and will become bewildered when he finds there is none.

The play should be the determining factor, though the writer should be urged to keep his cast small if he hopes to receive a production of his work. Large casts cost money and, unfortunately, the commercialized aspect of dramatic media demands economy in staging a play.

A good rule for the dramatist is to eliminate everybody he possibly can, no matter how interesting or picturesque or lovable a character may be. If he can be spared from the play's action, he should be omitted, but not if this will injure the play as a whole. There is a still better reason for keeping casts small. The more characters the writer must handle within the confines of the script the less time he will have to spend with his "real people." The playwright only restricts his own creativity by peopling his play with large numbers. True, when you have a large cast you can get greater variety by contrasting different people, but when these persons, of necessity, become more or less episodic, appearing only for short scenes, one must work more quickly and broadly to make them stand out sharply.

There is a direct relationship between the number of people in a play and the problem of "real people" versus "warm bodies." There can be more human characters in the small cast, because you can show more than one side of the individuals. To fit sixteen or seventeen characters into a play is akin to working with a jig-saw—each role has to be pared down until it fits into place snugly.

Van Druten's attitude toward the problem of numbers is one most new playwrights should adopt: "I have used as few as three, and as many as twenty-two. I prefer to use as few as possible, if only for the fact that the longer one has with a character, the better one is able to descend into and analyze him. The more characters one has, the quicker one will have to be in establishing them." [7]

Avoid the Stock Characters

The sure sign of the hack writer, the writer who lacks imagination and creativity, is a play peopled with stock characters. The tendency is understandable but not very admirable. All policemen, especially those mounted on motorcycles, are not Irish, and all clothing merchants are not Jewish. All librarians are not prim old maids who blush if smiled at, nor are all bookkeepers mousey individuals perched on high stools.

The various dramatic media are full of offerings with stock characters. There is the big, burly truck driver type, the sharp-tongued mother-in-law type, the sadistic criminal type, and, of course, the true-blue hero type, among many others. All these characters are to be avoided. They are shallow and lack dimensionality. Their mechanical creation makes a mockery of dramatic writing as an art.

THE EXIT OF CHARACTERS

In real life people wander in and out of rooms. They may excuse themselves, with an "I'll be back in a moment," or they may remain silent and just walk into another room. An audience, however, will not accept such apparently unmotivated movements. They need to know where the character is going and for what purpose or they will

---

[7] *Ibid.*, p. 92.

be wondering about his abrupt departure while the scene continues without him.

Many beginning dramatists have trouble motivating the exit of their characters from the scene of the action. Sometimes they want to get rid of a character and lacking a logical reason for an exit have the character suddenly dart off to write a letter, make a long distance telephone call, or to talk to a neighbor. Such exits when staged appear as contrived as they really are.

Unless the playwright carefully plans the exit of a character around the action of the play, he is going to be in for trouble. A character's exit should be logically connected to his reëntrance to the play's action. For example, in *Solid Gold Cadillac* when McKeever, the industrial tycoon, storms out of the office of the board of directors after failing to save Mrs. Partridge's job, we are prepared for his entrance into Mrs. Partridge's office in the next scene.

In a sense, the exit of a character should bear the same relation to the audience as the act curtain does to the plot. Every time a person leaves the stage the audience should know why he is leaving. However, it is perfectly normal for them to wonder what effect his offstage action will have on his next appearance. Audience interest in a character does not cease the moment he is out of sight.

The problem of character creation cannot be cleanly divorced from the task of constructing a plot or writing the dialogue. Therefore, much of the material in the chapters on plot, dialogue, and language will be an expanded treatment of the process of creating believable and dramatically compelling characters.

9

Plot Construction

A plot is merely the pattern on which the story is arranged.
—SOMERSET MAUGHAM

The story is necessary in any case and will be the main interest for many of the audience, but it will not necessarily be the main interest for the author.
—A. A. MILNE

PLOT is story arranged and amplified in terms of the author's purpose. As indicated in previous sections of the text, the author's purpose which dictates the arrangement of a story into a plot is often a subconscious one. As creation progresses the purpose may rise to an objective existence as the play's theme.

It is certainly possible for plot and story to be the same, though this occurrence is highly unlikely in modern drama. If ten writers were to take the same story and each write it as a play, in all probability each play will have a plot distinctly different from the others. Each playwright will intuitively arrange the elements of the story to reflect his own viewpoint. He may elect to begin at the beginning of the story and allow it to unravel chronologically or he may choose to begin near the middle or close to the end and reveal what has gone before through exposition. How he decides to reveal his story is plot construction. As stated in the previous chapter, it is difficult to divorce the creation of character from the more mechanical task of constructing a plot, since the play's story will at the same time be unraveled by and will spring from the characters in action.

THE IMPORTANCE OF PLOT

It must be remembered that when the Greek critic-philosopher Aristotle listed plot as the foremost element of the drama he was drawing his observations from witnessing the effect of Attic drama upon its viewers and their interest in the play's action. Since drama issues from characters in action, it is probable that the playwright is more concerned with the creation of the characters, whereas the audience is more interested in what happens to these characters.

Of one thing we may rest assured: audiences of today have grown tired of the old wooden plots of other days. As George Kelly said, "The play of structure—that is, one which has everything plotted out in an easily recognizable pattern—is definitely out-moded. What they want today is the play of character—one in which the audience can never quite catch up with what a character is going to do next. This is the holding quality today." [1]

Though plays of character command the greater interest today, the play's plot and its construction must not be overlooked. A building will surely crumble if its structure of steel girders is weak or nonexistent. A modern skyscraper is considered by many to be a work of beauty as it towers over a city. Such a building, with its attractive and decorous facade, gives little hint of its structural elements to the naked eye. But they are all there in a strong and architecturally sound sequence. The building's true strength is revealed when it is battered by high winds, swaying as much as several feet without dislodging a single stone.

In the construction of a play's plot, the playwright is very much like the skilled engineer or draftsman who carefully and painstakingly plans out each girder's location in the total pattern. Such a task requires a very special talent. As John van Druten has said, "A good plot needs

[1] *New York Times,* September 26, 1936.

a special kind of brain to create it . . . It needs a kind of mathematical instinct, a power to tie pieces together, thread incidents so that they lead logically from one to another, and then turn the whole thing into a neat package for the ending." [2]

Art consists of the concealment of art. The art product of the dramatic engineer is concealed by the artful execution of the play's blueprint, or plot, into a finished drama.

STORY AND PLOT

The legend of Oedipus, the picturesque and impulsive king of ancient Thebes, is well known in literature. The story of the man who slew his own father and married his own mother has been told and retold through the ages in countless forms. The original story, as treated by Sophocles in his play *Oedipus Rex*, offers an excellent example of the basic difference between plot and story.

The story of Oedipus actually begins before his birth when a curse is cast upon the House of Cadmus. When Oedipus is born his parents learn of the prophecy that the child will one day slay his father and dishonor his own mother's bed. To prevent this happening they give the child to a shepherd to take into the hills and leave staked to a rock to die. Instead, the shepherd gives the child to another shepherd, one from a neighboring kingdom, who takes the child back to his king and queen, who decide to raise Oedipus as their own son. When the boy reaches manhood he learns of the prophecy regarding his future. Believing his foster parents to be his real mother and father, he impulsively attempts to take destiny into his own hands. After all, he reasons, if he leaves the country, the prophecy can never come true. He decides to sail to Thebes and escape the curse. Soon after landing he has an encounter with a warrior driving a chariot who refuses to yield the road. A battle ensues and Oedipus slays the Theban warrior. Later he arrives in Thebes and finds the city gripped by the terror of a sphinx who demands human tribute. Oedipus accepts the

[2] John van Druten, *Playwright at Work*, Harper & Brothers, 1953, p. 30.

challenge, defeats the sphinx, and becomes the hero of Thebes. He is offered the crown, which he accepts, and he later takes as his bride the city-state's widow queen. The prophecy has come true. The warrior killed at the crossroads was his own father and the bride his own mother.

When the play's action opens, however, Oedipus is in ignorance of what he has done. He only knows that his kingdom is beset by a great pestilence and he vows to drive out whatever is causing the city such dire discomfort. Sophocles elected to begin the story close to the end, to depict those horrible hours of Oedipus's discovery of his own guilt. In the course of the discovery the complete story of the Oedipus legend is unfolded in the play's action. Sophocles focussed upon Oedipus's struggle to discover the truth, and it is this action, springing from the character of Oedipus, that brings the tragedy to its ultimate conclusion.

A more recent example of skillful and compact plotting of a play's story is the dramatization of the Caine Mutiny in *The Caine Mutiny Court Martial*. The court martial occurs near the end of the novel, whose action has been unfolded for the reader chronologically—as the events occurred. In the play, set almost entirely in the courtroom, the complete story of the Caine Mutiny is telescoped into retrospective action. Before the final curtain, author Herman Wouk has, through exposition, retold the story line of his novel, with the exception of its romantic subplot.

THE ESSENTIAL ELEMENTS OF A PLOT

In the chapters on the playwright's audience and the finding of dramatic material, it was shown that for a play to exist dramatically the audience must polarize around a protagonist in quest of a desirable and worthy goal. If the goal is not worthy of attainment, the identification of the audience with the protagonist may be a painful association. If the goal is one the audience wishes the protagonist to attain, they will usually struggle with him.

The protagonist may be an individual or a group. In modern drama, which deals more directly with social problems and the struggles of certain groups to attain common goals, the protagonist is often a group rather than an individual.

First, however, there must be a protagonist and, second, there must be a goal. By classic definition, if the hero attains the goal, the play is a *comedy;* if he doesn't, it is a *tragedy.* Yet it is not always possible to reduce a comedy or a tragedy to fit the formula. It is only enough to recognize that often the audience is satisfied by the struggle though the goal may never be attained. This is the case in much of serious drama as well as in classical tragedy.

In the chapter on character creation the process of creating a like-able protagonist, one whom the audience will care about, was discussed. The protagonists must be driven by will, volition, or desire toward a goal the audience wants them to attain. But merely setting up a like-able protgonist and a worthy goal does not in itself create a drama. If there is nothing to prevent the protagonist from attaining the goal, there can be no play, for the play, comedy or tragedy, more properly depicts the protagonist's struggle to reach his goal. There must be a conflict of opposing forces that will constitute an obstacle for the protagonist to overcome. It is from this clash of opposing wills that the dramatic action will spring. The conflicts may arise within the protagonist or from without. They may assume the form of antagonists who desire the same goal and are therefore bent on preventing the protagonist from reaching it. The goal itself may set up obstacles for the protagonist to overcome. Whichever is the case, the essential elements in constructing a plot are the protagonist, the goal, and the obstacles which must be surmounted to attain it.

In isolation the above may appear to be an oversimplification of the basic needs of a plot. However, it only substantiates the belief that the total playwriting process defies the divorcing of a single element, such as plot, from the overall pattern. The discussions in the chapters on audience, dramatic material, and characterization have led inevitably to the above generalizations.

A STRUCTURAL OVERVIEW

Several modern playwrights have explained in a rather whimsical manner the process of constructing a play. Upon examination, however, the whimsicalness can be overlooked and the method pronounced fairly sound. First, you get your hero up a tree. Then you throw rocks at him. And finally you get him down out of the tree—if you can.

One need look no further than many of television's time-restricted dramas to observe the above method in practice. Unfortunately, these dramas often die in the third act, acutely revealing television's distinctive time handicap. In the first act, the audience learns to like or dislike the central figure, whichever the case may be. Before the act concludes the essential elements to interest the audience have been introduced. They know who the play is about and where they are headed. As the time for the first commercial draws near, the hero is neatly left "up a tree" or in "hot water." This is calculated to keep the audience before the television sets during the commercial in order to find out what is going to happen to the "treed" hero.

In the second act, the hero leaves the first limb of the tree and scampers higher up among the foliage as rocks are thrown at him. These are the obstacles facing the protagonist. Unfortunately, and too often, the rocks are boulders of such proportions that the poor hero finds himself on the highest branch when the second act halts for another commercial.

It is at this point that so many television dramas begin to die an unnatural death. A glance at the clock reveals that only ten or twelve minutes remain to get the hero down out of the tree. The playwright has spent too much time getting his protagonist in the tree and then moving him up it. To bring him down in the time remaining he is forced to resort to contrived gimmicks and clichés. How often has the criticism been leveled that a particular television drama's first two acts were compelling, only for the play to fall apart in the last act? Too often this is true, but it needn't be. A story editor for one of the better-known television series has said that many of the scripts crossing his desk had excellent third acts before the sponsor's agency representatives and the program's directors began to tamper with the finished product. Perhaps they were too concerned with maintaining audience interest through the first two commercials to care what happened to the drama in its important concluding stanza. The story editor should know, for in addition to being a successful television playwright himself, he has taught playwriting at an eastern university for several years.

The "up a tree, throw rocks at him, get him down" sequence is *not* offered to the beginning playwright as a formula for the writing of successful dramas. It is cited only as additional proof of the concern audiences have for what happens to the central figure with which it has identified.

CRISIS AND CLIMAX

The terms *crisis* and *climax* have caused confusion among dramatists since their first introduction into the canons of dramaturgical theory. It is said that a play may contain many minor crises and climaxes but should have only one major crisis and climax. Some theorists have even used the terms interchangeably as synonyms.

If we leave the realm of dramatic writing for a moment, the use of the terms cause little confusion. Turn to the realm of medicine, for example. There is a sick child. The issue of its recovery is in doubt and it is said to be passing through a *crisis.* Patiently the mother and father sit by the bed, helpless, and await the ultimate outcome. There is nothing they can do but wait. The doctors have done all that medical science has placed at their disposal to do. The minutes grow into hours until finally the doctor steps up to the bed. The parents lean forward, expectantly, fearfully. The doctor will do one of two things. He will either feel the child's pulse, then lift the sheet over its head, or he will turn to the parents and announce, "The crisis is passed. He's going to be all right." The prolonged *crisis* has reached a *climax,* instantaneous in its effect upon the participants.

What has happened? Well, the parents—and the audience—have passed from a state of not knowing to knowing. The issue is no longer in doubt, the outcome is known.

What is so different about the terms crisis and climax when applied to plot structure? Very little. As the protagonist struggles against the obstacles facing him, he passes through a series of crises, each climaxed by the knowledge of the encounter's outcome. Each of the various scenes or situations of a play may be said to have a crisis culminated in a minor climax of instantaneous knowing. The ultimate crisis and climax is naturally concerned with the basic issue that gave the play its *raison d'être*. The major question of whether the protagonist will attain the goal or will fail is finally answered. All of the action prior to this moment, all of the minor crises and climaxes, have been the rising action to the play's ultimate climax. All that follows will, of necessity, be falling action or *dénouement*.

PLOT CONSTRUCTION SHOULD BE COMPLETED
BEFORE WRITING BEGINS

As characters should be fully created before writing the play begins, so should the construction of a plot be completed.

Several playwrights have commented that they adhered closely to the mandate of completing plot and character before putting pen to paper. Owen Davis remarked that he never started writing "until I have solved every problem, drawn every character and completely laid out my story line." Another playwright has been quoted as saying that "certainly, in writing a play I should be lost, unless I had long labored at a plot, and had everything planned out in advance before writing a line of dialogue."

In the chapter on character creation, Miss Rachel Crothers was quoted as preferring characters to plot. It is interesting to note that she also said, "Before I write anything on paper at all, except brief memory notes, I see clearly what the end of the play will be."

How, then, do playwrights construct a plot before writing a play?

Well, one sure method is to write from a scenario. Avery Hopwood once declared, "I should say that writing a play before a completed scenario is done—simply by delving right into the dialogue—would be an incredibly difficult, if not impossible, task if anything producible is expected to emanate out of the result." [3]

WRITING FROM A SCENARIO

The scenario is the tool by which plotting and characterization is most often successfully achieved.

Most writers employ a scenario, sometimes detailed, sometimes sketchy, as a preliminary step. The form of a scenario and its use vary with individual writers but essentially the scenario is a narrative of the events and situations that are to transpire in the action of a play, and a guide by which the relationships of the characters and the plot are kept intact.

Whether the scenario is painstakingly written out or just an unwritten mental blueprint, the product of intensive reflection, the major portion of the playwriting task is completed when the scenario is in its final form. Planning the scenario is often drudgery because of its many mechanical aspects, and this tends to frustrate the creativity of many writers. But to the beginning playwright the scenario is often the key to successful dramaturgy.

A recommended procedure is first to put down on paper an outline narrative of the play in approximately 200 words. As the late Owen Davis once said, "If your story won't go into two hundred words, throw it away." The next step is to write several more outlines in *narrative* form, expanding the detail with each draft. Later the addition of a little dialogue, as the characters begin to take shape, is sometimes helpful. Detailed character sketches, or profiles, tracing the history of the character up to the moment he becomes a part of the play, are time-saving devices for writers who have only a vague acquaintance with their characters.

[3] John van Doren, "How to Write a Play," *Theatre Magazine,* October, 1921, p. 276.

Many beginning writers fall into the deadly trap of starting to write their plays without a scenario. It usually begins with the innocent act of inserting a clean sheet of paper into a typewriter, then writing something like: "JOHN (Standing by the window): It's a beautiful day, Mary." Unfortunately, these writers must write a responding speech for Mary and then find they have very little idea what will happen to John and Mary in the ensuing three acts, or 120 odd pages, but at least they can boast they have started. Most plays started in this manner never reach the final curtain and, if they do, the writer discovers that the Mary and John in the final scene bear little resemblance to the Mary and John who opened the play.

Some playwrights find it beneficial to tell their stories to friends and then observe their reactions and listen to their comments. This sometimes reveals many of the rough spots by the simple act of telling the story "aloud" to an audience. The drawback to this procedure is readily apparent. Who would listen? Another writer? And risk losing the story or having it elaborated for you, which may be all right if your "audience" is also your collaborator. Of course, if playwrights are married they can tell their stories to their spouses, who apparently have to stand for it, but there is always the possibility of losing a husband or a wife as well a good plot.

Charts showing character relationships may be helpful to the writer having a story with a large cast. The chart can show exactly where each character is, what he says and what he is thinking about at each moment of the play's action. Winchell Smith had such concern over the activities of his characters he would often write as much as forty pages of dialogue of what happened to them between acts.

No one can be told how to write a scenario, probably because each playwright is not only his own architect, but unless he collaborates, he is his own contractor and his own crew. He not only lays the foundation, erects the sidings, and partitions the rooms, but he is his own bricklayer and landscape artist as well; and when he has finished, the lawn is in, seeded, and the real estate agent, or broker, is showing the prospective buyer, or backer, through the rooms. From beginning to end the playwright-architect-contractor-workman follows a master plan.

PLOT PROBLEMS

Since plot is so interrelated with the other elements of the playwriting process it is difficult to isolate its various factors for analysis. The basic attitude and approach to plot has been indicated in the preceding pages. Perhaps a more penetrating understanding of plot can be obtained by examining specific problems that often arise when constructing a play.

Action Consistent with Character

Since plot is the natural result of the impulses which lie in the hearts and minds of the characters as they have been conceived, one would imagine that all actions demanded of the character by the plot would be consistent with the characters as they have been established. This is often not the case, since the dramatist, especially the beginning one, frequently alters the plot arbitrarily to obtain a desired effect. There is nothing wrong with this so long as he does not require a character to contradict himself as he has been revealed to the audience.

To require a character to commit an act of violence, for example, demands that his capacity for violence first be revealed. It is the duty of the playwright to make his audience feel that his character's actions are in harmony with his temperament. They should be made to feel that the actions arise logically and naturally from previous actions together with the temperaments and previous known actions of the other characters in the play.

"The only truth of which the dramatist need be certain," said A. A. Milne, "is truth to character." So long as the actions of the characters demanded by the plot remain consistent, then truth to character is observed.

Preparation and "Plants"

In a one-act play published in 1946 and subsequently rather widely produced on high school stages, the leading character is required to die on stage while taking a nap. In 1945, an earlier draft of the play had been given an experimental production at the University of Texas. After the presentation the audience was invited to comment. One comment stood out above all others: "Why did the girl die of a heart attack?" The playwright then recognized his play's major weakness. He had made something happen to a character that the audience would not willingly accept.

In real life it is not unusual for a man suddenly to keel over without warning and die. This may happen while he is seated in the barber chair, or attending a conference, or while delivering a speech. If we witness the event we are naturally disturbed at seeing a man's final exit. It is the suddenness that is most disturbing. To realize that one moment a man is alive and active and the next moment dead, startles us with the realization that death is constantly imminent. On the other hand, we have known people who died suddenly and yet it came as no surprise. When a man with a history of heart disease dies, we understand it. In a sense we have anticipated the act.

The work of the one-act playwright was cut out for him. He had to make the audience willingly accept the sudden death of a young woman of 22, who a moment before her heart attack appeared to be in the best of health. His task was two-fold: first, he had to establish the fact that the girl had a heart condition and, second, he had to do it in such a manner that the audience did not say, "Ah-hah, that girl is going to die before this play is over."

The playwright made the following changes. As the play opened the family doctor, a close friend of the family for many years, is visiting the girl's mother. In a scene keynoted by light interplay between the doctor and the girl, it is established that the girl has been under medical treatment for several years. The scene ends with the doctor assuring the girl that having her husband back from the war would be the best medicine she could have. At no time was the heart condition treated seriously, yet its existence was clearly established. In a subsequent production the effect of the scene's humor was to allay any suspicion by the audience that the girl was to die before the play ended, yet when her death occurred it was plausible.

Preparation in the plot to make a subsequent act appear believable requires the utmost skill. If certain facts are presented as a natural outgrowth of the play's action—without attracting unnecessary attention to their presence—then when the subsequent act occurs it may come as a surprise and yet still be accepted as a natural consequence.

In the early American comedy, *Fashion,* the audience is prepared for the scene between the fraudulent Count Jolimaitre and the French maid, Millinette, for in the first act they have seen Millinette almost drop a glass of water when she first meets the Count in the Tiffany home. To spring the third act scene of jealousy upon the audience without any previous indication that a relationship existed between the maid and the count would have been a difficult situation to accept.

The problem of motivating the actions of the characters through preparation in the plot structure is a persistent one. Many writers believe that a playwright is obligated to furnish the motives for any action a character may perform. Motivation is the act of providing the "why" for anything a character may do or say.

Unity of Action

The concept of unity of action confuses many writers. Simply stated, it is the process of eliminating the unessential from the plot. In other words, every scene and every character should have a dramatic function that clearly furthers the forward progression of the play's action—or it should be eliminated.

In the chapter on character the problem of handling "warm bodies" was discussed. There the writer was warned not to make a character interesting and important to the audience if, after performing his dramatic function, he is to be dropped from the play. Again we see the close relationship between plot construction and character creation.

Kenneth Macgowan summarized the problem well when he wrote, "If a play has unity, it is not cluttered with scenes unrelated to the story that it tells and to the characters it needs to tell the story. There should be a minimum of discursive or intrusive material, and this minimum can be permitted only because it entertains without distracting. The play *might* be better without it; so make sure that such material does not bewilder or distract. Above all, there must be no scenes or even speeches that may arouse false expectations or lead an audience astray." [4]

Unity of action requires that there should be only one major plot in a play. If there are two plots of equal strength, one will be in conflict with the other. An audience cannot be asked to divide its attention between two plots of identical importance. There may be, and often are, minor plots or story lines that run concurrent with a play's major action. These are subservient to the major plot, yet either contribute to its forward progression or are actually effected by its outcome.

The Obligatory Scene

In modern drama much is made of the obligatory scene, that scene in the action of the play anticipated by and, in a sense, demanded by the audience. Such scenes, however, should not be artificially superimposed upon the plot but arise as a natural outgrowth of the play's action.

For example, in the story of Cinderella (how often have we seen this one dramatized?) we look forward to that moment when the ugly sisters and their tyrannical mother realize that it is their Cinderella whom the handsome Prince loves. When the members of the audience have been let in on certain facts not known by all the characters it is inevitable that they will relish their ultimate revelation. Look how an audience anticipates with delight the moment when the man who has been treated as a hungry poor man is revealed as a millionaire in dis-

---

[4] Kenneth Macgowan, *A Primer of Playwriting,* Random House, 1951, p. 94.

guise. That moment should not be denied the audience, since they have been in on the deception from the beginning.

Marian Gallaway, in her book, *Constructing the Play,* uses a set of exercises to sharpen her students' abilities to determine the obligatory scene demanded by a given set of circumstances. For example, she describes the following situation: "The attractive but prudish protagonist constantly reprimands two delightful old friends of her father for taking a drink. She becomes engaged to a fine lively young man, the proprietor of a tavern." Miss Gallaway asks her readers, "What is the obligatory scene?" Of course, it is that moment when the protagonist must face her father's two friends after her fiancé's occupation has become known to them.

What is the obligatory scene in the following situation? Mr. A., after a hard day at the office, comes home, gets into comfortable lounging clothes, picks up the evening paper, glances at the sports page and remarks to himself, "That fight on television tonight is one I won't miss." What Mr. A. doesn't know but what we already know is that Mrs. A. has invited her parents to supper. The obligatory scene demanded by this situation is obvious.

Perhaps the most common form of obligatory scene grows out of the audience's identification with or polarization around the play's central figure. As the hero struggles to attain his goal he encounters various obstacles. Some of these may defeat him for the moment, sometimes in such a manner that we urgently want the obstacle to be encountered again and immediately surmounted. For example, Hollywood adventure films frequently introduce a scene in which the hero is held helpless by two hoodlums while a third, one of the chief antagonists, administers a brutal beating. The hero cannot resist. He must take the vicious punishment. Such scenes are calculated to make the audience's blood boil and demand that moment when the hero will catch up with the villain and give him the thrashing he deserves. Such use of the obligatory scene is rather obvious and possibly not very laudatory; however, it is only natural for the audience to want to see a villain, especially one who has used "foul" means, get his "come-uppance."

The Deus ex Machina

Aristotle condemned the ancient Greek theatre for its use of an artificial device to resolve hopelessly embroiled plots. The device was termed the *deus ex machina,* which literally translated means "god out of a machine." Greek playwrights were not above using this contrivance and, unfortunately, neither are their modern counterparts. Some writers get their plots so hopelessly entangled that they can't possibly unravel them without outside assistance. In the Greek theatre the assistance came from lowering a god in a basket down from the *skene* into the acting circle. He would step out of the basket, set things aright, then climb back into the basket and be pulled back to the "heavens" from which he had descended.

If a play's complications cannot be resolved by the characters entangled in the situation, through some direct effort of their own, then the play should not exist at all, especially if it becomes necessary to "lower a god" into the arena.

Melodrama of more recent vintage used the *deus ex machina.* At the precise moment the heroine's skull reaches the whirling blade of the buzz saw to which she has been strapped by the villain, who crashes through the door but the hero? And not a moment too soon. Heroes arrive in real life too, but often after the heroine's skull is already split.

The motion pictures have long used the *deus ex machina* to resolve otherwise hopeless situations. For example, the beleaguered frontier settlers are entrenched behind their wagon train. They have warded off two attacks by the marauding Indians. The third attack is expected momentarily. The settlers check their ammunition and discover it is almost gone. The next attack will be the last one. Wives and husbands embrace for what they feel will be the last time. Then, with blood-curdling yells, the Indians rush the wagon train. As they race toward the barricades the air is split by the sound of a bugle and over a far hill appears a regiment of United States Cavalry riding to the rescue. It has only been in recent years, with the emergence of the adult western, that the motion picture writers and producers have remained honest, allowing the cavalry to arrive after the final slaughter.

Yes, the *deus ex machina,* condemned in Ancient Greece by Aristotle, is still with us and still to be condemned. Yet, as long as writers persist in shoving their heroes so far up the tree that they can't get them down under their own power, we will continue to see the *deus ex machina* used in the various modern dramatic media.

STRUCTURAL ANALYSIS

The following appraisal form is derived in part from Samuel Selden's *Introduction to Playwriting* and the appraisal form used by George McCalmon at Cornell University. This form will not suit all writers, but perhaps as these writers grow in experience they will devise their own plot check list. Whether a writer uses this form or one of his own devising, he will be wise if he remembers that as the author of the work he is appraising, he can't help but be prejudiced.

DRAMATIC WRITING APPRAISAL FORM

A. Structural Considerations
1. *Introduction or Preparation:* Does it arrest attention and arouse interest? Is the necessary information skillfully presented? Are the initial character relationships clear? Is a feeling of milieu suggested?
2. *Attack:* Is the play's basic conflict precipitated decisively? Is it appropriately timed? Are the opposing forces clearly aligned?
3. *Rising Action:* Is it built of interesting complications and obstacles? Are the minor crises vital? Are the motives of conflict strong enough to sustain it?
4. *Main Crisis or Turning Point:* Is it fully realized in terms of the play's basic conflict? Does one force gain complete control over others? Is the play's problem crystallized?
5. *Climax:* Is it the peak of emotional intensity? Has the protagonist and/or the audience passed from a state of not knowing to knowing? Is it the result of the arrangement of forces within the main crisis? Is it worth all the preparation?

6. *Falling Action:* Does it move swiftly away from the climax? If there is a minor crisis, does it grow naturally out of the climax?

7. *Conclusion or Outcome:* Is it purposeful? Is it the result of the basic conflict? Does it indicate a future trend? Does it make a commentary on the problem?

B. Conceptual Consideration

1. *Theme:* Is the total pattern of the play unified? Has it been motivated by the central idea? Is the theme valid and acceptable to the audience as it is expressed? Is the theme implicitly or explicitly stated?

2. *Issue:* Is the issue in the conflict clear? Is it important and interesting? Is the issue too subtly handled? Would simplification yield greater clarity?

3. *Drive:* Is the desire of the protagonist definite and forceful, is it likely to win sympathy and hold the attention of an audience? Are the opposing forces of such a nature as to make their resistance worthy of the protagonist's struggle? Do the desires of the opposing forces generate the greatest amount of dramatic intensity consistent with the basic issue of the play?

The Dialogue

> From start to finish good dialogue is hand-made, like good lace;
> clear, of fine texture, furthering with each thread the harmony
> and strength of a design to which all must be subordinated.
> —JOHN GALSWORTHY

ONLY after the plot has been planned out to the last detail and all
of the important characters fully conceived is the playwright ready to
execute his play in dialogue. Everything that has gone before, the many
hours of inspiration and drudgery that transpired between the inception
of the initial idea and the completion of the working scenario, has been
preparation for the dialogue phase of the dramatic writing process. The
characteristic which most distinguishes a play from other forms of literature is dialogue, for it is through the dialogue and its attendant stage
business that a play is finally expressed by a playwright.

THE NATURE OF DIALOGUE

Dialogue is the quality which gives a play life and magnetism. It is
the vehicle through which everything must be conveyed, or, as Rachel
Crothers puts it, it is "that magic thing which is the blooming of all
the other elements in the play."

In describing the process of writing dialogue, Galsworthy said: "The
art of writing true dramatic dialogue is an austere art, denying itself all

license, grudging every sentence devoted to the mere machinery of the play, suppressing all jokes and epigrams severed from character, relying for fun and pathos on the fun and tears of life." [1]

This chapter's prefatory quote by John Galsworthy draws an analogy between dialogue writing and lacemaking. Crothers, too, remarks that in a play one scene flows into the other with a pace and rhythm that are electrical, like "many threads weaving in and out on that quick shuttle, never becoming entangled or confused—while we watch the tapestry woven swiftly before our eyes." [2]

Very few successful dramatists have assessed the qualities of dialogue as thoroughly as have Galsworthy and Crothers. "Good dialogue," according to Galsworthy, "is character marshalled so as continually to stimulate interest or excitement." Crothers says that "great dialogue flashes the light on characters as lightning illumines the dark earth— in flashes." Great dialogue does not stand still and analyze, it conveys so much in a few words that the actor holds "a great instrument in his hands and with it can make the audience know the depths of his being."

A flair for writing fairly good dialogue is the commonest gift found in all writing, and the most misleading. This flair has lured many into trying to write drama. This is unfortunate, for the flair that promises so much doesn't make a play. Again quoting Crothers, "Very great dialogue is the rarest gift, and is the flower, the crowning touch of drama."

Whenever the dramatist divorces his dialogue from the progress of events and the events which are significant of character, he is not making drama, though he may be making pleasing disquisitions. Every line of dialogue should contribute to the development of character or to the forward progression of the character's relationship to the plot.

---

[1] John Galsworthy, "Some Platitudes Concerning Drama," *The Inn of Tranquility,* Charles Scribner's Sons, 1912, p. 195.
[2] Rachel Crothers, "The Construction of a Play," *The Art of Playwriting,* University of Pennsylvania Press, 1928, p. 127.

Admiration of the Dialogue Form

Many of our outstanding literary figures have professed a great liking for the dialogue form of composition. Some even claimed they were lured to the field of drama by the appeal of dialogue. J. M. Barrie, for instance, said that dialogue fascinated him from the moment he fell into it and found he could swim. He even wrote many of his letters in dialogue and claimed that he would preach in dialogue if he were a clergyman, and write prescriptions in it if he were a physician.

What is there about dialogue that compels such interest among certain writers? Perhaps the interest, emotions and suspense that may be aroused by it. After all, the most telling things in Homer and later Greek poetry and philosophy were in dialogue. Even the profundities of Confucius and Christ have been preserved for us in dialogue.

John van Druten once said, "I know only that anything written in dialogue has always had an instantaneous appeal to me, so long as it reflected—or seemed to—the quality of real speech." [3]

The Importance of Dialogue

Dialogue, being the natural form for composing a play, is a natural resultant of the preparation and thought that goes into the development of either character or plot, or both.

Regardless of the plot's construction, an important problem of language arises in the writing of any play. Solving this problem is as important as the construction, since the reach and impression of a play must be immediate. The members of an audience can't go back, as they can when reading a book, and wonder about the meaning of what they have heard. They must realize the meaning of a line of dialogue the moment they hear it. Nor can an audience be asked to listen to language for its beauty of sound alone. Beauty in modern plays is not so much in the words as in the thought.

In the early decades of the twentieth century, dialogue was less

[3] John van Druten, *Playwright at Work,* Harper & Brothers, 1953, p. 11.

important than it is today. New York, the center of the professional theatre in America, was a "foreign" city because of its many immigrants. The melting pot was still in the process of homogenizing its people with their different mother tongues. The basis of many plays of that day was a good pantomime, so planned that the drama would be easily intelligible even to a spectator who was deaf. The purpose of dialogue in this approach was to illustrate or to enrich with overtones a composition which was already self-sufficient visually.

Almost all of the silent motion pictures were complete pantomimes. Though the film actors could be seen speaking, the number of dialogue panels flashed on the screen were few. It is difficult for the present generation, so accustomed to the interdependence of visual and aural action, to understand the widespread popularity of the silent movies.

Augustus Thomas, author of many plays of the 1900 to 1920 period, adhered to the predominance of visual action, especially as it pertained to the audience of foreign born. Thomas reasoned, with some validity, that "the eye is more educated than the ear. Communication through the eye is more direct. Ocular presentation is the thing itself; aural presentation is the thing in symbols, a message to be translated. Messages through the ear require the recipient to think, and thinking to feel. And so it comes that the limited vocabulary of the foreign born and the influence of the screen method, make for a faster play in the spoken drama." [4]

Motion pictures did not suddenly begin to speak because a scientist discovered how to synchronize a sound track to the film. Instead, the motion picture industry wanted sound, had to have it, in order to keep pace with the needs and wants of a changing audience. The novelty of moving pictures was wearing out. Audiences were again ready to listen to ideas as well as see actions. The "talking" picture was a logical development. Science merely satisfied the demand for sound.

Action by itself means little. It must be accompanied by keenly vivid

---

[4] Augustus Thomas, "Two Decades of American Playwrights," *Theatre Magazine,* May, 1920, p. 394.

dialogue. Today's public believes what it hears as well as what it sees. There is more listening in the theatre today and a more intelligent and subtle drama has emerged. Our modern drama relies upon the ear as much if not more, than the eye. Witness the success of such aural action plays as *The Crucible, The Lark,* and *Inherit the Wind.* Today there is an audience for this drama of dialogue *and* action, a more imaginative audience keeping pace with more imaginative dramatic writing.

Dialogue-Character Consistency

When a character says anything in a play, he must say it because it is his nature to say it.

The concept of dialogue being consistent with character was explored in the chapter on character creation. There it was suggested that once the characters are clearly and completely conceived, the playwright should allow them to act and react to whatever environmental situations may be encountered in the course of the plot and in a sense write their own dialogue. Of course, it is obvious that the success of this concept is directly proportionate to the completeness with which the characters have been created by the dramatist. One thing is certain, however. Dialogue must be consistent to character; a dramatist should never permit a character to say anything that would not be in accordance with his personality as it has been established or represented to the audience.

One reason for condemning the use of a character to sermonize or preach the author's point of view is that to do so may violate the character as he has been originally conceived. Characters cannot be expected to give voice to sentiments and opinions that are not theirs, unless it first has been established that they, as characters, would say such things.

Hesketh Pearson, one of Shaw's unauthorized biographers, says that in many of his discussions with Shaw he received the impression that Shaw wrote his dialogue without worrying about who would speak it and later fitted it to the characters. Therefore, Pearson one day asked Shaw if this were the case and received a resounding, "Certainly not," in reply. "My dialogue and characters are absolutely inextricable," said Shaw, "each being the essence of the other."

One final word on character-dialogue consistency. Owen Davis complimented Lillian Hellman for her play, *The Children's Hour,* which appeared on Broadway in 1934. In it, Davis believed he had found one of the best scenes in modern drama. Two young women who have been slandered by an older one call on her and demand to know her reasons for saying what she has. Of this scene, Davis said, "These three women were beautifully drawn and every word they spoke in a long, harrowing scene, was exactly what these three women under the same circumstances would have said. That, of course, should be true of every scene in every play, but it isn't." [5]

RHYTHM AND DIALOGUE

The quality of rhythm is as essential to a play's life as it is to the life of the human body. Without rhythm, the play, like the body, dies. Rhythm is not confined to the art of playmaking but is the essential quality of all art.

"What is Rhythm," asked John Galsworthy, "if not that mysterious harmony between part and part, and part and whole, which gives what is called life." Drawing the analogy to living matter, the concept of rhythm can best be grasped in observing how life abandons an animate creature when the essential relation of part to whole has been sufficiently disturbed. "This rhythmic relation of part to part, and part to whole," said Galsworthy, "is the one quality inseparable from a work of Art."

The rhythm of a play lies in the relation of a line of dialogue to another line of dialogue. Within one line there is the rhythmical relationship of word to word. Beyond dialogue, but brought about by it, is the

[5] Owen Davis, *My First Fifty Years in the Theatre,* Walter H. Baker Company, 1950, pp. 125–126.

rhythmical relationship of scene to scene and act to act. These relationships are clearly drawn and established in Crothers' description of the total process of rhythm within a play. "And in the acts are scenes—little acts within themselves; and in the scenes are speeches; and in the speeches are sentences; all building, climbing to a climax. And in these acts and scenes and speeches and lines is rhythm. Each can only carry so much—its own beat. A little too long and the effect of the whole is hurt." [6]

The parallel of rhythm in the drama to harmony in music is readily apparent. In both the drama and music a primary appeal is to the ear, though this in no way dismisses the importance of the visual rhythm of movement and action. But, since the ingredient of expression available to the dramatist is dialogue, we should be concerned, as writers, with the rhythmical qualities of the English language.

A playwright's words must have that strange power that will project them over the footlights. The two factors most concerned with this projection are a sense of rhythm and a sense of timing. Each depends upon the playwright's "ear," a knowledge of when to increase and when to decrease the speed of his writing, to know when a scene needs to move fast and when it must be slowed down. This ability is akin to a director's sense of tempo in playing a scene and will come to the dramatic writer through practice and from the practiced ear. Van Druten offers the new playwright this advice, "An author, having written his scene, will do well to read it aloud, to try and hear it in a theater, even to try and direct it in his head so that it will be a simple and not a complicated thing for the real director when he comes to it." [7]

Few persons realize how vital instinctive timing is to a play. There are many scripts, especially comedies, that make little sense when you read the words, but when heard in production they come to life and thrill the audience. This thrill will be due to the instinctive timing of the playwright in composing the lines of dialogue. Owen Davis even

[6] Crothers, *op. cit.*, p. 132.
[7] van Druten, *op. cit.*, p. 150.

felt that it is impossible for anyone "without the instinctive feel of the born dramatist to learn how to time a speech or pitch a climax and without this all the rest is useless." The feeling for the rhythm of words is due to inborn sensibility and a musical ear.

John Galsworthy felt that a sensitivity of the ear and a perceptiveness of the mind to lyric expression is necessary for the dramatist to interest the audience to whom he directs the dialogue. "Take Shakespeare's 'Out, out, brief candle!' Why is it charmed?" he asked. "Because of the vowel sounds? Or the dramatic unexpectedness of 'brief' applied to 'candle'? Or the image of the human spirit burning like a little flame, and blown into nothingness? Because of all three, I think, and in about equal proportion." [8]

Eugene O'Neill in a memorandum to Lee Simonson admitted that he was "a bug on the subject of sound in the theatre." He stated that he always wrote primarily by ear for the ear, and that most of his plays, even down to the rhythm of the dialogue, had the definite structural quality of a musical composition. This purpose in utilizing sound, said O'Neill, "is the principal reason why I have been blamed for useless repetitions which to me were significant recurrences of theme." O'Neill considered the sound of the dialogue to be a structural part of his plays. Somerset Maugham also concerned himself with the sound of words and objected to writers who put two rhyming words together or joined "a monstrous long adjective to a monstrous long noun." Maugham also objected to the practice of placing "between the end of one word and the beginning of another . . . a conjuncton of consonants that almost breaks your jaw."

Words have weight, sound and appearance and it is only by considering these that we can write a sentence that is good to look at and good to listen to. Using archaic and affected words is all right when they sound better than the blunt, obvious ones, but they must be true to the character who uses them.

[8] John Galsworthy, "On Expression," *Candelabra*, Charles Scribner's Sons, 1933, p. 181.

George Bernard Shaw felt all playwrights should have the attributes of Shakespeare, who "was extremely susceptible to word music and to graces of speech; he picked up all sorts of odds and ends from books and from the street talk of his day and welded them into his work." Shaw offered the playwright practical advice for the handling of rhythm of dialogue in his "Rules for Directors": "The director must accordingly take care that every speech contrasts as strongly as possible in speed, tone, manner, and pitch with the one which provokes it, as if coming unexpected as a shock, surprise, stimulant, offence, amusement or what not. It is for the author to make this possible; for in it lies the difference between dramatic dialogue and epic narrative. A play by a great poet, in which every speech is a literary masterpiece, may fail hopelessly on the stage because the splendid speeches are merely strung together without provoking one another, whereas a trumpery farce may win an uproarious success by its retortive backchat." [9]

Words have the ability to produce a rhythm of their own. The "well" and "yes, but" that start almost every other speech in the plays of beginning playwrights who are trying to capture the quality of real speech can hold up a manuscript as often as the needless repetition of such phrases as "I think" and "I believe." With reference to these standard phrases of conversation when they are applied to dramatic writing, John van Druten said, "They can also weaken the character that speaks them, and they can end by becoming a personal and irritating habit of the author's, started once to try to break down the set speeches of an earlier type of dialogue and turn it into a nearer kind of vernacular, ending now by reducing it to a tepid form of chatter." [10]

The dialogue of a play, as the medium of expression for the dramatist, must have an integral rhythmical relationship which builds from line to line, scene to scene, act to act, to a dramatic climax. The rhythm of the parts may differ, as does the relationship of notes and chords in

---

[9] George Bernard Shaw, "Rules for Directors," *Theatre Arts*, August, 1949, p. 9.
[10] van Druten, *op. cit.*, pp. 151–152.

music, but each "harmonizes" into a totality of effect, which, in itself, contains a basic rhythm. So long as the essential relation of the parts to the whole is not disturbed, then rhythmically speaking, the play has an opportunity to succeed.

THE FUNCTIONS OF DIALOGUE

There are three major functions of dramatic dialogue. The first is the furthering of the plot, its progression; the second is the revelation of character; and the third is the aiding of a play technically during its production.

Every speech must help the play forward, even the exposition, which by throwing light on the past clarifies events of the present and the future. Drama means moving forward all the time, through inevitable action and speech, to an inevitable conclusion. There can be no stopping along the way. Every scrap of dialogue should lead toward the one big climactic scene.

Any dialogue that does not have a direct bearing upon the evolution of the drama being enacted, any piece of business that does not directly aid that evolution, is unnecessary and should be eliminated. Some lines may be pure plot dialogue, others will throw a character into perspective; often dialogue performs both functions at the same time. The playwright should watch his scenes, see that they go to their objective in one direct line. If a minor or subsidiary point is an interesting one, it should be taken where it is natural to do so, but it should never be interjected or superimposed. If you allow the dialogue to digress from the main line, you are in danger of losing the flow and the main point altogether and, especially, of losing the attention of your audience.

Expository Dialogue

The exposition within a play imparts to the audience the information they will need to understand the action they are witnessing. Primarily, exposition is concerned with what has happened before the play begins, relating that which will have bearing on what happens to the characters in the ensuing action. However, exposition occurs throughout the play, revealing what has happened to characters while they are off-stage and explaining the action that occurred between acts.

In the not-too-distant past, expository material was imparted by prologue, aside, soliloquy, and even through the use of program notes. Today, it is woven into the action of the play and unfolds as the drama itself unfolds.

Fifty years ago it was considered obligatory to let the audience know through dialogue between two persons already on the stage the characteristics and relevant facts and history of every important character before his initial entrance. That obligation accounted for the perennial butler and housemaid who opened the play with a discussion of what has happened and to whom. George Broadhurst, in ridiculing this method, offered the following example of the expository device.

BUTLER: I say, Mary, that was a 'ot old row the governor and the missus 'ad last night, eh?

MAID: That's right, Mr. Tootleham. Hi wouldn't be a bit surprised if she did a botl with Lord Herringwater. 'E's been 'anging round 'er quite a lot, 'e has.

BUTLER: I'll be sorry for 'er if she does. You know 'Is Lordship's reputation, don't you, Mary? A Don Jewan, that's what he is.[11]

No one can deny that the essential facts have been revealed about the principals of the play's action through this device. Nor can one deny that these facts have been artificially revealed. As early as 1896, Shaw condemned this method of exposition as being trite. In a criticism of the opening performance of *The Queen's Proctor*, a play by Herman Melville, which was adapted from *Divorçons* by Victorien Sardou and E. de Najoc, Shaw said, "First, we had the inevitable two servants gossiping about their employers' affairs, their pretended function being to expound the plot, their real one to bore the audience sufficiently to make the principals doubly welcome when they arrived." [12]

[11] George Broadhurst, "Some Others and Myself," *Saturday Evening Post*, November 6, 1926, p. 28.

[12] George Bernard Shaw, *Our Theatres in the Nineties*, II, Constable & Co., Ltd., 1932, p. 149.

Perhaps one of the most difficult tasks for the dramatist is getting the audience informed as to the existing situation. Prior to the modern period there was the prologue and the device just cited. With their disappearance the necessary expository material had to be imparted somehow in the first act without seeming to be pasted on. The device of the gossiping servants had been worn out, yet the exposition still had to be accomplished.

In the modern play the exposition must come indirectly and through the action and dialogue of the characters themselves. All explanations must be made as the play progresses. Van Druten suggests that the influence of Ibsen was responsible for this change of approach to exposition. "From Ibsen our playwrights learned the trick of communicating what the characters were thinking without having to fall back into soliliquy and asides. People stopped reading letters aloud to themselves on the stage." [13]

Many dramatists struggle with this effort to be entirely natural while wasting no unnecessary time in getting information across to the audience. George M. Cohan once described this struggle as he experienced it in writing *Get-Rich-Quick Wallingford*. In the third act Wallingford had been placed in his office, and at the opening of the act Cohan wanted Judge Lambert to come in and tell Wallingford that he had received a visit from the Board of Directors of the Tack Company, and that they had just left his office with the avowed intention of coming directly to Wallingford's establishment to denounce him. The presence of Judge Lambert ahead of the members of the board of directors who left his office ahead of him presented Cohan with a genuine problem of exposition. Cohan relates that the solution kept him guessing for several days, but after rereading the scene as he had written it, he solved it by making Judge Lambert say to Wallingford: "Yes, they left my office five minutes ago, but I took the short-cut through Pearl Street." A minor problem, perhaps, but such problems of exposition often defeat the beginning dramatist.

In a lecture at the University of Pennsylvania Rachel Crothers said

[13] van Druten, *op. cit.*, p. 38.

that the further on in the story the plot actually begins, the better the play will be. A construction problem is immediately presented, however, since the opening lines of the play must reveal the situation, the people, and their relationships to each other. Crothers said these things are not to be revealed to the audience through explanation but "by the natural impulsive speech of the characters telling each other things they do not know but want to know." She insisted that the dialogue of the characters must be "always advancing, not going back and recalling to each other things which of course they do know in order to tell the audience." For example, it is perfectly natural for two old maid aunts to tell their nephew's fiancée what their nephew was like when he lived with them, but it would be rather absurd if the aunts are shown telling one another what they both already know just to inform the audience.

In the modern drama, the device of heralding the arrival of the "star" by building up to the key character's entrance is rapidly losing favor. No longer will the audience accept the artificial device of someone rushing to the window and saying, "Look, here he comes now," at which other characters come to the window and comment on the character's wonderful appearance and the cut of his clothes. Then the character would be heard entering the house and speaking to the butler in a voice loud enough to be heard three blocks away, followed by an anticipatory pause climaxed by his regal entrance greeted by thunderous applause from the audience. Unfortunately, we still see the "star build-up" in many modern plays, but fortunately, writers are becoming more imaginative in getting the play's chief character onstage in a logical manner consistent with the play's action.

Expository dialogue, incorporated within the action of the play, can indicate the time of day, the season of the year, the condition of the weather and many other things. The secret today, however, is to wed the exposition to the natural flow of the action, never intruding it as an obvious imparting of information.

There is a danger, however, in understressing highly significant expository material, especially when it is necessary to impart the information in the opening moments of the play. The noise and confusion caused by late arrivals rushing to their seats during a performance of the roadshow of *A Hatful of Rain* illustrates the problem. The play concerns a boy hopelessly addicted to narcotics. In the opening scene it is very matter-of-factly established that he became addicted to narcotics while under treatment in an Armed Services hospital. This very important piece of information was lost in the noise made by the members of the audience settling down into their seats. Consequently, it was difficult for them to sympathize with the boy's plight. He was seen, not as a victim, but a product of his own weakness. If the highly important exposition concerning the drug addict's war experiences had been more pointed in the dialogue, then the audience would have had a true understanding of his plight. This could have been done without injurying the play's logical progression.

Creating Mood and Atmosphere Through Dialogue

The use of dialogue to establish atmosphere or to set mood is an intrinsic function of the spoken lines. Upon analyzing the dialogue of a play to discover just which lines or what words are responsible for the establishment of a mood or the creation of an atmosphere, one will soon discover that the task is similar to trying to determine which raindrops are responsible for the noise of a rainfall. Each drop by itself is imperceptible, but acting together and collectively, the atmosphere of "rain falling" is immediately established. So it is with the creation of mood and atmosphere in a play. The specific words and lines of dialogue, standing alone, cannot claim credit for creating mood or atmosphere, but when operating collectively, they undeniably function as an atmosphere or mood-establishing agent.

The beginning playwright would do well to inspect J. M. Synge's classic one-act drama, *Riders to the Sea,* and Eugene O'Neill's *Emperor Jones.* These two plays show atmosphere and mood creation at its finest. An examination of these plays will also reveal that atmosphere is achieved through totality of effect, not through individual lines of dialogue. Atmosphere cannot be seen. It is felt. Atmosphere is what is done and said. The mood for a scene is set by all the words which the author has given his characters to say. Good dialogue, well written, is the perfect clothing of mood.

Dialogue and the Machinery of the Play

The playwright is expected to assist, through his dialogue, the overcoming of certain technical difficulties in the execution of his play in performance. However, the dialogue employed to solve such mechanical problems should also sustain the forward progress of the play's action.

Some of the technical problems overcome through dialogue are: (1) the focussing of attention away from the setting to allow time for set changes, (2) the prolonging of scenes to enable actors to make entrances on certain lines, (3) in live television the covering for an actor while he moves from one set to another, (4) the allowing of time for costume changes, and (5) compensating for a delay in dropping the curtain at the end of an act or to conclude the play. Many more could be suggested.

The stage setting, the scenery, should never attract attention away from dialogue. David Belasco, who considered the purpose of the theatre to be that of holding a mirror up to nature, felt this purpose could be achieved only through a balanced relationship of setting and dialogue. Encompassed within Belasco's total concept of stage setting were the more intangible elements of light and color as creators of a life-like force within the scene. This producer-director-playwright thought it was his duty to seek in light and color the same interpretative relationship to spoken dialogue that music bears to the words of a song. The establishment of this interpretative relationship, said Belasco, is the "real art, the true art, of the theater."

The playwright should not make his scenes difficult to produce. On a stage he cannot call for a camera, as he can in television, to dolly in for a closeup and thus eliminate the background. His characters must play their scenes in front of whatever the designer has set behind the action. On the stage it is seldom advisable to place comedy scenes which depend upon witty dialogue in an exterior setting. Most exterior settings suggest too great an expanse for the dialogue to overcome. The eyes of the audience tend to wander from the words to the scenic surroundings. Most comedy scenes placing stress on witty dialogue are best done in an interior setting. Of course, there are exceptions to this, but it is a good rule of thumb to keep scenes highly dependent on dialogue indoors and away from expansive settings.

Owen Davis, who began his playwriting career as a writer of popular melodrama, felt that his early background helped him acquire what he termed "a very difficult trick of mechanical dexterity." Rapid scene changes were as often called for 50 years ago as they are today, and Davis regarded his handling of the old melodrama changes as expert.

The old melodramas employed many devices still used in modern drama. One of these was the use of a blackout to cover a scenic change, such as the removal or addition of a prop, the dropping of a new set, while a spirit of continuing action is still maintained. Then, as today, it was necessary to bridge the gap of the blackout in some manner. Davis climaxed such scenes with "some sure-fire 'belly-laugh' or bit of heroic bunk that would be sure to bring a yell of delight from the audience." This yell, or laugh, would then be sustained by its own momentum through the scenic change.

Dialogue to cover a character's off-stage action is a common problem facing dramatic writers. When John Galsworthy first wrote *The Silver Box* he discovered that he had to lengthen the dialogue in a certain scene to allow a key character time to get a cab and return at a certain point in the dialogue. As originally written, the reëntrance appeared ludicrous. The dialogue was lengthened for no other purpose except to make the passage of stage time seem believable. However, as you read this scene, you are struck with the fact that all of the dialogue between the character's exit and his return is essential to the play's action and to the revelation of its characters. In rewriting the scene, Galsworthy added dialogue organically, thus enabling him to account for the lapse of time without bringing his play to a temporary standstill.

Another, and more obvious, technical function of dialogue is its relationship to costume changes. The dramatist should remember that costume changes take time for which he must allow in his script. He should not consider the covering dialogue as padding but instead anticipate the problem in his construction of the play.

Shaw had an amusing experience during the production of *Too True to Be Good* which illustrates another technical function performed by dialogue. In the early performances of the play they could never get the curtain down in time to choke off an oration being delivered by Sir Cedric Hardwicke. Shaw provided an additional set of lines to be used by the actor to cover the curtain's being late, thus avoiding an embarrassing pause or forcing the actor to ad-lib lines not in keeping with the original speech.

REALISTIC DIALOGUE

The modern theatre has been keynoted as a period of realistic drama. Much confusion arises in explaining what the playwrights, the critics, and the public conceive to be stage realism. One often-heard explanation is that realism should be a faithful and photographic portrayal of incidents, characters, and conversation drawn from actual life. This is a myth and has been exploded even by those playwrights so closely associated with the "naturalistic movement" of the early part of this century, David Belasco and John Galsworthy.

Actions in the dramatic media are calculated to give impressions of realism rather than being real. All dramatic timber, to be sure, should be hewn from real life, but almost never can a section of life be sawed out bodily, as it stands, to make drama. Naturalist disciple Belasco thought the audience would rebel against seeing an *actual* transcription of life on the stage. He reasoned that the impression of actual reality is brought about through the selection of representative moments and details, and these, in turn, create the impression of reality. He recognized that the art of drama, in common with all of the other arts, consists first, last, and always in the exercise of an exquisite faculty of selection and rejection.

A play is not real life. This fact must never be forgotten. It is real life presented selectively and with a purpose. As van Druten has said, "That ugly fellow in the gallery knows all about that; it is your job, as playwright, to make him forget it."

Photographic representation of real life actually appears untrue in the dramatic media. The playwright does not reproduce life. He attempts to *represent* reality, creating an impression or illusion that what is happening dramatically could actually transpire in real life. The aim of the dramatist writing realism is to create an illusion of actual life that will compel the viewer to pass through an experience of his own, to think, and talk, and move with the people he sees thinking, talking, and moving in front of him. Stage realism is an idealization of reality, the application of selectivity to actual life in order to create an illusion of reality.

A realistic play must give an *impression* of reality, not a copy. There is no such thing as objective realism in the theatre. The only truth that matters is the truth of the characters to themselves. The dramatist selects and presents the truth so that it will appear real for the moment to the audience.

"A work of art, after all, is not reality," asserts Elmer Rice. "It is merely the artist's attempt to represent reality by the use of symbols." According to him, success of the playwright, the artist, is "exactly to the degree in which the selection and arrangement of his symbols makes his meaning intelligible to those who conceive reality in similar terms." [14]

The Qualities of Realistic Dialogue

Realistic dialogue should appear to be true to life, as people really talk, yet not in the form of conversation—a heightened, selected

[14] Elmer Rice, "Introduction," *Two Plays,* Coward-McCann, 1935, p. vi.

speech revealing character and situation. It is not difficult to *reproduce* exact conversation and actions. It is, however, very difficult to *produce* perfectly natural conversation when each phrase must contribute toward the development of a drama and also reveal, phrase by phrase, the essential traits of a character.

A. A. Milne felt keenly about the matter of realistic dialogue, saying that "real conversation is too inconsequent, too dull, too allusive, for the stranger at the window to follow it with comprehension for three-quarters of an hour."[15] To illustrate his point more fully, Milne penned a scene from life, as he found it, showing the inadequacy of real conversation, as it is spoken, for inclusion in a play. The scene is quoted in its entirety.

HUSBAND: Well, what do you think?
WIFE: I don't know. (*Thinks for a minute.*)
HUSBAND: It's for you to say.
WIFE: I know. (*After a long pause.*) There's Jane.
　　(Colonel in third row of stalls strikes match to see who Jane is. She isn't in the programme. Who the devil is Jane? He never knows.)
HUSBAND: You mean the Ipswich business?
WIFE: Yes. (*Telephone bell rings.*) That's probably Arthur.
　　(Clergyman in fifth row of stalls strikes match to see who Arthur is. He's not in the programme either.)
HUSBAND: Monday. Much more likely to be Anne.
WIFE: Not now.
HUSBAND: Well, you anyway.
WIFE: Oh, all right. (*Exit for ten minutes while husband reads paper.*)
HUSBAND: (*As she comes back.*) Anne?
WIFE (*in a voice*): "Give my love to the dear boy."
HUSBAND: "No darling, *not* like chickens."
WIFE: Of course. What are you doing on Friday?
HUSBAND: Trevors. Why? (*He sneezes.*) Damn, I haven't got a handkerchief. (*He gets up. At the door he says:*) Oh, by the way, I'd better ring Morrison. (*Exit. Wife writes a letter and then picks up paper. Husband returns.*)
WIFE (*from paper*): Myrtle's engaged! Fancy!

[15] A. A. Milne, *By Way of Introduction*, E. P. Dutton & Co., 1929, p. 108.

HUSBAND: Yes, I meant to have told you. I saw John at the club.
(*Two old gentlemen strike matches.*)
WIFE: It's difficult. (*After a long pause.*) Oh, well, let's—
(*Enter Maid.*)
MAID: There's a policeman downstairs, sir, wants to see you.
HUSBAND: Oh Lord! (*He goes out for five minutes while the audience waits breathlessly. Now the drama is moving. He returns.*)
WIFE: Car?
HUSBAND: Some fool turned the lights off. Let's see. *What* were we talking about? Damn, I left my pipe downstairs. (*He goes out.*)
(And if the audience goes out too, who shall blame it?)
That is how real life is lived. It is clear that natural behavior, natural dialogue, must be dressed up before it can recommend itself to an audience.[16]

A play which depicts modern life should be written in the simplest language, suggestive of the clippings and cuttings certain people habitually make, and containing grammatical errors, if a character portrayed would normally make them. The dialogue should appear to be like natural speech, but never become so realistic that it approaches the type of speech in Milne's example. Robert E. Sherwood said, "It ought to be obvious that the wholesale slaughter of illusions would be disastrous to the theatre, which survives solely because of its ability to create and sustain the illusion of reality." [17]

The distinction between realism and reality is that realism, as we know it in dramatic writing, is the *illusion* of reality. Good dialogue is not what it would be in real life; it can only sound as if it were.

POETIC DIALOGUE IN THE MODERN PLAY

From the earliest beginnings of the theatre, poetry has been closely associated with dramatic art. In fact, so close has been the association that many of the early treatises concerning the theory and technique of writing for the theatre were entitled, with some variations, "The Art of Poetry."

[16] A. A. Milne, *Autobiography*, E. P. Dutton & Co., 1939, pp. 292–293.
[17] John Mason Brown, *Upstage*, W. W. Norton & Company, 1930, p. 13.

An examination of Homeric drama and the plays of the Age of Pericles will reveal the widespread use of poetic dialogue. From the days of the Greek dramatists, such as Aeschylus, Euripides, Sophocles, and Aristophanes, through the works of the great Latin playwrights, Plautus and Terence, down through the golden and highly productive Elizabethan age, plays were primarily expressed in dramatic poetry. However, in the theatre of the twentieth century, modern plays containing poetic dialogue have rarely found popular success. Why is this? Is there an apathy on the part of the general public toward the use of poetry in the theatre? If so, it is the first such mass expression in over two thousand years of dramatic history. The early audiences, composed of people from every walk of life, from noblemen to prostitute, enthusiastically received the plays of the Greek and Elizabethan poets.

Maxwell Anderson, who believes, with Goethe, that dramatic poetry is man's greatest achievement, is not the only modern playwright who has utilized poetic dialogue. T. S. Eliot and Christopher Fry have received some *critical* acclaim, but only Anderson has received popular acclaim at the box office.

The Language of Emotion

Poetry, as a way of using language, impels the user powerfully toward emotional utterance. By the same token the use of poetry impels the user *away* from the commonplace. Apparently the modern playwright, as did Shakespeare, may employ both prose and poetry in the same play. Anderson feels that prose is the language of information and poetry the language of emotion. Prose can be stretched to carry emotion, but only in the cases of such playwrights as Synge and O'Casey can prose occasionally rise to poetic heights by substituting the unfamiliar speech rhythms of an untutored people for the rhythm of verse. Anderson felt the problem so keenly that he endeavored to become a poet, for, as he looked about him, he reasoned that under the strain of an emotion the ordinary prose of the modern drama breaks down into inarticulateness, just as it does in life. Because of the inability of the contemporary playwright to express his emotional peaks in poetic dialogue, Anderson rationalized the existence of what he called the "cult" of playwrights writing realistic dramas, "in which the climax is reached in an eloquent gesture or moment of meaningful silence." [18]

If, as Anderson thought, prose is the language of information and poetry the language of emotion, there must, necessarily, be an emotional jumping-off place where it is natural for a character, under emotional stress, to speak in lines of poetic dialogue without appearing unnatural.

Clayton Hamilton reported that after the triumphant opening night of Anderson's *Mary of Scotland,* he asked the author why he had begun the play in prose and ended it in verse. Anderson's reply was very simple. "Until a play has risen to a certain level of emotion," said Anderson, "it seems most natural to write the dialogue in prose; but, after this level of emotion has been superseded, I find it impossible to restrain myself from writing verse. Verse is much more natural than prose as a medium for expressing high emotion. Furthermore, since all the really greatest plays in history have been written in verse, I can see no reason for rejecting this tradition, even though it appears to be unfashionable at the present time." [19]

Some playwrights believe poetry is the inspiration of beauty. However, in dramatic writing it must not be the poetry of literature if the playwright expects a large audience. It must, instead, be the poetry of human feeling. As Samuel Shipman, who longed to write in poetic dialogue but never succeeded, said, "It is no use playing Beethoven on a church organ in the Theatre, even if you are a fine organist, when the hand organ will inspire a wider poetic appeal."

[18] Maxwell Anderson, "Poetry in the Theatre," *Off Broadway,* William Sloane Associates, 1947, p. 48.
[19] Clayton Hamilton, *"So You're Writing a Play!"* Little, Brown & Company, 1935, p. 227.

Poetic Tragedy in a Modern Setting

One reason for the lack of poetry in modern dramatic writing was found by Anderson, who, returning to the world's storehouse of dramatic literature, discovered that poetic tragedy has never been successfully written about its own place and time.

"There is not one tragedy by Aeschylus, Sophocles, Euripides, Shakespeare, Corneille, or Racine," said Anderson, "which did not have the advantage of a setting either far away or long ago." With this admonition in mind Anderson wrote *Elizabeth the Queen* and a succession of historical plays in verse, some of them highly successful. The key term employed by Anderson is "poetic tragedy," since poetic satire on contemporary affairs in a contemporary setting has been successfully expressed ever since Aristophanes attacked the existing order of Greece through satiric poetry.

Anderson was not willing to accept the tradition of the great masters and so began a period of experimentation in which he attempted to treat modern themes in a modern setting. *Winterset,* which won for him the New York Drama Critics Circle Award for 1935–1936, was his initial attempt to establish a new convention. Anderson said of this attempt: *"Winterset* is largely in verse, and treats a contemporary tragic theme, which makes it more of an experiment than I could wish, for the great masters themselves never tried to make tragic poetry out of the stuff of their own times. To do so is to attempt to establish a new convention, one that may prove impossible of acceptance, but to which I was driven by the lively historical sense of our duty—a knowledge of period, costume, and manners which almost shuts off the writer on historical themes from contemporary comment. Whether or not I have solved the problem in *Winterset* is probably of little moment. But it must be solved if we are to have great theater in America." [20]

The reason so many critics deplore the lack of verse in the Ameri-

20 Anderson, *op. cit.,* p. 54.

can theatre is that they can think of few serious prose plays that have survived the generation that gave them birth. In justifying his own prose plays as being a concession to public demand, van Druten claimed that "most readers prefer the newspaper to a literary classic and most playgoers visit a theatre not in the hope of seeing a beautiful work of art." However, many of the people who condemn the extreme realism of many modern prose plays hold that the chief value of verse dialogue is that it delivers a play from sober reality. Many writers who would not ordinarily employ poetry do not rule out its use. Poetry has its place in modern dramatic writing so long as it is the natural culmination of a character in the stress of an emotion.

HUMOROUS DIALOGUE

Genuine comedy usually depends for its value upon the skillful portrayal of character. The humor and warmth derived from, or originated by, a genuine character is one of the attributes of successful comedy characterization.

Some dramatists feel that comedy and farce are more exacting in their demands upon the playwright and, therefore, more difficult to write than more serious drama. Since the humor of comedy dialogue often lies in the subtlety of lines, the audience, of necessity, must be more discriminating. Comedy presupposes a considerable degree of intelligence. Avery Hopwood commented, "Of course, it does not require the brain of a Spencer or a Descartes to respond to the comedy of a clown falling over a chair. But it does require a certain discrimination and intelligence to grasp a comedy line or situation of some subtlety." [21]

It is even possible that the playwright has to be more active or agile, intellectually, when he writes a comedy than when he writes a more serious drama. Few people seem to realize the exhaustive drain writing dialogue for a comedy or a farce makes upon one's inventive powers.

[21] Avery Hopwood, "Why I Don't Write More Serious Plays," *Theatre Magazine*, April, 1924, p. 10.

The technique of writing for a laugh is an exacting procedure demanding a keen comic sense on the part of the dramatist. The writer cannot depend upon the excellence of his actors to provide the necessary twist to a line of dialogue, for while many comedians possess a sense of the comic they often lack a sense of humor. Therefore the technique of writing for a laugh becomes so exact as to be almost a science. After all, comedy is not achieved when the audience laughs only at the actors and not at the play.

S. N. Behrman feels that the playwright should approach all forms of drama with a sense of humor and that a line of humorous dialogue sometimes can be more revealing and penetrating than any dramatic explanation. "The ability to laugh at its own pretensions and shortcomings," wrote Behrman, "is the true mark of the civilized nation, as it is of the civilized man."

It is very difficult to cite examples of humorous dialogue from successful comedies. But this is good. It shows how impossible it is to isolate a sequence of lines from the total context of a comedy and still reveal humor. Since true humor emerges from a character's reaction to a situation, not to show the character's complete development prior to his saying the isolated lines of dialogue may rob them of any real humor.

It is the element of unexpectedness which often makes a line of dialogue humorous. However, this can best be demonstrated by placing the line in context. In the opening scene of F. Hugh Herbert's *The Moon Is Blue*, Patty O'Neill meets Don Gresham on the Observation Tower of the Empire State Building. They are strangers. In the ensuing conversation Don tries to talk Patty into going out to dinner with him:

PATTY: I love spaghetti, don't you?
DON: Frankly, I prefer a good steak.
PATTY: (*Hesitates, stalling*) It's early. I'm not hungry.
DON: Fine. We'll go to my place first and have a drink. How about it?
PATTY: (*Looks him over for a long time*) Would you try to seduce me?

Patty's last remark, of course, has the quality of unexpectedness, yet it is perfectly in keeping with her character, for frankness and bluntness are two of her most pronounced traits. For example, Don's reaction to Patty's question is one of amusement as he replies, "I don't know. Probably. Why?" To this Patty says matter-of-factly that a girl wants to know:

PATTY: (*Bluntly*) Look, it's very simple. Let's face it—going to a man's apartment almost always ends in one of two ways: Either the girl's willing to lose her virtue—or she fights for it. I don't want to lose mine —and I think it's vulgar to fight for it. So I always put my cards on the table. Don't you think that's sensible?

That's Patty and the comedy emerging from her dialogue actually stems from her character as she reacts to the situation facing her.

A line of humorous dialogue is often used intentionally to bring relief and relaxation from a play's mounting tension. Just as Shakespeare introduced the grave digger's scene into *Hamlet* as a comic relief device, so modern playwrights give their audiences an opportunity to catch their breath before taking them to even higher peaks of intensity. An audience can stand just so much suspense, intensity, and emotional strain. It needs relief, and if the playwright doesn't provide the opportunity, it will make its own. This is what happens when a nervous laugh is heard in the wrong place or at an inopportune moment. The viewer needs an outlet and having none he will laugh at the first out-of-the-ordinary act or word that comes along. Nervous laughter during serious scenes can ruin a performance. It is a wise playwright who leads the members of his audience step by step up the emotional ladder, allowing them to pause and recover before carrying them to the top.

Examples of comic relief lines of dialogue are much easier to isolate since they stand out in relief to the seriousness of a scene. For instance, in the closing scene of *The King and I*, the King is dying. Anna, the English schoolteacher, has just changed her mind about returning to England.

ANNA: Louis, please go down and ask Captain Orton to take all our boxes off the ship. And have everything put back into our house.

(*Louis runs off eagerly. The children break into shouts of joy.*)

KING: Silence!

(*At the note of anger in his voice, the children, wives, Lady Thiang— all fall prostrate.*)

Is no reason for doing of this demonstration for schoolteacher realizing her duty, for which I pay her exorbitant monthly salary of twenty . . . five pounds! Further, this is disorganized behavior for bedroom of dying King!

This is followed by a scene between the King and his son who is made to tell what he will do when king. The boy does this with difficulty and when he is finished the King's head sinks back on the pillow and he is dead. The King, who has charmed Anna and the audience for two and a half hours, has died in character.

The Use of Epigrams, Wisecracks, and Jokes

The use of epigrams, wisecracks, and jokes in the dialogue of a play is extremely hazardous, since they may endanger the harmony and strength of a play's design. There is a tendency to employ such humorous elements merely for their own comic value, completely severed from character and situation. Being severed, these epigrams and jokes cannot contribute to the forward movement of the play's action.

Part of the art of writing true dramatic dialogue consists in the suppression, by the playwright, of all jokes and epigrams severed from character. The modern reaction against the use of epigrams is a rebellion against a dramatic tradition inherited from the nineteeth century. The comedies of that day had to have epigrams—the audiences expected them. Oscar Wilde was the darling of the theatre because he popularized the smart and universal generalizations about life. The epigram was so popular that authors might well have carried notebooks in those days to jot them down when they occurred to them, for an audience was immediately prepared to laugh when they heard a character start off a line with "All men" or "Any woman" or "The conventions of society are." Today, however, audiences are not as prone to laugh at the dragged-in joke or snappy epigram which has no connection with the characters or philosophy of the play.

Noel Coward, in discussing his own development as a dramatist, singled out his play, *Hay Fever,* as the crucial turning point in his transition from an immature to a mature writer of comedy. Prior to this particular play he had emphasized the comedy value of actual lines rather than the comedy values stemming from character and situation. It was with some reluctance that he became aware of his changing attitude, for he wrote, "I expect that when I read through *Hay Fever* that first time, I was subconsciously bemoaning its lack of snappy epigrams."

The day of epigrams is behind us. Lines that are truly funny by themselves are rare, for humor comes most naturally from the characters and their relationships to the situations of the play. The beginning dramatic writer often assumes that in a comedy every line deserves a tongue-in-cheek wisecrack as a reply. He should look at any popular modern comedy and find the lines that can be extracted from a scene and remain funny. It is likely that he will have to extract entire scenes, since the characters and the situation have to be present for the line to be humorous.

On the other side of the ledger, epigrams, wisecracks, and jokes may be used in a modern play if the playwright has carefully established their use as an integral part of a character's natural conduct. To place epigrams or jokes in the mouth of a character it must be established clearly and early that such an outburst is a normal method of expression for the character using them.

DIALOGUE PROBLEMS

Many dialogue problems have already been cited in the preceding sections of this chapter. They are not offered as examples of problems the dramatist will encounter, but merely as perplexing situations that have confronted successful playwrights in the past. The following problems are of a similar nature.

An amusing dialogue problem arose for J. M. Barrie in connection with the first performance of *Peter Pan*. Barrie was besieged by irate parents the day after the play's opening. It seems that many of the children in the audience had gone home and attempted to fly from their beds as the children had done in the play. Unfortunately, their efforts to duplicate the feat of flying, realistically performed on the stage with the aid of piano wire, resulted in several very serious injuries which required surgical attention. When made aware of what his play had indirectly caused, Barrie immediately agreed to write additional dialogue to dissuade children from trying to fly. "I had to add something to the play," said Barrie, "about no one being able to fly until the fairy-dust had been blown on him." The added dialogue apparently served its purpose since no additional accidents were reported during the London run.

Addressing himself to the specific problem of handling the dialogue of a play set in Biblical times, Bernard Shaw struck out at the inconsistency of mingling simple, modern language with the vernacular of a bygone day. In a review of *The Daughters of Babylon,* by Wilson Barrett, Shaw attacked the mixture of modern Old Bailey English with the obsolete use of the second person singular. Attacking the playwright's inconsistency, he said, "Pray observe that I should not at all object to the wording of the whole drama in the most modern vernacular, even if it were carried to the extent of making the Babylonian idol seller talk like a coster. But modern vernacular seasoned with thees and thous and haths and whithers to make it sound peradventurously archaic is another matter." [22]

Shaw recognized the tendency to borrow from the language of the Elizabethan period, noting that it was then that the Bible received its most famous translation. Many of the present objections to the *Revised Standard Version of The Holy Bible* are based on its departure from the language which many generations have assumed to be authentically biblical. The King James translation of the Bible was a modern render-

[22] George Bernard Shaw, *Our Theatres in the Nineties,* Constable & Co., Ltd., 1932, p. 45.

ing into the best speech of its period. What is so unusual about a translation that again places the Bible into the vernacular of the present? However, we must recognize that the objection exists and many writers attempting to capture the flavor of biblical drama fall back on the use of the obsolete second person singular. Shaw refutes the effectiveness of such language, calling specific attention to such lines in Barrett's play as, "Who is he that biddeth against me for this woman?" Would it not be more understandable to a modern audience to say, "Who are you?" Is the meaning lost?

Telephone scenes are very popular with actors, since they afford an opportunity for a solo piece of acting. Several academy awards won by actors playing such scenes has not diminished their popularity in the least. Edmund O'Brien was the most recent winner of a supporting Oscar. He had his big dramatic moment at the telephone in *The Barefoot Contessa.* Writers should be very careful in composing such solo scenes, for if they have been written well and executed well, the actor may get a round of applause from the audience. Whenever an audience is moved to express its appreciation for an excellent piece of acting, then it has had its attention focused upon the actor rather than the character in relationship, or in proper perspective, to the play.

Channing Pollock discusses in his autobiography a problem that arose in a play in which he was attempting to treat four stories. He was trying to make each sufficiently, though superficially, dissimilar, yet find a way to remind the audience that basically the different stories were the same. He contrived to do this by three devices: first, by using an object, or property, easily identifiable and recognizable, in each story; second, by employing a sound effect which would be used in each story; and, third, by using dialogue as a *leitmotif,* or reminder. "The third and most ingenious device," wrote Pollock, "was an adaptation of Wagner's *Leitmotifs.* You will remember that when Siegfried's sword is laid by his dead body in *Götterdämmerung,* for a few bars the music is identical with that accompanying his father's withdrawal of the sword from the tree in the first act of *Die Walküre.* Thus we are reminded that this is the same sword, and of its history. In my play I did my reminding with dialogue, using, for the same purpose, a few identical phrases in each repetition of what was fundamentally the equivalent outcome." [23]

Dialogue is to the dramatist what paints are to the artist and clay to the sculptor. Each sees clearly in his mind's eye that which he will create. The painter roughs in his plan with charcoal, the sculptor shapes his trusses, and the playwright constructs his plot. The painter then uses paints to communicate his total concept. The sculptor molds clay to the trusses to achieve his desired effect. The playwright uses dialogue to give his play life.

[23] Channing Pollock, *Harvest of My Years,* The Bobbs-Merrill Company, 1943, pp. 239–240.

Language Difficulties

THE composer of music expresses himself by a series of sounds represented by symbols—notes drawn on white paper with bars, rests, and also signs. The composer works with notes, the dramatic writer with another symbol of sounds—words. The chief difference between music and drama is that the symbols used by the composer of music are usually those of sound alone, whereas the symbols employed by the dramatic writer represent ideas as well as sounds.

Being a playwright implies a mastery of language, a concern for the choice of words, their arrangement, and their meaning and effect upon an audience. Words are, after all, the only tools the writer has to build with.

THE TECHNICAL LIMITATION OF ENGLISH

A major language problem facing the dramatic writer is the inability of written English to convey exact meanings. Take the phrase, "He saw me." Here are three words, two pronouns and a verb, a total of seven letters, all apparently combined to convey a certain meaning. But what is that meaning?

By stressing each word in turn, different meanings are conveyed. "*He* saw me" may be a positive identification of the man who did the seeing. "He *saw* me" stresses the fact that he was seen and had better not deny it. "He saw *me*" affirms who was seen. By using a rising inflection with each word in turn we get another set of meanings. "He (?) saw me" questions that the man said to have done the seeing was actually the man. "He saw (?) me" questions the act of being seen, though it may admit the presence of both the man said to have done the seeing and the person said to have been seen. "He saw me (?)" questions not only who was seen but can even suggest that it must have been somebody else who was seen.

Of course, the "He saw me" example is an oversimplification of a problem much larger in scope. How can the writer be sure of the meaning that will be conveyed when he writes out his thought in words, symbols to be used for speech? Bernard Shaw always insisted upon being in attendance at all rehearsals of his plays so that he could interpret what the language could not convey. "I have of course been compelled to omit in the printed version of the play many things that a stage representation could convey," said Shaw, "simply because the art of letters, though highly developed grammatically, is still in its infancy as a technical speech notation: for example, there are fifty ways of saying Yes, and five hundred of saying No, but only one way of writing them down." [1]

The dramatic writer must be constantly aware that the thought he has so well conceived may find difficulty being expressed in written language. Whatever he can do to eliminate confusion, he should do, whether it is underscoring certain words, indicating hesitations, or explaining in parentheses the attitude or emotion desired when the actor is delivering a line of dialogue.

THE MEANING AND EFFECT OF WORDS

Words continually change their meaning and do not always mean the same thing to everyone who hears them. Almost every word in general use has two or three distinct meanings. It is the wise playwright who attempts to know them all.

[1] George Bernard Shaw, *Plays Pleasant and Unpleasant*, I, Constable & Co., Ltd., 1931, p. xxi.

An excellent example of the multiple meaning of a word is the word *word*. What abuse *word* receives! The first sergeant barks at his troops, "All right, you guys, I'm going to give you the *word*." How many times have we heard the expression, "I wish you'd put in a good word for me." And then there is the Biblical phrase, "The word of God." People still say, "May I have a word with you," "Upon my word," "I give you my word," and "My word is my bond." Of course when someone says, "You can take my word for it," you may wonder which word in the English language is his word.

Another word with innumerable significations, most of them essentially American, is *run*. A run in baseball is a score, yet in football it is the action of advancing the football. A woman has a run in her stocking, a bomber makes a run on its target, and there is the run on a bank. Then there is the run of a play, a run for the money, and a man uses a canoe to run the rapids. A man controlling his own affairs is said to run his own business, a newspaper may run a story or an advertisement. A candidate may run for public office and yet be run by his political party. Certainly the words *word* and *run* illustrate the multiple meanings words may possess.

A single word or a series of words may have an effect upon the audience and upon the play. In a dramatic speech a single word can easily make or mar a scene. John Galsworthy contended that a "false phrase, a single word out of tune, will destroy the illusion of the play as surely as a stone heaved into a still pool shatters the image seen there."

An image is inherent in any word or group of words which appeals to the senses. Sensory appeal to an audience results from the use of a word or a combination of words that calls up an image response. The image may be a simple representation such as "a saloon" or it may be a more complex association such as "I saw him hanging there—still— like a side of beef in a meat market."

In dramatic dialogue, image stimulus comes from a word or group of words rather than from an object. The word-stimulus strikes the listener's ear, which in turn transmits the received symbol to the brain, which then makes an image association to the object symbolized. Only rarely does an image appeal to just one of the senses. What are these senses which are appealed to through word-stimuli? Most authorities agree that there are eight basic senses. Images that appeal predominantly to the sense of sight are called *visual*; to the sense of hearing, *auditory*; to the sense of taste, *gustatory*; to the sense of smell, *olfactory*; to the sense of touch, *tactual* or *tactile*. A feeling of heat or cold is said to be a *thermal* sense. *Kinetic* imagery is an appeal to the motor sense. A response to muscle tension or relaxation or a response to height or distance is said to be *kinesthetic* imagery.

Imagery often operates at two levels. At one level it recreates a thing in terms that can be readily perceived by the senses, but at another level, it can weld intellect and emotion together into a single concept. The dramatic writer, of course, operates at both levels.

CHOICE OF WORDS

The standard to be applied in choosing a word is in its clarity of thought and its ability to gain understanding from an audience. But at the same time, the playwright must be true to the emotion he is attempting to convey, not just by one word, but by all the words in any given scene.

One major misconception that may bother the dramatist is the confusion between the complexity of a thought or concept and its expression in language. Hollywood, for example, has been criticized for directing motion pictures toward an intellectual level of 13 years of age. Do these critics mean that the language is at a level comprehensible to the 13-year-old mind or do they mean the concepts directed toward an audience are at a 13-year-old level? There is a difference. Simplicity of expression in no way means simplicity of thought. Many of the profoundest thoughts can be stated simply and in language understood by a widespread audience. One of the purposes of dramatic communication is to take complicated ideas or concepts and make them understandable by the receiver to whom they are directed. The mistake often made is to express in simple language correspondingly simple and inane thoughts.

The vocabulary of the receiver of a drama is just as important to its successful communication as is the vocabulary of a reader of a novel. The reader, however, holds an advantage over the auditor and viewer, since he can stop and look up any strange words in a dictionary. Channing Pollock once said, "Generally speaking, the man who attempts to write or produce something a bit better than is demanded encounters resentment rather than mere indifference." He felt that next to love, the most universal sentiment is "hatred of the 'highbrow'."

The playwright who can reach his audience is the playwright who can address his audience in language they can understand. Stating things in simple, comprehensible words in no way eliminates what a playwright may say nor the effectiveness with which he may say it. He should avoid words, however, which are unfamiliar or vague or which may have special connotations, unless their use makes them correspondingly clear to the audience.

Playwrights should have a regard for the actors who will give utterance to their words. From an actor's point of view, short, simple, straightforward sentences or phrases are easier to deliver than complex sentences with long and unusual words. Long words convey formality and are more unusual to the auditors.

If a writer has an unerring sense of the vernacular, he will find that not only is he able to communicate well, his character will achieve greater dimensionality and believability when presented to an audience. Current slang, however, should be avoided unless it is necessary to the establishment of a character. Originally, slang was considered to be the special vocabulary, or professional jargon, of vagrants and thieves, but in recent decades slang has come to be considered the peculiar use of popular but unauthorized language by all professional groups.

There are several good reasons for avoiding the use of slang in the modern play. Slang dates a play and limits its universality. Slang vocabulary changes constantly, varying from decade to decade, and in many cases from year to year. The use of slang also limits the possibility of being translated from English into a foreign language.

Of course it would be almost impossible to build up many modern characters without having them speak in colloquial English. As a matter of fact it would not be amiss to claim that there is a colloquial American language and if a playwright is to communicate effectively to an audience he will become an expert in the field. Many persons can be characterized only by the language they use and Americans use words in a peculiar manner.

Americanisms are words or phrases that differ in meaning or form from the expressions that would commonly be used in England to mean the same thing. They may or may not have originated in the United States, but they are the American way of expressing a certain idea. Obvious Americanisms are *apartment* for *flat* and *hood* (of an automobile) for *bonnet*. These, however, are seldom considered words that would characterize an individual.

Different people use different words to mean the same thing. The following synonyms for *abnormal* would certainly characterize the persons using them. One man may say that a man is "mixed up," while another will call him "pixilated." Others will employ such descriptive terms as "screwball," "screwy," "disturbed," and "souped-up."

Americanisms also include distinctly modern terms such as "AWOL," a military term meaning absent without leave, or additional meanings to old words like "blackboard jungle" to describe classroom conditions so violently unruly that teachers cannot perform their duties. Once coined, phrases in the news pass into the language as Americanisms to be broadly applied. An example of this is the term "brainwashing." Also look how Quisling, the Norwegian betrayer during World War II, has had his name pass into the language as a noun to describe a citizen who goes over to the side of the enemy, especially to become a high-ranking official in a puppet government. Then there are popular idioms like "brushoff" and "bobbysoxer." Of course slang expressions must be considered, but with care. "Baloney" is a slang expression for "nonsense" but only certain characters would use the term.

The evolution of words from coinage to acceptance usually follows the route of slang or vulgarism to colloquial American and finally into acceptable literary diction. When writing plays employing historical characters it is wise to use only acceptable literary diction. Robert E. Sherwood, for example, in later years was dissatisfied with his first stage hit, *The Road to Rome,* complaining that in it he resorted to the cheapest sort of device—making historical characters use modern slang.

THE USE OF PROFANITY AND TABU WORDS

A perplexing problem in modern dramatic writing is the handling of profanity and tabu words. Only recently have the dramatic media been able to use "socially objectionable language," and then in only a limited sense. What the individual can use in his own vocabulary and what he can read in novels in the privacy of his own library, is often the first to be condemned by him when it is spoken in a theatre or from a motion picture screen.

A social self-consciousness seems to possess people when they see and hear things as members of a group. A sort of embarrassment prevents some of them from accepting what they would ordinarily accept when alone.

Profanity for profanity's sake, divorced from character creation, is never wise. It is using words for shock effect, and, as such, should never be permitted. There may come a time in the rising intensity of a play, however, when a character, acting under great emotional stress, expresses himself in extreme terms. This is most natural and not nearly as objectionable, even to those most opposed to profanity of any kind. In some situations any other words but profanity would be neither appropriate nor believable.

For example, a certain actor became so affected by the situation he was facing that in a speech of great emotional intensity he ad-libbed a "God damn." The actor was Lloyd Bridges, the play was a television drama, *Tragedy in a Temporary Town*. The play is set in a trailer camp of migrant workers. A girl has been kissed in the nearby woods. This act is amplified by the indignantly righteous workers into an attempted rape. Actually, it was merely a teen-age boy professing his adolescent feeling toward an attractive girl of his own age. Unfortunately, it was dark and the boy and his true intent went unrecognized. The workers become an unruly mob and interrogate each male member of the "temporary town." Suspicion shifts from one trailer to the next. A Puerto Rican family has a boy about the age of the supposed attacker. Prejudice drives the mob to seize him. But before they can carry out their lynching, the truth comes out, largely through the efforts of the character portrayed by actor Bridges. It was a highly emotional scene as Bridges castigated the mob for their blind stupidity. The speech builds to a peak and Bridges capped it with, "You God damn pigs!" Later it turned out that Bridges hadn't been aware that he had even inserted the "God damn," he had been so carried away by the emotion of the scene he was playing. Nonetheless, the network received quite a landslide of mail, some condemning the "slip," but, and more important, some praising the program for having allowed an actor to say what the character would have said in such an extremely emotional situation. The slip was unfortunate, but the reaction to it demonstrates that a mature audience appreciates emotional honesty in the handling of profanity in the dramatic media.

Not too many years ago actor Bridges would have faced legal action for such a slip of the tongue. Radio and television, the dramatic media open to the public at large, number in their audiences many children and people who would never willingly pay to hear profanity. Legally, the airwaves are public property and thus subject to some regulation as to what is or is not said. The attitude toward profanity, which is *not* to be mistaken for *obscenity,* is understandable, but at the same time the writer must deplore it when it restricts what a carefully created character would logically say in a certain situation. Certainly such use of profanity is not profanity for profanity's sake, but instead profanity of dramatic necessity. Obscenity, the use of language to make vulgar allusions, is never justifiable.

The history of modern American drama reflects a changing attitude toward strong language uttered publicly. Early in the century the use of "damn" or "hell" on the stage was enough to arouse in an audience the laughter which is an outward manifestation of shock or embarrassment.

An historic occasion in the annals of American playwriting occurred in the year 1909 when "God damn" was first heard from an American stage. The play was Clyde Fitch's *The City,* which was posthumously produced. Rice, referring to this first use of the phrase by an American playwright, concluded: "Indeed, it is not the least curious thing about all of those tabu expressions that almost everybody is thoroughly familiar with them and they are frequently to be heard in the street, in the school-yard, and around the dinner-table. It is another evidence of the conservatism of the stage that it surrenders its reticences much more slowly than do its sister arts, poetry and fiction or, for that matter, than do the individuals who comprise its audiences." [2]

Channing Pollock, in his autobiography written in 1943, referred to Fitch's use of "God damn" in 1909 and said, "We were shocked but no more so than we should have been by plain 'damn' a decade before." A decade prior, 1899, was the year Fitch's play, *The Cowboy and the Lady,* opened in London. The curses contained in the dialogue never went beyond "hell" and "damn" but Fitch reported that "*The Telegraph* was brutal toward me about the swearing."

Fifteen years after *The City,* came the dialogue of *What Price Glory?* which made the Clyde Fitch epithet sound like baby prattle. This famous and realistic play about World War I, by Maxwell Anderson and Laurence Stallings, utilized the language of men in wartime serv-

[2] Elmer Rice, "Sex in the Modern Theatre," *Harper's Magazine,* May, 1932, p. 669.

ice. Making its appearance on the New York stage in 1924, *What Price Glory?* contained the lustiest language yet to be utilized in a play. So intent at not being misunderstood by their liberal use of profanity, Anderson and ex-Marine Stallings inserted a note in the program to the play and later insisted that it should be included as a preface to any printed version. This short note explained that it was not the authors' intention to shock, but to be highly realistic. Anderson and Stallings felt it was impossible to characterize men under wartime pressure as speaking parlor English. Because of its significance as a landmark in the development of the modern American play, the program note is quoted in its entirety.

> *What Price Glory?* is a play of war as it is, not as it has been presented theatrically for thousands of years. The soldiers talk and act much as soldiers the world over. The speech of men under arms is universally and consistently interlarded with profanity. Oaths mean nothing to a soldier save a means to obtain emphasis. He uses them in place of more polite adjectives.
>
> The authors of *What Price Glory?* have attempted to reproduce this mannerism along with other general atmosphere they believe to be true. In a theatre where war has been lied about, romantically, effectively—and in a city where the war play has usually meant sugary dissimulation— *What Price Glory?* may seem bold. The audience is asked to bear with certain expletives which, under other circumstances, might be used for melodramatic effect, but herein are employed because the mood and truth of the play demand their employment.[3]

The general tenor of many of the plays subsequent to the initial appearance of *What Price Glory?* included more and more profanity. This trend was justified by what some playwrights termed a more widespread use of expletives by all members of society. For example, Willard Mack noted that crude language was beginning to permeate all strata of society. "Our social conversation, our tea-table talk, our card-game comments are all more or less punctuated with adjectives of

---

[3] Maxwell Anderson and Laurence Stallings, *Three American Plays,* Harcourt, Brace and Company, 1926, p. 3.

masculine crudity," said Mack, "profanity has become a matter of common usage, and the most delicate intimacies of the boudoir are discussed with blatant familiarity." [4]

Not all playwrights succumbed to the use of profanity. George M. Cohan condemned the trend of the 1920's, saying that "bar room conversation is like a prayer meeting compared with some of the dialogue in present-day stage production." His first objection was based on the increasing presence of children at dramatic performances. The second, and to Cohan a much more valid objection, was the use of questionable language to swell the box office lines. In Cohan's own words, "I've talked to several playwrights and to some of the producing managers about all this unnecessary profanity being slung at the theater-going public, but it's all a waste of words to get them to eliminate these objectionable words, because they seem to think that when the word gets around that there are certain nasty words spoken in a play, the words on the signboard in front of the theater read 'Standing Room Only.' " [5]

Elmer Rice dealt at length with words considered tabu. He considered it remarkable that the mere utterance of a syllable or a combination of syllables should have the power to provoke in the listener an intense emotional state. He felt it was insufficient to explain such phenomena by saying it was not the word but its connotation which aroused the emotion.

Rice set forth to prove his contention that it was the word, not the connotation, which was objectionable. First, he pointed out that often two words having exactly the same connotation will find one word permissible on the stage while the other is tabu. For example, said Rice, "prostitute" and "whore" mean exactly the same thing, yet the use of "whore" is frowned upon on the stage, despite its frequent occurrence in the English Bible and throughout English literature gener-

[4] Willard Mack, "The New Realism of the Stage," *Theatre Magazine*, April, 1927, p. 21.

[5] Ward Morehouse, *George M. Cohan, Prince of the American Theatre*, J. B. Lippincott Company, 1943, p. 225.

ally. Again, said Rice, whereas the use of such an expression as "sexual intercourse" would undoubtedly shock many people in the audience, it would certainly be permissible in the theatre of today, "whereas the use of certain other words and expressions which have precisely the same meaning would result in storms of protest from the auditors." [6]

The explanation of such hairline distinctions is best left to psychologists and etymologists. Many words that are tabu for the dramatic media are sexual in their connotation; however, many are not. Some relate to the anatomy and physiology of the reproductive system while others are closely allied to other bodily functions. Some tabu words are racial or religious in their connotation. Others are tabu, yet their exact meaning is obscure. That the problem is genuine witness this paragraph's omission of the very words it discusses. Unless it becomes absolutely essential dramatically to use some of the so-called tabu words, the writer should omit them. When words offend, the offense usually acts as a barrier to effective dramatic communication.

It must be admitted that the inconsistency with which words offend an audience is difficult to comprehend. Many of the world's masterpieces of dramatic literature, for example, contain scenes, expressions, and allusions that rightly should shock the staunchest reformers, yet they usually remain silent concerning these transgressions because the plays are considered "classics." It is difficult to find plays as rich in sexual connotation as Aristophanes *Lysistrata* and Shakespeare's *Taming of the Shrew*. Almost every year the Broadway scene is treated to at least one successful play stressing sex, such as *The Seven Year Itch*, but these plays are actually few in number when compared with the plays that find a stronger appeal in theme, character, and action.

CHARACTERIZATION THROUGH LANGUAGE

If the playwright has concerned himself with what a character will say in a certain situation all that remans is how he says it. This is the final culmination of the dramatic writing process. No one can prescribe formulas for characterizing people through language. It remains to

---

[6] Rice, *op. cit.*, p. 668.

the writer to find the best way of putting appropriate words into the mouths of his characters, words that will reveal the character and at the same time forward the progression of the plot. Dramatic literature is rich with illustrations of how successful playwrights have characterized their people. This storehouse is as varied as it is rich. Playwrights should study it not for characterizations to be imitated, but for examples of how dialogue may be written to convey styles and rhythms of speech. Much can be learned from dramatic literature about characterizing people of varied ethnic heritages, economic levels, and professional classes.

For example, both John Howard Lawson and Elmer Rice attempted to express native idiom in many of their plays. Lawson's *Processional* portrayed heterogeneous Americans of foreign origin who work beneath the earth's surface in the nation's coal mines. For instance, the character of Psinski says: "A fool that walks on asphalt among electric lights, what can you know about people born in the dark, a lonely bitter people in the mountains, an' to them come a stream of mystic foreigners—the Pole, the Greek, the Italian—" At this point the character of Phillpots interjects, "That's all right, but they all turn into Americans," to which Psinski replies, "They turn into dirt, the earth is their mother an' she calls 'em."

Lawson's characters are not only picturesque, their manner of speech portrays their longings, their frustrations. Old Pop Pratt, the Civil War veteran is heard to say, "Yes, friends, in them days sinful pride leaped up an' we fought our brothers, American blood to water American earth . . . (*Tapping wooden leg with stick*) That's what my flesh done; fertilizer. My leg went to make the flowers grow on Gettysburg. We fought our brothers, we did." Lawson has a way of arranging words for maximum character revelation. The character Slop says, "I wish Jim Flimmins was here; he's the guy got music inside him comes out natural like the foam off beer." [7]

Elmer Rice's *Street Scene*, set against a tenement front in lower New

---

[7] John Howard Lawson, *Processional*, in *Contemporary Drama* edited by E. Bradlee Watson and Benfield Pressey, Charles Scribner's Sons, 1941, pp. 849–886.

York, is peopled with characters of different foreign origin. An excerpt of dialogue, a conversation between neighbors living on the street, reveals Rice's keen ear for the sounds of language. Note carefully the way he writes each character's speeches to reveal their feeling and to indicate their racial origin:

KAPLAN: Eet's de folt of our economic system. So long as de institution of private property exeests, de verkers will be at de moicy of de property-owning klesses.

MAURRANT: That's a lot o' bushwa! I'm a woikin' man, see? I been payin' dues for twenty-two years in the Stage-Hands Union. If we're not gettin' what we want, we call a strike, see?—and then we get it.

LIPPO: Sure! Ees same wit' me. We gotta Musician Union. We getta pay for da rehears', we getta pay for da overtime—

SHIRLEY: That's all right when you belong to a strong union. But when a union is weak, like the Teachers' Union, it doesn't do you any good.

MRS. JONES: (To Mrs. Fiorentino) Can y'imagine that?—teachers belongin' to a union!

KAPLAN: (Impatiently) Oll dese unions eccomplish notting wotever. Oll dis does not toch de fondamental problem. So long as de tuls of industry are in de hands of de keptalist klesses, ve vill hev exploitation and sloms and—

MAURRANT: T'hell wit' all dat hooey! I'm makin' a good livin' an' I'm not doin' any kickin'.

OLSEN: (Removing his pipe from his mouth) Ve got prosperity, dis country.[8]

Rice has certainly enabled the director and the actor to grasp the basic speech rhythms of his characters. He has, through misspellings, omissions, substitutions, and intrusions, captured the quality of his character's ethnic origins. He has also endowed them with distinct personalities.

Eugene O'Neill often wrote about people he encountered in his adventures as a sailor before he turned to playwriting as a career. O'Neill's characters are well drawn and his methods of characterizing them are excellent models for the new playwright wondering how to

[8] Elmer Rice, Street Scene, Samuel French, 1929, pp. 50–51.

impart a certain flavor to a character's speech. Witness the following speech of Yank in *The Hairy Ape*:

YANK: (*Standing up and glaring at Long*) Sit down before I knock yuh down! (*Long makes haste to efface himself. Yank goes on contemptuously*) De Bible, huh? De Cap'tlist class, huh? Aw nix on dat Salvation Army-Socialist bull. Get a soapbox! Hire a hall! Come and be saved, huh? Jerk us to Jesus, huh? Aw g'wan! I've listened to lots of guys like you, see. Yuh're all wrong. Wanter know what I t'ink? Yuh ain't no good for no one. Yuh're de bunk. Yuh ain't got no noive, get me? Yuh're yellow, dat's what. Yellow, dat's you. Say! What's dem slobs in de foist cabin got to do wit us! We're better men dan dey are, ain't we? Sure! One of us guys could clean up de whole mob wit one mit . . .[9]

O'Neill has certainly captured the character of Yank, a lusty stoker, more animal than man. His speech reveals his background, his outlook, and most of all his brute-force leadership of the boiler room.

Contrast the above speech from *The Hairy Ape* with the following speeches from *The Emperor Jones*. Brutus Jones was an uneducated negro, a former railroad porter who fled the United States to an island where he has set himself up as emperor. The natives are all under his heel. His foil is Henry Smithers, a cockney trader.

SMITHERS: (*With curiosity*) And I bet you got yer pile o'money 'id safe some place.

JONES: (*With satisfaction*) I sho' has! And it's in a foreign bank where no pusson don't ever git it out but me no matter what come. You didn't s'pose I was holdin' down dis Emperor job for de glory in it, did you? Sho'! De fuss and glory part of it, dat's only to turn de heads o' de low-flung, bush niggers dat's here. Dey wants de big circus show for deir money. I gives it to 'em an' I gits de money. (*With a grin*) De long green, dat's me every time! (*Then rebukingly*) But you ain't got no kick agin me, Smithers. I'se paid you back all you done for me many times. Ain't I pertected you and winked at all de crooked tradin' you been doin' right out in de broad day? Sho' I has—and me makin' laws to stop it at de same time! (*He chuckles.*)

---

[9] Eugene O'Neill, *The Plays of Eugene O'Neill*, vol. III, Random House, 1948, p. 212.

SMITHERS: (*Grinning*) But, meanin' no 'arm, you been grabbin' right and left yourself, ain't yer? Look at the taxes you've put on 'em! Blimey! You've squeezed 'em dry!

JONES: (*Chuckling*) No, dey ain't *all* dry yet. I'se still heah, ain't I? [10]

The dialects of O'Neill's characters are unmistakable. The skilled actor would have little difficulty capturing the rhythms suggested in the above excerpt of dialogue.

There is an unmistakable similarity between the folk drama of Ireland and the regional drama of the United States. The Irish playwrights have succeeded in sharply characterizing the people of every walk of life—so have the American folk dramatists, Paul Green, E. P. Conkle, Kermit Hunter, etc. The new writer will learn much from a study of the Irish drama, especially the works of J. M. Synge, Lady Gregory, Lord Dunsany, Sean O'Casey, Paul Vincent Carroll. Such a study will also reveal that people are frequently characterized by the rhythm of word arrangement as well as the way individual words are pronounced.

Sean O'Casey in *Juno and the Paycock* even tried to capture the dialect. For example, he has Mrs. Boyle say, "Isn't it terrible to have to be waitin' this way! You'd think he was bringin' 20 poun's a week into the house the way he's going on. He wore out the Health Insurance long ago, he's afther wearin' out the unemployment dole, an', now, he's thryin' to wear out me! An' constantly singin', no less, when he ought always to be on his knees offerin' up a Novena for a job!" [11]

Lady Gregory, in portraying the characters of the little town of Cloon in *Hyacinth Halvey,* is satisfied just to capture the rhythm of the speech without trying to indicate word pronunciations. Take a portion of the scene in the post office between Mrs. Delane, the postmistress, and Miss Joyce, the priest's housekeeper:

MRS. DELANE: Good evening to you, Miss Joyce. What way is his reverence to-day? Did he get any ease from the cough?

[10] *Ibid.,* pp. 177–178.
[11] Sean O'Casey, *Juno and the Paycock,* The Macmillan Company, 1925, pp. 5–6.

MISS JOYCE: He did not, indeed, Mrs. Delane. He has it sticking to him yet. Smothering he is in the night-time. The most thing he comes short in is the voice.

MRS. DELANE: I am sorry, now, to hear that. He should mind himself well.[12]

These women speak as it is their natures to speak. When Mrs. Delane inquires as to the priest's health, it is natural for her to say, "What way is his reverence to-day?" just as it is natural for Miss Joyce to arrange her words in replying, "Smothering he is in the night-time." The way each woman phrases her words imparts an unmistakable rhythm to their sentences.

Perhaps the most famous one-act play written is *Riders to the Sea* by J. M. Synge. Many authorities attribute its greatness to its uncanny revelation of completely dimensional characters in a brief span of time. This trait, when coupled with a powerful and all-pervasive mood atmosphere, provides an excellent model for study.

Note the charm of the Irish speech in the play's opening scene between the old woman's two daughters:

CATHLEEN: (*Spinning the wheel rapidly*) What is it you have?

NORA: The young priest is after bringing them. It's a shirt and a plain stocking were got off a drowned man in Donegal.
(*Cathleen stops her wheel with a sudden movement, and leans out to listen.*)

NORA: We're to find out if it's Michael's they are, some time herself will be down looking by the sea.

CATHLEEN: How would they be Michael's, Nora? How would he go the length of that way to the far north?

NORA: The young priest says he's known the like of it. "If it's Michael's they are," says he, "you can tell herself he's got a clean burial by the Grace of God, and if they're not his, let no one say a word about them, for she'll be getting her death," says he, "with crying and lamenting." [13]

American playwrights dealing with strictly American subjects have managed to capture the same quality the Irish have in their plays. For

[12] Lady Gregory, *Hyacinth Halvey,* G. P. Putnam's Sons, 1909, p. 33.
[13] J. M. Synge, *The Complete Works of John M. Synge,* Random House, 1935, pp. 81–99.

example, Robert E. Sherwood and E. P. Conkle both wrote plays about Abraham Lincoln. Sherwood's Lincoln reflects his frontier background and his down-to-earth attitudes. In *Abe Lincoln in Illinois*, the character of Mentor asks, "You think a lot about death, don't you?" The reply:

ABE: I've had to, because it has always seemed to be so close to me—always —as far back as I can remember. When I was no higher than this table, we buried my mother. The milksick got her, poor creature. I helped Paw make the coffin—whittled the pegs for it with my own jackknife. We buried her in a timber clearing beside my grandmother, old Betsy Sparrow. I used to go there often and look at the place—used to watch the deer running over her grave with their little feet. I never could kill a deer after that. One time I catched hell from Paw because when he was taking aim I knocked his gun up. And I always compare the looks of those deer with the looks of men—like the men in New Orleans— that you could see had murder in their hearts.[14]

Now compare this speech with the following one from Conkle's *Prologue to Glory:*

ABE: I reckon no one's got more sympathy for the sore-oppressed than me. But we can't afford to make up our minds till we know the facts. Southerners would stand to lose millions if they were freed. Seems to me whether slavery is or is not wrong depends on whether the slave is or is not a *man*. I think—I—don't rightly keer to talk of it now, Stranger.[15]

Sherwood and Conkle both captured Lincoln's character. The speech patterns are not identical, yet the totality of effect of each is that we are witnessing a true dramatization of Lincoln as he actually lived.

There are countless examples in dramatic literature of every conceivable type of character. The cleverness with which our dramatists have created characters, endowed them with traits of personality, thus making them real people of true dimensionality is remarkable. One

---

14 Robert E. Sherwood, *Abe Lincoln in Illinois*, Charles Scribner's Sons, 1939, pp. 11–12.
15 E. P. Conkle, *Prologue to Glory*, Samuel French, 1938, p. 92.

instance is Lady Kitty, the chatterbox, in Somerset Maugham's *The Circle*. Witness how her chatter reveals her character:

LADY KITTY: I'm never nervous. I'm a born actress. Of course, if I had my time over again I'd go on the stage. You know, it's extraordinary how they keep young. Actresses, I mean. I think it's because they're always playing different parts. Hughie, do you think Arnold takes after me or after his father? Of course I think he's the very image of me. Arnold, I think I ought to tell you that I was received into the Catholic Church last winter. I've been thinking about it for years, and last time we were at Monte Carlo I met such a nice monsignore. I knew Hughie wouldn't approve, so I kept it a secret. (*To Elizabeth*) Are you interested in religion? I think it's too wonderful. We must have a long talk about it one of these days.[16]

The late Sidney Howard's play, *The Silver Cord*, is a remarkable portrayal of a woman who refuses to break the symbolic umbilical cord that ties her to her sons. Her possessiveness is very evident when she talks to a daughter-in-law about a photograph album:

MRS. PHELPS: I never counted. I used to study their photographs, month by month, just as I did their weight. I wasn't satisfied to watch only their bodies grow. I wanted a record of the development of their little minds and souls as well. I would compare the expression of Dave's eyes, for instance, at nine, with their expression at eight and a half, and see the increased depth. And I was never disappointed.[17]

In the previous chapter on dialogue the problem of writing poetical dramas was discussed. There it was observed that frequently prose and poetic dialogue may be found in the same play. Maxwell Anderson's *Elizabeth the Queen* is an example of the skillful blending of prose and poetry. The guards in the opening scene, of course speak in prose:

THIRD GUARD: What say you of the queen?
FIRST GUARD: Of the queen? I say she is well-known to be the virgin queen; I say no more.

[16] W. Somerset Maugham, *The Collected Plays of Somerset Maugham*, vol. III, William Heinemann Ltd., 1954, p. 26.
[17] Sidney Howard, *The Silver Cord*, in *Contemporary Drama*, edited by E. Bradlee Watson and Benfield Pressey, Charles Scribner's Sons, 1941, p. 938.

SECOND GUARD: But do you think she is a virgin?

FIRST GUARD: She doubtless has been a virgin, bully, for all women have been virgins, but the question is: First, when . . . and, second, where?

SECOND GUARD: Where?

FIRST GUARD: Where, bully, where?

THIRD GUARD: Would you not say, in the proper place?

FIRST GUARD: No. I would not say in the proper place. Because it is hard to say if there is a proper place wherein to be a virgin . . . unless it be in church, and, God defend me, I do not go to church.

Now compare the language of the guards to the poetic expression of Elizabeth and Essex. In the following excerpt, Elizabeth has just made reference to Sir Walter Raleigh and his silver-plated armor.

ESSEX: He'll wear no more
      Silver at your door.

ELIZABETH: What have you done . . . come, tell me.
      I knew this silver would draw fire. What happened?

ESSEX: Nothing . . . but the fashion's gone out.

ELIZABETH: No, but tell me!

ESSEX: He happened to be in the way
      When the upstairs pot was emptied.
      He's gone to change his clothes.

ELIZABETH: You shall not be allowed
      To do this to him. . . .

ESSEX: (*Moving toward her*) You shall not be allowed
      To mock me, my queen. (*He kisses her*)

ELIZABETH: Isn't it strange how one man's kiss can grow
      To be like any other's . . . or a woman's
      To be like any woman's?

ESSEX: Not yours for me,
      No, and not mine for you, you lying villain,
      You villain and queen, you double-tongued seductress.
      You bitch of brass!

ELIZABETH: Silver, my dear. Let me be
      A bitch of silver. It reminds me of Raleigh.

ESSEX: Damn you! [18]

[18] Maxwell Anderson, *Elizabeth the Queen*, in *Contemporary Drama,* edited by E. Bradlee Watson and Benfield Pressey, Charles Scribner's Sons, 1941, pp. 1069–1075.

If a playwright is to achieve any success in the dramatic media, he will of necessity become a student of language, for only through the combination of what a person says with how he says it can he be characterized for dramatic presentation. The examples cited above represent only a very small portion of the wealth of examples student playwrights should inspect and study. Such study will reveal how much like the composer's task is the playwright's; only the symbols are different.

12

Writing Procedures and Practices

PLAYWRIGHTS, like any other artists, rarely conform to a predictable pattern. Anyone who attempts to formulate a standardized approach to the playwriting task will quickly discover that an individual intuitively seeks out and pursues the method which for him is the easiest and most natural.

This chapter describes various approaches to the strictly mechanical procedures, from writing out the dialogue to getting the play into final manuscript form. The methods are many and varied and it is only hoped that from this discussion beginning playwrights and teachers of playwriting will find information that may be helpful in solving personal problems encountered in writing plays.

ACTING OUT THE DIALOGUE

As was indicated in the chapters on dialogue and language, difficulties frequently arise in getting words in correct juxtaposition so they will sound right when delivered. Actors sometimes find that a certain combination of words prescribed by the playwright will not "marry on the tongue."

The writing of "actable" lines, those that will effectively capture the author's meaning yet will be easy to deliver, can often be insured by the playwright's reading aloud his lines or acting out the scene. In this way the writer will convey the proper meaning and reveal the correct nuance of emotion. Chapter 4, "Developing the Playwriting Ability," recommended acting as a helpful pursuit in preparing the playwright for his task. It was this basic difficulty of authoring actable lines that inspired such a recommendation.

The written line and the spoken line sometimes have far from the same effect. A playwright writes for the theatre, not the reader, and he will do well to try to hear his plays as they might be heard in a theatre and even to try to direct them in his head so that he does not burden the director with an impossible task.

WRITING STAGE DIRECTIONS

There are two points of view regarding the writing of stage directions. Some playwrights feel it essential to incorporate the description of the visual actions demanded by the play while writing the dialogue, and others hold to the opinion that it is best to write all of the dialogue and then go back and fill in the stage directions. Whichever method is employed will in almost every case be determined by which method is the best for the individual writer.

Those who take care to insert stage directions with dialogue feel that if they write the dialogue first and then return to fill in the stage directions, the fresh, spontaneous understanding of the situation has disappeared. Some writers find their stage directions mechanical and artificial if they are written after the dialogue has been written. Those who hold this opinion usually feel that stage directions are as much a product of creativity as is dialogue.

Miss Rachel Crothers, author of *Susan and God* and many other successes a few decades ago, subscribed to writing dialogue and directions simultaneously. To aid her she carefully drew ground plans of the stage arrangement of doors, chairs, tables etc., before writing the dialogue. Though these directions were probably changed in production, Miss Crothers was able to visualize more completely the action of her play and the stage relationships of the characters.

The argument for writing stage directions *after* all the dialogue is completed is essentially that the stage directions require such a different style of writing that it intrudes upon the creative process necessary for a spontaneous flow of dialogue. A. A. Milne, the English playwright, always wrote the dialogue first without a single stage direction and then, as he put it, "reluctantly turned novelist." Milne is typical of the writers who find that though there is a certain amount of fun to be had in describing characters and hinting at their emotions, it is dreary work to record the position of a window or a fireplace, and the number of telephones on a desk: "With the opening scene of Act II bubbling over in one's mind one cannot impede himself with upholstery."

Regardless of the method of writing stage directions elected by the beginning playwright, he will eventually settle upon the method that contributes most to his ability to create effective theatre.

Stage directions present no real handicap to the professional playwright who also directs his own manuscript in production, for then he can execute the action in accordance with what he visualized while writing the dialogue. George M. Cohan's method of writing plays illustrates this and also reveals an unorthodox approach to play making. Cohan was once charged with plagiarism. At his trial he told the plaintiff's counsel that he wrote his plays one scene at a time and that he would begin rehearsing the scene before he had an act and would then build up the play during rehearsals. The jury found Cohan not guilty of the plagiarism charge. Neither the beginning nor the practicing playwright of today will probably have the opportunity to try Cohan's method, unique and interesting though it may be.

MOOD AND ENVIRONMENT FOR WRITING

Mention should be made of the problem of proper mood and environment for writing. Many would-be writers procrastinate but do not write. Such excuses are offered as, "I'm not in the mood," or, "I can't write here—there are too many distractions," or better still, "I'm an artist and I must feel creative." Such remarks are absurd. If one is a writer, one writes. Such excuses as cited may be justifiable, but in most cases they are attempts to rationalize one's inability to be productive.

Before it is assumed that "honest-to-God" problems of mood and writing environment do not exist, it should be declared emphatically that some writers do encounter such problems, but if they seek a solution they can usually find it. If one is not in the mood, then he should attempt to establish the proper mood. If one feels that he cannot possibly write in a certain location he should seek the right location. In both cases he should act, not procrastinate.

Sustaining a mood that one is hoping to capture in a play poses a problem for some writers. If the play demands a certain mood and the writer is one who must submerge himself in the mood in order to reproduce it, then he has little choice but to sustain it through mood-evoking activities. These activities vary with the individual and often with the type of mood to be captured. Some do it by reading plays of a similar genre, or by listening to certain musical selections. Others find recreational pursuits helpful. For some strange reason, the concentration required to play golf or tennis affects certain people in a peculiar manner. An abundance of energy is released yet the mind continues to sustain the creative mood. Others walk in the rain, while still others perform rather odd rituals in order to capture the "right" spirit.

Edward Knoblock, for example, chose a mood-evoking procedure for each play. He has described the method he used in preparing himself for the writing of *Kismet*. Writers who have no difficulty capturing the mood may consider this method amusing and some may even find it insane, but Knoblock approached it with deadly seriousness at the time. In his book, *Round the Room,* he wrote: "I now rose every morning at dawn, put on my Arabian robe, which I had bought at Tunis, and solemnly performed the genuflexions prescribed by Mohammed before I set out to work. This will sound silly to others. It does so to me, now, too. But I was terribly in earnest. This play should prove a success or I would have to give up all thoughts of ever becom-

ing an acknowledged playwright. I felt by going through the Moham-
medan prayers that I was throwing myself into the proper mood. It
prepared me for my day's task. It was a rite necessary for my spirit to
approach my subject unafraid." [1]

No one can prescribe a sure-fire method for evoking mood. It is
enough just to indicate that a problem exists in capturing and staying
in a mood appropriate to the play upon which one is working. Working environment or conditions is another matter. Generally speaking,
the best work can be done in a quiet place, removed from outside
contact with the world. While actually working one should isolate
himself from such interruptions as those occasioned by the telephone
or the doorbell. If an environment is to be conducive to thinking and
writing, it must be relatively free of distractions. Unfortunately, writers
are sometimes considered peculiar for isolating themselves, since quite
often, of necessity, they become antisocial during periods of creation.

Many writers caught in the zeal of constructing a scene will write
through lunch and dinner hours and miss business and social appointments. Owen Davis, in reviewing his own long career as a dramatist,
humorously suggested to the beginning playwright that he not let anyone bother him when writing and advised: "If the phone rings, don't
answer it, and if your wife rebels, divorce her." It is not recommended
that one break with one's spouse over quiet hours, but nothing and
nobody is important when thoughts are boiling. After all, nobody
really expects a dramatist to be a reasonable member of society.

The playwright requires time for "introspective placidity, a weighing
of inner values," as Charles Klein once described it, and this may be
found as easily in New York or any other metropolitan area as in the
remotest corner of the country. The author must be internally insen-
sible to the tide and turmoil outside while creating, a complete re-
versal of his existence while gathering dramatic material. He must not
become involved in factional disagreements in the commercial or
professional world, for such involvements invariably cause worries that
preclude creation.

1 Edward Knoblock, *Round the Room*, Chapman & Hall, Ltd., 1939, p. 111.

Distractions may occur in the country as well as the city. Edna Ferber has said that she is continually distracted while writing on a farm for "a cow is always having a calf." Some people, such as Augustus Thomas, who was a working newspaperman, can work anywhere, but, generally speaking, most creative artists require a peaceful, quiet atmosphere in which to work. The college student of playwriting has a real problem in finding such a place. The crowded conditions of the modern campus prevent a student from living alone and therefore he must always consider the wishes of others. It is amazing, however, how few students discover the quiet confines of the university library, where the surroundings are usually most conducive to creative thinking.

WRITING HOURS

When should a playwright write? Should he wait until the urge possesses him or should he restrict himself to regularly scheduled working hours? Actually it is a matter of finding the best method for the individual, though it is strongly recommended that regular working hours be observed.

An inquiry into the writing habits of some of the successful Broadway playwrights reveals a vast range of working hours. Some write all day long; others prefer to limit themselves to a few hours at a stretch. Still others find they do their best writing at night. There are those who write only when they feel they can produce something, and make no attempt to regulate the hours into a working day. Then again there are those who adhere to a strict schedule and are able consistently to write plays of merit. Clyde Fitch, for instance, limited himself to three hours a day but wrote every day. Another playwright places himself on a rigid schedule, working from nine to twelve-thirty and from one-thirty to four every day. Channing Pollock wrote every day from eight in the morning until three in the afternoon and reported in his autobiography that on the day of his mother's death he wrote from eight until luncheon and would probably do so on the day of his own demise.

There is much to be said for maintaining a regular writing schedule even when one feels nonproductive. A man who has no other master because he works for himself must learn to be his own. This type of writer must learn to set up a time clock in his brain and punch it as though it hung in a factory and his job depended on it. He should write whether he feels like it or not and no mere headache or other distraction should ever intervene. With this attitude it is better to write and throw the result in the wastebasket than to break the habit. As the habit becomes fixed, it will be discovered that less and less manuscript ends up as scrap paper.

It is more than implied here that the playwright should regard his work as a job and that a working schedule is a good habit which, when established, actually aids productivity. Maugham takes the view that a professional writer cannot afford to write only when he feels like it. In discussing writing habits, he says that if the professional writer "waits till he is in the mood, till he has the inspiration as he says, he waits indefinitely and ends by producing little or nothing." According to him, the professional writer creates the mood. "He has his inspiration too, but he controls and subdues it to his bidding by setting himself regular hours of work. But in time writing becomes a habit, and like the old actor in retirement, who gets restless when the hour arrives at which he has been accustomed to go down to the theatre and make up for the evening performance, the writer itches to get to his pens and paper at the hours at which he has been used to write. Then he writes automatically. Words come easily to him and words suggest ideas. They are old and empty ideas, but his practiced hand can turn out an acceptable piece. He goes down to luncheon or goes to bed with the assurance he has done a good days' work." [2]

WRITING THE MANUSCRIPT

Playwrights use several methods of transcribing their plays onto paper. Some prefer to dictate, others use longhand or a typewriter and

[2] Somerset Maugham, *The Summing Up*, Doubleday, Doran & Company, 1939, p. 181.

some both. It is up to the beginning playwright to discover the method that best suits him.

Only the successful or wealthy writer can afford the luxury of dictating to either a stenographer or a dictaphone. For years, many playwrights have dictated their plays. David Belasco learned much of his playwriting skill by taking dictation from Dion Boucicault. Later on he himself used two stenographers, since one soon tired of the pace he maintained when working.

It must be remembered that Belasco acted out his dialogue and business as so many playwrights do today. He would also watch the stenographer as a representative of his audience of a year or six months hence. In reviewing his writing method he reflected, "If I say, in a scene with my wife in the play, overbearingly, 'Helen, how dared you do that?' there is no response. The stenographer is thinking that I have been too stern with the wife. 'Helen, how could you have done this?' I say, pleadingly, and my audience at the typewriter looks up in pleased recognition. I know then that there is the right line, and it stays." [3]

Of course, unless a writer is married to an understanding woman, the problem of dictating whenever something is ready to be transcribed may be difficult to surmount. There is, of course, the possibility that the aspiring playwright could propose to his prospective bride in the following manner: "Do you take dictation? Can you type? Will you marry me?" However, that specific line of questioning may be grounds for a refusal. It is not known if A. A. Milne, the English playwright-author, used this approach in proposing to the woman who became his wife, but it is known that she would accompany him on his strolls in the woods, or, for that matter wherever he went, in order to transcribe his dialogue.

Noel Coward's choice of method for writing his manscript is determined by availability. If he has a typewriter handy, he uses it, but he will proceed with longhand if necessary. Then there are those writers who use both methods of transcription purposefully, the dialogue being roughed out in pencil or pen and later transferred to the typewritten page. The writer is then able to fuss as much as he pleases with a line yet get a general idea of the whole by having a clean typed sheet in front of him. This method is strongly recommended to the beginning playwright. Maugham once said, "I have never found a typewriter through which the subconscious seemed able to penetrate, but it seems to flow right through a fountain pen."

On the other hand, some writers find it impossible to write creatively in longhand, finding that a pen or pencil is like a shovel in their fingers. The creative flow seems to be paralyzed unless it can flow freely and rapidly. Such people should, of course, use a typewriter. It is, after all, a matter of personal preference and individual efficiency.

TIME REQUIRED FOR PLANNING AND WRITING A PLAY

Teachers of playwriting are often asked how long it takes to plan and write an acceptable play. Unfortunately, there is no pat answer, since there is no standard length of time for putting a play down on paper. There are so many variables to consider, the most important being the working habit of the individual playwright. Some dramatists plan their plays for years, then write them in ten days; others evolve an idea in a day and then spend three months writing it into a play.

There is a wide diversity of time necessary to compose a play. For example, George Broadhurst planned *Bought and Paid For* for seven years before he wrote a line of it. However, when he got down to it, he wrote it in a matter of weeks. Moss Hart once told an interviewer that his time varied from play to play. One thing he was sure of, that he worked steadily until he had completed the task. Sometimes it would move along rapidly and at other times it would come slowly, but he would always keep at it, regardless of the difficulties involved. Maugham claims that he spent six or seven years thinking about a play, though it never took him more than six weeks to get it down on paper. These examples appear to confirm the contention advanced in earlier chapters that the major portion of the playwriting process, the real work, is in the planning and preparation, not in the writing of the dialogue and business. If the superstructure of a building is sound, the façade can always be added later.

There are, however, playwrights who work rapidly from the moment of conception until they write "curtain" on the final scene. Robert E. Sherwood, for instance, took only five weeks to conceive and write *There Shall Be No Night,* and only four to complete *The Petrified Forest.*

The student playwright, unfortunately, cannot take years or even months to plan a play. The confines of a semester's course demand that he work more rapidly. This is probably why so many playwriting courses require only the composition of a one-act play. It is possible, however, for the student playwright to turn out an acceptable piece in ten or twelve weeks, the average length of a course, if he applies himself. In addition, if he is really serious about his writing and will note carefully the criticism of his instructor and classmates and then observe the play in its test production, he will usually set out to rewrite it even though he is no longer required to meet a classroom obligation.

Playwriting is so much a product of the creative faculties that each playwright must find the writing procedure that best suits his own temperament. It is hoped that the preceding paragraphs on writing procedures will suggest possible approaches to the more mechanical phases of the process. Through trial-and-error experience each playwright will ultimately find his own approach and, oddly enough, it will be the best.

Writing in Collaboration

IF the number of hits is any indication of the success of a playwright, then George S. Kaufman is perhaps the most successful American dramatist on the contemporary theatre scene. Over twenty highly successful plays have been written by Kaufman, but, strangely enough, only one, *The Butter and Egg Man,* was authored without the assistance of a collaborator. Such well-known theatre writers as Marc Connelly, Edna Ferber, Ring Lardner, and Moss Hart have all worked with Kaufman—and it may be said that they became famous playwrights because of their collaboration.

The literary marriage of two or more writers has become an accepted practice on Broadway in the past fifty years. Of course, it has always been customary for lyricists, composers, and playwrights to join talents in developing musicals and musical comedies. The most notable modern example of such collaboration can be found in the team of Richard Rodgers and Oscar Hammerstein, II, with *Oklahoma, Carousel, South Pacific,* and, more recently, *Pipe Dream.* But the trend has extended through the years to the realms of comedy, farce, and serious drama. Comedy- and farce-writing teams, such as Howard Lindsay and Russell Crouse, have given the stage such successes as *Life With Father, State of the Union,* and *The Great Sebastians*; Kaufman and Hart created modern classics with *You Can't Take It With You* and *The Man Who*

Came to Dinner; and George Abbott and John Cecil Holm collaborated to write *Three Men on a Horse.*

In a more serious vein, Maxwell Anderson teamed with Laurence Stallings to produce the realistic war play, *What Price Glory?* Who can ever forget the melodramatic, yet hilarious, *Front Page* of Ben Hecht and Charles MacArthur, or the light, yet serious, treatment of academic freedom in *The Male Animal* by James Thurber and Elliott Nugent?

In more recent years the combination of Arnaud d'Usseau and James Gow has written such hard-hitting dramas as *Tomorrow the World* and *Deep Are the Roots*; Jerome Lawrence and Robert E. Lee enticed Paul Muni out of retirement with their version of the Scopes "monkey trial" entitled *Inherit the Wind*; and Henry Denker and Ralph Berkey startled the 1955–1956 season with *Time Limit!* the story of an American soldier on trial for giving aid to the enemy in Korea.

The motion picture industry has long held the philosophy that two or more heads are better than one. Scenario writers in Hollywood are accustomed to pooling their talents in developing a picture. The practice on Broadway is becoming more evident each season. It is difficult to understand why teachers of playwriting have ignored the area of collaboration, especially since it has proved to be both financially rewarding and critically successful. Perhaps collaboration entails such a secret meeting of minds and writing personalities that it cannot be analyzed and taught. However, certain advantages and disadvantages to writing in collaboration are readily apparent. Many successful collaborators have described their methods of working together. There is much to be learned from investigating the mysteries of coauthorship.

THE ADVANTAGES OF COLLABORATION

To understand the advantages of collaboration it would be well to recognize that this partnership is akin to the marriage contract. "In neither case," quips H. R. Popper, "would a sensible man undergo so demanding a pattern of concession and compromise if he thought he could do as well on his own." [1] And as marriage is marked by disagreement and making-up, so the collaboration process is highlighted by argument and resolution.

Collaboration provides each playwright with a critic, an audience where each can sound out the other and test ideas and lines of dialogue. The good partner will be quick and frank to condemn what is irrelevant and immaterial or what is not really dramatic or comic, whichever the intention may be. Left to himself a man must be both creator and critic and, as Guy Bolton comments, "that is rather like playing a game of chess by oneself; every move you make has to be viewed from opposite sides." Collaboration, on the other hand, provides two chess players, two critics for the game of playwriting. In collaboration the creator is always sure of his critic because there he sits opposite him, waiting to discover any error that may have escaped him in the fine fervor of invention.

David Belasco, in commenting on William DeMille as a coauthor, claimed that they had always been successful because of their frankness in criticizing one another. Harriet Ford, who made it a practice to form writing partnerships with men, recommends a formula to insure frankness of criticism from collaborators. "If you are good-tempered," says Miss Ford, "you must choose a bad-tempered collaborator. If you are bad-tempered, choose a good-tempered one, of course. There is no way to write a successful play except by quarrelling about it. Anger is necessary to stimulate thought and exasperate invention." [2]

Collaboration is always stimulating and it takes some of the lonely curse off writing. There is something about getting one's own ideas into contact with those of somebody else that sharpens them, makes them clearer, more vivid. Russell Crouse once described this process to a correspondent of the St. Louis *Globe-Democrat:* "We just stay here and bounce ideas back and forth for hours, or as long as we feel that

---

[1] H. R. Popper, "Collaborators on Broadway," *Theatre Arts,* October, 1946, p. 599.
[2] *New York Times,* December 13, 1914.

some sense is going to come out of the nonsense. I'm so ashamed of some of my ideas that I'm afraid to tell them to myself, but I don't mind telling them to Howard. He'll venture an improvement and I'll venture another. We throw everything we have at each other and it works." [3]

Another advantage to collaboration emerges in the partnership of a playwright who may excel in plotting with another who may be more talented at writing dialogue. Belasco and Kaufman are both more renowned as dialoguists than as storytellers. Some writers dislike the job of plot construction, finding it tedious and so objective in nature that to go through the plotting process is a real chore. Bolton, for example, dislikes the task of plotting and asserts that the chief advantage of collaboration is that the playwright who is weak or otherwise dislikes one of the tasks may shift that duty to his partner. "I am able to dialogue with some facility," he says, "and, therefore, in practically all my collaboration, this has been my task."

At times a writer may find himself unable to develop a good idea to a successful ending and it may be advisable to call in expert help. It may be argued that the merger of two artists, each skilled in one or more of the elements of playwriting, increases the chance for a successful play, whereas by going at it alone neither may ever make the grade. Winchell Smith gave excellent testimony to this advantage of collaboration when he said: "Suppose I have a particular knack of mapping out plots, and suppose someone else has a corking idea, but can't seem to get a good play out of it. This man comes to me with his good idea and poor play. We go at it together, each one putting into our pooled assets the work at which he is especially adept. The result may be an extremely successful play." [4]

When the personalities of the writers meld and each is performing what he can best do, the time factor in turning out plays is greatly

---

[3] George Beiswanger, "Lindsay and Crouse," *Theatre Arts,* February, 1944, p. 80.
[4] Winchell Smith, "Take Some Kind of a Plunge," *American Magazine,* December, 1918, p. 110.

reduced. Like many businessmen, most dramatists are in a hurry—usually not to turn out art but to write sure-fire box office hits. This advantage of collaboration may appear to be of low motive, but the majority of professional writers who feel they must express themselves are somehow consciously or subconsciously motivated by the possibility of a generous return on their investment of time, effort, and creativity. After all, it is their profession, and success in most lines of endeavor has its rewards.

A novelist who sees a great play in his work of fiction often seeks out a competent theatre craftsman to work with him in translating his fiction to the stage. In some cases, such as *Mister Roberts,* the approach may be made by the playwright. Joshua Logan, an accomplished director and a dramatist of ability, convinced Thomas Heggen that there was an excellent play in his novel. When Logan's knowledge of the theatre and its special requirements combined with novelist Heggen's understanding of the sea and its men, one of the comedy sensations of the post-World War II period was produced. Heggen had spent three of his four years in the Navy on sea duty and knew whereof he wrote.

Mister Roberts also points out another advantage to collaboration. It often happens that one writer's experience may be limited to a certain sphere of activity and knowledge, yet, his partner's contacts with a different way of life broaden the viewpoints and understanding of each and thereby enable the combination to produce a sounder, more believable play. Maxwell Anderson, for instance, was a newspaperman, a literary critic, yet when he teamed with Laurence Stallings who had served in France with the Marines during the first World War the two were able to produce the exciting and realistic *What Price Glory?*

Many Broadway producers are reluctant to take a chance on an untried playwright's manuscript. It is an old adage that it "takes experience to get experience." But how does one get produced who has never had a play on the boards professionally? The answer is not simple and collaboration is not necessarily the answer, but many of Broadway's successful playwrights gained their entry to the profession as collaborators with established playwrights. As Smith indicated, the professional dramatist often welcomes the man with a good idea but a poor play. This has apparently been the case with Kaufman and others. Of course, financially, the royalties will be half what they would be if only one writer produced the script. This disadvantage is cancelled out by the increased potential of the established playwright as he minimizes the possibility of "draining himself dry" by sharing the task of creation. Furthermore, most collaborators who have succeeded remain together as a team and in the long run are able consistently to turn out more plays which will receive box office approval than many of the playwrights who prefer to write alone. Consequently, the income of proven teams such as Lindsay and Crouse, Rodgers and Hammerstein, becomes proportionately larger.

Occasionally writing teams have been composed of members of the opposite sex. The success of Bella and Sam Spewack, Betty Smith and Robert Finch, Joseph and Marijane Hayes, Walter and Jean Kerr probably indicates that *occasionally* is a poor choice of words. Is there an advantage to the writers being of opposite sex? Harriet Ford, who wrote plays with Joseph Patterson and Harvey O'Higgins, seemed to think so. She once told a feature writer: "In case you are a man, let your collaborator write all the men's parts, so that they may be convincing to women. And if you are a woman, let your collaborator write all the women's parts, so that they may be convincing to men." [5]

Perhaps there is some truth to the idea that women think they understand men and, of course, all men naturally believe they understand women. But it was Miss Ford's belief that it is a common mistake in collaboration to let the man write the men's parts and the woman the women's. It is not necessary to accept Miss Ford's edict as a rule, yet it seems logical that in a collaboration between the sexes each will severely criticize any apparent inconsistency in the characters of their

[5] *New York Times,* December 13, 1914.

respective sex and any incredulity in the actions or speech of their opposite.

THE DISADVANTAGES OF COLLABORATION

Collaboration is not without its pitfalls and beginning writers should weigh the problems carefully before attempting a coauthorship. The moment a playwright begins to collaborate he encounters the major difficulty of achieving unity of impression in so far as the creation of characters and the maintaining of a mood are concerned.

Owen Davis, who won the Pulitzer Prize for 1922–1923 with *Icebound,* later collaborated with his son Donald on several plays. "To me," declares Davis, "a play is so essentially a mood and it is so impossible for two human beings to enter into the same exact mood that all such collaboration is started under a very real handicap." [6] It is Davis' argument that, though it is possible for two writers to agree upon details of plot and even upon shades of characters, the mood which would compel certain reactions from the characters, which must of necessity propel them along the narrative line in a certain way, cannot dominate two writers at the same moment.

Collaboration merely for the sake of collaboration is not good. There is apt to be a lack of unity of impression in the total work. There is the distinct possibility that the points of view of two dramatists might cloud the original idea. As a rule, one thinks it out and the other endorses the idea and perhaps augments and improves it, but there is always present the danger of the original idea becoming obscured when too many minds are at work upon it. The personalities of the individual playwrights must be subordinated to the total work, or the personality of one author may shine through the fabric in one place and that of the other in another and produce an uneven surface.

Though each season introduces new writing teams to the stage there are few playwrights with a real gift for collaboration. Often the result may be a watered-down version of what one playwright could have written brilliantly. This may have been the reason for the failure of

[6] Owen Davis, *I'd Like to Do It Again,* Farrar & Rinehart, 1931, p. 189.

Tennessee Williams' and Donald Windham's *You Touched Me,* the only attempt by Williams at collaboration.

Different writers have different methods or systems of working out their plays and sometimes the literary marriage of such writers must end in an annulment. Speaking from personal experience, having written a play with Guy Bolton, Somerset Maugham declares that he has never taken very comfortably to collaboration, finding it "more and more difficult to work in harmony with collaborators." Unfortunately there is no personality test or method of analysis that can predict whether two writers will succeed together. But, then too, there is no certainty about marriage. You never know until you have tried it.

METHODS OF COLLABORATION

J. M. Barrie once admitted to being puzzled as to how "real collaboration . . . is done." He had attempted two plays in collaboration, neither of which succeeded. These efforts were with close friends, Marriott Watson and Conan Doyle, and Barrie wondered for years afterwards just how writers really collaborate.

In Chapter 12, it was suggested that playwrights should select the method or approach best suited to their temperaments and the procedure that will be the easiest for them. The foregoing discussion of advantages and disadvantages of collaboration revealed that the basic problem here is the adjustment of personalities and methods to discover the best and easiest approach for both writers. The initial problem has therefore been doubled. However, there are only three basic methods of collaboration employed by modern playwrights. There may be variations as to how each method is practiced, but, fundamentally, the chosen method will conform to one of the three. Nor is it necessary to use the same method. Often with one collaborator a certain process will be selected whereas a different approach may be adopted in working with another collaborator. As Moss Hart has said, "The essence of collaboration is fitting your own working method into that of your collaborator."

The first method of collaboration employs a distinct division of duties. One writer draws up a detailed scenario of the action and the other writer executes the dialogue. The system has been used successfully but it presents definite problems of achieving unity of character. It is impossible to plan a scenario without revealing definite traits of character. As was explained in the chapter on characterization, it is impossible to divorce character from action since well-conceived characters will only perform those acts consistent with their characters as they have been presented in the development of the plot. Conversely, as the character becomes established through action and dialogue, it is disastrous to assign an act or line that will violate or contradict a believable pattern. Therefore, it is safe to say that, though on the surface it appears to be a distinct division of duties, the link of characterization binds the two tasks together.

In the second method of collaboration the two playwrights agree on the plot and the characters, draw up a careful scenario, then separate, each assigned to write certain scenes or acts. When this has been done they get together again, revise each other's work, and eventually, after several drafts the scenes or acts appear to be in harmony and possess unity of impression. Edward Knoblock described his use of this method when writing *Milestones* with novelist Arnold Bennett. "In the afternoon I would go over to Bennett's and we would each read to the other what we had written during the morning," says Knoblock. "Our method was this. He would take my scenario and write a scene of it. We would then confer. I would rewrite or tighten it up the next morning and bring it back to him in the afternoon, when he would be ready with another scene." [7]

Miss Ford followed this second method when she wrote *The Fourth Estate* with Patterson. Edna Ferber and George V. Hobart also used this approach in writing *Our Mrs. McChesney*. Marc Connelly and George S. Kaufman utilized the process in writing *Dulcy, Merton of the Movies* and *Beggar on Horseback*. They would discuss everything together and after they had decided on the plot and the trimmings one

[7] Edward Knoblock, *Round the Room*, Chapman & Hall, Ltd., 1939, p. 153.

would say to the other, "I'll start on this act and you do the second." These two craftsmen made it a practice to work out a good architect's blueprint of what the whole ground plan of the play would be. "After we've parted, written and met again," says Connelly, "the newly finished scenes come up for discussion and unification." [8] Belasco and John Luther Long also adhered to this method when they wrote *Darling of the Gods* and *Andrea* together.

Dr. George McCalmon, a professor of playwriting and now director of the University Theatre at Cornell, employed this method as a teaching device. It is to be recommended to teachers with advanced and mature students who are seriously trying to master the techniques of dramaturgy. Though stressing collaboration, the mutual benefit in acquiring an understanding of basic problems of plot, character, and dialogue is beyond measure.

In one such experiment at Florida State University in 1952, McCalmon chose a unique group of playwriting students. One had won several playwriting awards in national competition and had mastered the intricacies of the three-act form. Another was basically a one-act play craftsman, having written many plays of this type for college and high school use. The third member of the group was a nonwriter but an accomplished director in educational theatre. The fourth participant was an undergraduate who had displayed evidence of playwriting skill in writing scenes for the acting class. McCalmon, himself, became the fifth member.

For four months the group worked under McCalmon's supervision. First, they decided on an initial idea. Being a presidential election year, and probably remembering the success of Lindsay's and Crouse's *State of the Union,* it was decided that politics should be the topic. Then the "what if?" period commenced and possible situations were batted back and forth. For a central character, the group picked what they felt was the most unlikely candidate for President, a professor of horticulture.

---

[8] Katharine Sproehnle and Roi Cooper Megrue, "The First Three Acts the Hardest," *Saturday Evening Post,* January 16, 1926, p. 58.

But how to get the professor nominated as his party's presidential candidate? Recognizing the similarity between national education association meetings and party conventions, it was decided that *if* the two meetings were happening simultaneously and *if* the professor and his colleagues were assumed to be delegates and *if* they mistakenly ended up on the floor and *if* . . . and the method of evolving a plot through collaboration was underway.

Care was exercised to generate genuine conflict and to erect obstacles to prevent the protagonist reaching his objective and finally a scenario was completed. There just happened to be five scenes in the proposed play so each member of the group was assigned a unit of the scenario. As the assigned scenes were completed the group would meet again to discuss and analyze the results. Then the scenes were reassigned and rewritten along the lines of the discussion. This process was repeated extensively for several months until a unity of impression began to emerge. The characters became dimensional and the live action became crystal clear. The final step was to assign the entire play to one of the playwrights to write the final draft, thus imparting the finishing touches to unify and integrate a comedy on politics.

The third method of collaboration places the two writers together throughout the process whereas the first two methods find the writers separating for large portions of the work. Here the playwrights work together from start to finish, one usually seated at a typewriter and the other roaming the room, thinking and acting out possible lines of dialogue while his partner serves as a sounding board, an editor, or another actor.

Though Miss Ford favored the second method with Patterson, she and Harvey O'Higgins subscribed to this third method in writing such plays as *The Argyle Case, The Dummy,* and *Polygamy.* Miss Ford would sit at her desk and O'Higgins would walk around the room and if one of them thought of a line of dialogue upon which both would agree then it would be written down. Though Kaufman and Connelly followed the method of dividing the work and separating, in collaborating with Hart and Ferber, Kaufman followed this third method. With both writers, Kaufman either "paced" or "stalked" about the room while his collaborator sat at the typewriter recording the dialogue. Belasco, like Kaufman, was on many collaborating occasions an actor. In all of his many collaborations with DeMille, Belasco "acted out the dialogue" while DeMille sat at the typewriter and acted as a weather vane, writing down that which "rang a bell."

Regardless of the method chosen by collaborators it is essential that their final product possess such unity of technique that it appears to be the product of a single mind. As a director will not tolerate inconsistency of performance from an actor so the audience will adversely react the moment they sense the existence of a dual technique within the total structural pattern. The individuality of the playwright must be so immersed in the collaboration process that he will find it difficult to recognize his own contribution. "You know," says Russel Crouse, "we have tried to figure out which lines in *Father* each of us wrote. We can't do it. We don't remember. Really, we just don't know. Perhaps it *was* written by one man." This is the ultimate aim and only really satisfying result of collaboration.

Collaboration has been and will continue to be one method of professional playwriting. Whether the teacher and students of playwriting can master the process is not known. It is both an intriguing and hazardous experiment—one that may not only sharpen their instincts for dramatic writing, but may well lead to successful literary marriages and financially rewarding careers.

Dramatization and Adaptation

WHEN is a play original? Why is there such care to label new offerings on Broadway as "original plays"? In the chapter on finding dramatic material it was noted that though plays are frequently derived
from characters and incidents known by the playwright, the final
product is almost always considered "an original play." Even when it is
based on the life of an actual historical character, as is Sherwood's *Abe
Lincoln in Illinois,* the play is said to be an original.

Originality is a relative term. In theory, "an original play" implies
that the story, plot, characters, and theme have originated with the
playwright. In fact, however, the term describes a work of dramatic art
whose elements and their arrangement or presentation are sufficiently
unlike any other work of fact or fancy for the playwright to assume
full credit for what he has authored.

CONFUSION IN LABELING A PLAY'S ORIGIN

There seems to be much mystery and confusion surrounding the
labeling of a play's origin. For example, Maxwell Anderson's tight
pulling-together of William March's novel, *The Bad Seed,* is called a
dramatization, whereas Herman Wouk's transference to the stage of
Part VI of his novel, *The Caine Mutiny,* as *The Caine Mutiny Court
Martial* is carefully labeled an *adaptation.* Sidney Kingsley's prize-

winning *Darkness at Noon* lists as its source, "Based on the novel by Arthur Koestler."

The origin of the present-day musical play sometimes rivals Hollywood's scenario credits in complexity. *Carousel* is a musical play adapted by Benjamin F. Glazer from Ferenc Molnar's play, *Liliom*, with music by Richard Rodgers and a book and lyrics by Oscar Hammerstein II. The popular musical play *Fanny* is by S. N. Behrman and Joshua Logan but *based* on the trilogy, "Marius," "Fanny," and "Cesar" by Marcel Pagnol, with music and lyrics by Harold Rome. More recently *My Fair Lady* began breaking box office records. The credits of this musical list it as *adapted* from Bernard Shaw's *Pygmalion* with book and lyrics by Alan Jay Lerner and music by Frederick Loewe. Confused? Then there is the problem of listing translations from a foreign language. Such terms as "translated and adapted," "the English version," and "suggested by" are often found affixed beneath a play's title.

Plays not truly original are most often derived from works of fiction. Chapter 2 compared and contrasted the playwriting and novel-writing processes and it was suggested there that the essential difference between the two is that playwriting is a time-art, whereas novel writing is not. This concept was fully explained in that section and it is only necessary here to state that the distinction between the two processes apparently constitutes the major difficulty in properly attributing the credit due an original work, since the playwright's function is to translate the novel in some degree into the time-art medium of the stage.

WHY FICTION IS DRAMATIZED OR ADAPTED

To what degree of faithfulness should the play adhere to the original work? To answer this question it is first necessary to know why playwrights approach material in other media in search of plays. This can best be understood by recognizing the occasions for such translations of form from the nondramatic to the dramatic.

There are three classifications of those who dramatize, adapt, or base plays upon other sources. Some playwrights are commissioned by producers to provide a dramatization or adaptation of a book. The producer feels he has discovered a piece of fiction that has dramatic potentiality. Next, some playwrights unintentionally encounter a novel that suggests a play. In this case the playwright stumbles upon the potentiality and does not go searching for it. This is perhaps the largest group. Last, there are those writers who constantly search literature for stories which lend themselves to dramatic presentation. For the most part these are the children's-theatre playwrights who believe that familiar stories from literature are most suitable for an audience of children.

THE PLAYWRIGHT'S FREEDOM OF APPROACH

The treatment of a work of fiction by a playwright may vary from faithful adherence to the original story to liberal interpretation in which the writer borrows as much or as little of the material as he chooses in terms of his own specific purpose. Some story material, such as the court martial scenes of Wouk's *Caine Mutiny*, contain elements which make them suitable for almost literal transference to the dramatic media, while other works of fiction lend themselves to dramatic presentation in only some respects. In the latter case, the playwright must treat his material more liberally in order that it may be made to serve his own purpose.

Suppose a playwright upon reading a novel decides that it would make a good play, but a study of the work indicates that it will need altering to fit his requirements. He may take this liberty but he should properly label it. Perhaps the novel is not suitable for one of the dramatic media because of the scope of its production demands; certain changes will have to be made to accommodate the staging limitations of the medium. On the other hand the material may be lifted literally from its context with a minimum of alteration and be suitable for the dramatic media. In every case the alteration should be in terms of the playwright's purpose in using the borrowed material.

CLARIFICATION OF LABELING TERMINOLOGY

Confusion arises when the dramatic writer attempts to determine his degree of indebtedness to the original and to label it accurately. Much of this confusion arises from an absence of clearly defined terms with which to describe the degree of adherence to original material. The following definitions are offered as guides for properly labeling a playwright's indebtedness to material from nondramatic sources.

Dramatization implies faithfulness to story and characters and the taking over of the thematic purposes of the original work. If the material lends itself to literal transference the playwright accepts the plot, characters, and theme *in toto* and gives them dramatic life.

Adaptation implies that the purposes of the playwright may supersede those of the author. Since a story seldom lends itself to literal transference, an adaptation is somewhat more faithful to the original material, but the playwright may take greater liberties with plot, character, and theme in terms of dramatic feasibility.

Based upon is a term applied by the playwright to a play which takes as its basis portions of an original story and its characters. More liberal changes in plot, character, and theme are made in accordance with the purpose of the playwright.

Suggested by is a term used when an idea or ideas expressed in an original work are borrowed and amplified and in all probability lose their original identity in the plot of the play.

THE BORROWING OF PLOTS

Even the greatest playwrights borrowed their plots, usually to apply them to their own purposes. Shakespeare's *Comedy of Errors* is a retelling of Plautus's Roman play, *The Menaechmi*. The Hamlet legend was in existence prior to the Bard's version. The Faustus story was told by both Marlowe and Goethe.

In more recent times, it has been common practice to take from the literary realm stories possessing potential dramatic life and to breathe into them the necesary ingredients for dramatic existence. Joseph Hayes perhaps had this in mind when he scored his triple sweep with *The Desperate Hours*—a novel, a play, and a motion picture. First, he wrote the novel, which was also serialized in *Collier's Magazine*. Many playwrights saw a play in this work, but Hayes had already written the play and a motion picture scenario as well. The play opened shortly after the novel was published. As it was in its waning weeks on Broadway the motion picture version, filmed months before, was released. There is no other assumption but that the clever Mr. Hayes knew where he was going before he wrote *The Desperate Hours* in its initial fictional form.

THE GREATEST OBSTACLE—THE AUDIENCE

The audience's attitude toward the "translation" of art forms is perhaps the greatest obstacle for the playwright to overcome. J. M. Barrie, who was both a novelist and a dramatist, once said, "When a man dramatizes his troubles begin." In the first place, the novel chosen for adaptation is usually well known to the reading public and the audience expects the stage version to amount to a staging of the novel. The audience invariably makes a comparison between the two and, unfortunately, this attitude on the part of the public constitutes a distinct disadvantage. A "borrowing" from an original work of fiction should be judged on its own merits as a play, a work of art in itself, without any attempt to compare it to the novel.

THE *Diary of Anne Frank* CONTROVERSY

A controversy arose prior to giving the 1955–1956 Drama Critics Circle Award to *The Diary of Anne Frank* as the best American play of the season. The question in the minds of the critics was whether or not this play could be rightly considered an American work. There was a real diary kept by an authentic Anne Frank describing her adolescence, which was spent hiding from the Nazis in a loft in Amsterdam during World War II. A spirited discussion developed among the critics over the classification of the play. While the authors, Frances Goodrich and Albert Hackett, were Americans the source material dramatized was of foreign origin.

By a vote of nine to four, however, the critics ruled that "Any play written by an American based on a foreign work, but not on a foreign play, could be considered as an American play in the voting." By this ruling the leading New York drama critics established a precedence in evaluating the indebtedness of authors to original source material. *The Diary of Anne Frank* was allowed to stand on its own merit as a play by American authors and thereby won the award as the best *American* play of the season.

The importance of this decision cannot be minimized; but it should be carefully noted that the critics specifically excluded the translation and adaptation of foreign plays for the Broadway audience, since their original existence is dramatic rather than fictional or factual. The wisdom of the critics was apparently confirmed several weeks later when the Pulitzer Prize selection committee chose *The Diary of Anne Frank* as the best play of the season. It had previously won the Antoinette Perry award, thus giving the play a triple sweep in the honors department.

THE PROBLEM OF LENGTH

The length of a novel usually prohibits literal transference. The average stage play runs two and a half hours and the playwright, unfortunately, is expected by his audience's attitude to include everything of importance in the novel in that short period of time. Needless to say, this is an impossibility, yet the playwright sometimes succumbs to public pressure and the ensuing stage piece is weaker than it was in book form. This is not necessarily true, but in treating a popular novel there is a general tendency to crowd in extraneous material because it was in the book.

This in itself is sufficient reason not to follow a work of fiction too closely. If the playwright is overly familiar with the book, he often will select too much to be placed in a 20,000-word manuscript, and he will also have the tendency to use dialogue, incidents, and characters that were appropriate in a 100,000-word book but are without sufficient dramatic merit to be transferred literally to the stage. As was explained in Chapter 2, the novelist may leisurely develop a character in a chapter or more, devoting many pages to an explanation of motives and tracing the workings of a character's mind. This task is doubly difficult in the compressed theatre medium.

THE OBLIGATION OF THE PLAYWRIGHT IS TO HIS PLAY

There is no doubt that deriving a play from an original piece of work restricts the creative freedom of the dramatist. George M. Cohan placed his finger on a key problem when he declared that if a playwright sticks too closely to the original work, he cannot express his own opinions, create his own characters, but must reflect the opinions and characters of the author of the story.

Naturally, much of the blame must be placed on the audience, which demands close adherence to the characters and their language as known to them in the novel, thus burdening the playwright with the task of creating characters and lines in the style of the novelist instead of the playwright. This, incidentally, Cohan always refused to do, even in his stage version of Earl Der Bigger's *Seven Keys to Baldpate*. Instead, he performed an adaptation which was referred to in the theatre world as "Cohanizing a script." Granted, he took the plot and the essential characters of the story, but from that point on he was on his own.

Cohan rightfully declared that his responsibility ended with the *adoption* of the plot and chief characters. From then on he felt he was obligated only to create a work of the theatre, a play which would stand or fall on its own merits as a drama and not on its faithfulness to an original novel or story.

THE USE OF ADAPTATION IN PLAYWRITING COURSES

This tendency of an audience to judge the play as a transferral of a book is to be deplored. If the stage version is a success, the novelist often gets the credit, whereas if it is a failure it is put at the door of the adaptation. Deriving a stage piece from another work is as difficult as writing an original play. Knowing this, it is strange that so many playwriting courses in colleges and universities introduce the students to adaptation as a means of getting them started in dramatic writing. The assumption that removing the necessity of creating a story or characters will reduce the problems facing the student playwright is a mistake. Without sufficient experience, the student dramatist invariably attempts to *dramatize* the fiction whereas he may be better off *adapting* or *basing* or merely letting an incident of the novel *suggest* a possible drama.

This is not an attack upon the current practice of many college teachers of playwriting, but merely an attempt to place the problem in its proper perspective. The adaptation method can be employed successfully, but the writer's background in the realms of both fiction and drama should be determined first. One thing is certain: it is a mistake to make an adaptation or dramatization assignment on the ground that it will make the writer's task of learning the playwriting process easier.

ADAPTATION IS FOR THE ADVANCED PLAYWRIGHT

Five recent master's degree projects in playwriting at Michigan State University demonstrate that the various forms of adaptation are perhaps best reserved for the most advanced students. Two of these studies focussed upon the need of the children's-theatre movement for new plays: one was the writing of a children's play based on Thackeray's *The Rose and the Ring*; the other was an intensive exploration of local American folklore to discover tales and legends suitable for transference in some degree to the children's-theatre stage. Both studies were concerned with deriving children's plays from other sources. Both were conducted by experienced writers. It is doubtful that either project could have been achieved by the beginning playwright in a college course.

The three other graduate projects were also concerned with adaptation. One student dramatized Guy de Maupassant's "The Necklace" and then adapted the dramatization to television. After the production a kinescope recording was analyzed and an estimate of the writing problems involved in the transfer process was made. "Noon Wine" was the subject of another project in which Katherine Anne Porter's short story was dramatized and adapted to television. The final study on deriving plays from other sources was a reconstruction of a late sixteenth century *commedia dell' arte.*

THE DIALOGUE PROBLEM

How far should the playwright go in using the original dialogue of the novel? This dialogue, with its accompanying narrative description, is often not suitable for literal translation to the stage—the inadequacies have to be removed first. But what should you do about those passages in famous novels that have become household words to the faithful? The dramatist should please himself as to how much or how little of the original dialogue he takes, but when he encounters well-known passages he should do one of two things, either use the exact dialogue or omit the passage altogether. One thing he should not try to do is to *improve* the familiar passage, however dramatically necessary this may seem.

With most novels it is possible to choose some speeches, some sentences, and upon occasion, some whole scenes, but as a rule the playwright should be prepared to breathe dramatic life into these borrowed elements, since they usually will be cold and flat when delivered from a stage without the accompanying narrative.

THE "POINT OF VIEW" DIFFICULTY

A basic difficulty encountered with some novels is the point of view from which they have been written. Owen Davis, who with his son, Donald Davis, was commissioned to dramatize Edith Wharton's novel, *Ethan Frome,* encountered this problem. The father-and-son writing combination read the novel carefully. Profoundly affected by the story and the skillful characterization, they felt their task would be comparatively easy. However, upon closer examination of the novel, they found the point of view of the storyteller to be a real handicap.

The story line of *Ethan Frome* was clear enough, and the characters were all well drawn and so real that they seemed actually to be alive; but Mrs. Wharton had written the story from the point of view of a stranger who had seen "poor old Ethan, crippled and broken, dragging himself along the village street." It was the story of something that had happened 20 years before and none of the characters in the book told any of it. "What they had done was clear enough," commented Davis, "but what they had said, it was up to us to write."

The two playwrights were faced with the task of supplying all the dialogue for characters skillfully created in the novel without the use of direct dialogue. For example, Owen Davis recorded the following in his book, *My First Fifty Years in the Theatre*: "Ethan Frome, his wife Zenobia, and little Mattie were glowing with life upon Mrs. Wharton's canvas, but she had given them no voice at all. It was a story of a very tender love, and of a hate so bitter that it could end only in a dreadful tragedy, but nowhere in the book was there a record of one single angry word. What Zenobia had said, and what Ethan had said, was sometimes briefly written down, but always in the words of some neighbor who was repeating it, but Mattie was only told about; what she said and how she expressed herself Donald Davis and I had to work out ourselves." [1]

It is certainly possible in handling most novels to blend the dramatist's dialogue with that of the novelist. Though the playwright is writing for a distinctly different medium, the audience of both book and play should not be able to detect where the novelist's dialogue ends and the playwright's begins. If the playwright is skillful, it is possible for the two styles to be equal to each other simply because they are equal to the same thing; namely, the way the actual people would have talked

[1] Owen Davis, *My First Fifty Years in the Theatre,* Walter H. Baker Company, 1950, p. 136.

in their particular station or way of life and in the situations they would normally encounter.

CHARACTER DEVELOPMENT IN THE ADAPTATION

The author of the play should take the characters and situations of the novel and develop them as fully in his own mind as if he were the author of the novel. Since he is not a novelist, but a dramatist, his process of character development will be toward the dramatic rather than the narrative. When his task is completed the characters will be in harmony with the novel and also capable of carrying the story to its dramatic conclusion.

The principles of character creation formulated in Chapter 8 are valid in developing characters in an adaptation. Only the starting point is different; the process is the same.

The practice of translating fiction to the stage is widely accepted in the commercial and educational theatre. It will continue to be so but it is hoped that the future will see the playwright freed from the audience's unreasonable demand that he duplicate on the stage that which they knew in the novel.

LIMITATIONS OF THE TELEVISION MEDIUM

The basic elements of the dramatic-writing process do not change when applied to television. However, because of the demands and limitations of the medium itself, television writing does require special techniques.

The television stage is in the form of a cone, wide at the back and tapering to a point at the camera lens. Theatre action, framed by a proscenium arch, is predominantly parallel to the curtain line, while television action is more likely to be staged in depth. In the theatre the individual member of the audience sees the stage only from the vantage point of his seat in the auditorium. The television stage, however, changes every time the director cuts from one camera to another, thus providing the viewer with the choicest seat in the house. When writing for television, the dramatic writer must write with pen, paper, *and* camera.

In Chapter 2, "The Play and Fiction," we saw the play as an art form restricted by time. Not only must television plays start on time, they must end on schedule, since broadcast time is usually purchased by the sponsor in time-segments of 30, 60, or 90 minutes. Since the advertiser is interested in selling his product, the playing time of the drama is actually less than the total time-segment purchased. The half-hour play is usually only 23 minutes of playing time, the hour play, 50 minutes, and the hour-and-a-half play, 70 to 75 minutes. The play must also be structured to provide for one, two, or three commercial announcements during the course of the unfolding action.

Considering the rigid time restrictions of television, it is apparent that any adaptation will require extensive condensation. This is why television adaptations, even of short stories, are more often for the 60- and 90-minute time-segments. When the dramatic writer is condensing a long prose work or a stage play into the television format he should think first of what he can show visually before he concerns himself with the play's dialogue. As Edward Barry Roberts says, "Sight is the short-cut in your task of condensation, of distilling the essence of the drama from the story you have selected."

Perhaps the most frustrating limitation to the dramatic writer endeavoring to adapt a novel to television is the cast-size restriction. Small casts are demanded by production costs and the difficulty of developing many complete characters within the time limitations. The National Broadcasting Company even states in its interdepartmental correspondence to writers doing adaptations for NBC Matinee Theater that they are limited to ten full parts. Since two small parts of five lines of dialogue or less equal one full part, the cast can include more than ten actors, but the combination of full parts and five-line characters must not exceed ten. For example, an adapter may cut the number of characters in his dramatization to seven full parts and six five-line parts and still be within the maximum total allowed by the producers.

A recommended procedure for adapting fiction and stage plays to television is to first write out the basic story using only those characters absolutely essential to its telling. Next, through structural analysis, discover the scenes necessary to tell the basic story. Make sure all subplots are eliminated or as many of them as can be and still keep the basic story intact. At this point it is possible to determine if the number of characters and scenes necessary to tell the basic story will fit into the time and cast-size restrictions of the medium.

Another basic consideration is that live television cannot present the panoramic or spectacular scenes so inherent to motion pictures. Filmed television shows do cover more territory but even here the scope is greatly limited. Medium-long and long shots become minute on 17-, 21-, and 24-inch picture tubes. The vaster the setting the smaller the people. A sharp contrast between motion picture and television films is immediately evident when motion pictures are telecast. As long as the action is close-up, the audience has little difficulty in following the action. But when the action is shown through wide and sweeping long shots much of its impact is lost to the television viewer. The playwright must write with one eye on these limitations if he is to be produced.

LIMITATIONS OF THE RADIO MEDIUM

The radio dramatic writer shares the same problem as the novelist. Both appeal to individuals in isolation. Both enlist active collaboration with the individual since their end products can exist only in his mind or imagination. Some of the problems already discussesd in adapting fiction and stage plays may be applied to radio. However, the characteristics of this medium provide additional limitations to be considered.

Radio shares the same time limitations imposed upon television. In both media the action of the play must get underway swiftly. Since the audience unit is thought of as one person, it is not necessary to unify audience interest as in stage or motion picture presentation. Abrupt beginnings, fatal in the theatre, are more acceptable in broadcast media.

Since the radio listener is not regimented he is fairly free to react individually and therefore it is possible for radio drama to possess a faster rhythm. Small casts are as necessary on radio as they are on television. There is an additional reason for small casts in radio drama: The listener is trying to imagine the action in his mind's eye, and he cannot be asked to keep track of many characters. For the same reason there is a general elimination of subplots.

In radio the writer must learn to hint, suggest, to stimulate the imagination. In the other media a character may be seen striking a match, opening a door, mixing a drink, etc. In radio these nonplot activities take place but they are only suggested through the use of sound effects. The listener creates for himself the image of the physical activity accompanying the unfolding of the drama.

There is more freedom of movement in radio than in any of the other dramatic media. The action may jump around the world in a matter of seconds without worrying about production costs. The radio dramatic writer has access to scenes unconstructable by the most ingenious scenic artist of stage or screen. Radio is under no compulsion to localize its action. Its scenery cost nothing and shifts easily. Radio has the privilege of moving or of not moving. An entire play can be set in one small place with little physical action and the listener will accept it, whereas the viewer-listener may find it tedious.

Use of a narrator moves radio closer to the form of the novel. Radio drama may be in the first person singular, told from the viewpoint of the protagonist. The protagonist-narrator may comment, explain, or even plead with his audience. The theatre of the mind is a versatile collaborator. It is amazing how actively it will cooperate with the writer when stimulated by speech, sound effects, and music.

LIMITATIONS OF THE MOTION PICTURE MEDIUM

When adapting fiction or plays to the motion picture medium the playwright has many of the advantages offered by the other dramatic media and only a few of their disadvantages. The motion picture form is still restricted by time, but like the stage play, it runs its course without the fear of running into a closing commercial which haunts the writer adapting to the radio and television media. There still must be condensation, however, for the auidence cannot be asked to sit still while the continuous action of the complete novel is presented to them. Production budgets may restrict the scenarist but he doesn't have to worry about his action being too large or epic for the smallness of a television screen. Since motion pictures are filmed in large studios or on location there is greater camera mobility than is possible in live television.

The most apparent difference between the motion picture and the stage is the mode of presentation. The story is told in a succession of images flowing upon a large screen in a darkened auditorium. In addition, the sound effects so important to the creation of action in radio are present but always in relationship to their physical activity or atmospheric cause.

A motion picture scenario is so filled with technical instructions that it often makes dull reading, since the scenarist, unlike the television playwright, prepares a shooting script, complete down to the angles of the shots he wants from the cameras.

John Howard Lawson, in describing the differences between the novelist's technique and the screen writer's, touches upon four basic points. These have already been covered in previous discussion. First, says Lawson, the film has to show visual activity. So does the stage and television. The motion picture has an advantage in exploiting this factor, however. Second, film conflict cannot be embodied in generalizations expressing the author's views of life and society. If necessary, they must be translated into the language of the film and directly related to the action of the screen. The other dramatic media are faced with the same problem. Third, the film must personalize the conflict. The events on the screen must be identified with people who are either observing the activity or participating in it. This is also true of the other dramatic media. Fourth, film conflict achieves a visual tension which is not necessary in the novel. Stage and television conflict must be shown in the same way.

15

The Play in Rehearsal and Performance

"PLAYS are not written, they are rewritten," said Dion Boucicault, popular Irish-American dramatist of the nineteenth century. Every experienced playwright knows this adage to be true. Regardless of the care with which a play is constructed, the characters created, and the dialogue executed, there is always room for improvement.

That even our most brilliant playwrights agree with the Boucicault adage is evidenced by Eugene O'Neill's remark, "I confess, though, that I have never been completely satisfied with anything that I have done and I constantly rewrite my plays until they are produced and even then I always see things which I could improve and regret that it is too late to make more changes." [1]

REVISING THE INITIAL DRAFT

Since the initial draft has been completed by following the pattern of alternate production from subconscious bursts of inspired creativity and conscious deliberation over what has been written, the playwright should continue the process through the rewriting stages.

As the construction of the working scenario was more or less a conscious, deliberate task, the rewriting phase also begins at the con-

[1] S. J. Woolf, "Eugene O'Neill Returns After Twelve Years," *New York Times Magazine*, September 15, 1946, p. 62.

scious level with a structural analysis of the total work. The experienced playwright does this instinctively and has devised his own method. The beginning dramatist, however, is usually at a loss as where to begin and what procedure to follow. The following method may be helpful since it is effectively employed by several outstanding teachers of playwriting and many prominent professional writers.

First, break the play down into its component scenes or units of action. This is called "French-scening a play," since action units are frequently delineated by the arrival or departure of key characters. However, many scenes may transpire continuously with the same characters present throughout.

Second, make out an index card for each scene or action unit with the names of the characters and a brief description of the action. In the index card's upper left-hand corner label the scene's primary purpose or function. Is it a unit primarily designed to be expository? Or to reveal character? Or to establish motivation? Is it a key scene in the unfolding of the plot? Whatever its function, label it clearly. Next, indicate in the upper right hand corner of the card the scene's length in terms of pages and page fractions.

Third, arrange the cards in act sequence on a large table. Now the playwright has a structural overview of his initial draft.

This procedure can be invaluable to the beginning dramatist. It enables him to discover if he has too many expository scenes grouped together and unbroken by an action scene. It also reveals the scenes that have been given too much stress or importance as well as those that haven't been given enough. The card arrangement also locates the climactic scenes in relation to the scenes leading up to and away from them and enables the writer to determine if they have been given proper weight. He may on the basis of his analysis decide to rearrange some scenes, eliminate others or introduce new scenes where they will strengthen the overall presentation of the play's action.

This procedure is obviously mechanical and highly conscious, but it gets the dramatist started. The index card method may be called a retrospective scenario.

PREPARING THE MANUSCRIPT FOR PERFORMANCE

The playwriting process does not end with the delivery of the finished manuscript to a producer. Since the lifeless manuscript does not truly become a play until it is produced, the professional playwright is expected to be present at all rehearsals and pre-Broadway tryout performances to make whatever revisions are found necessary. It is during this period that a playwright often does his most significant rewriting. As Moss Hart put it, "Things can't always be worked out in practice as they are imagined on the typewriter. One readjusts in rehearsal." George Bernard Shaw also noted that "only rehearsal can tell what should stay and what should not."

The value of the rehearsal period experience to the development of the beginning dramatist must not be underestimated. The necessity of being produced has been emphasized in many of the previous chapters, for only through production can the dramatic-writing process be completed. The playwright's development also remains incomplete until he witnesses his work in rehearsal and performance. The dramatic-writing programs of many major universities are designed to give student playwrights production experience. Whether it is a formalized theatre reading, a laboratory presentation, or a full scale production, the writer will learn as much from it as he would in an entire semester's work in a playwriting class if not more.

What should be the attitude of the playwright as he faces this important phase of his experience? How should he conduct himself at rehearsals? What should be his working relationship to the director and his cast?

THE PLAYWRIGHT AND THE DIRECTOR

Perhaps the most common relationship on the New York professional stage and on the better television series has the playwright in attendance at all rehearsals and working closely with the director on matters of interpretation. He is also there in case a line or a scene or an act is in need of revision.

The concern for one's "created child"—the raw manuscript—perhaps accounts for the beginning playwright's hesitancy to release his child to another's guardianship. However, the playwright who is neither established nor already a competent stage director should leave the staging of his work to another. The beginning playwright is much too close to his play to serve objectively as its director, for as the director, he will unfortunately remain a playwright trying to organize his concept into a production entity.

There is much to be gained by working with a director, watching him as he approaches the work and interprets it. The good director instantly sees the dead script as live action and quickly recognizes the qualities which the actors can best convey and the audience most readily accept. The director usually welcomes the playwright's presence, especially to clarify vague situations or to interpret difficult lines. But a ship can have only one pilot and when a playwright turns over command to a director he must assume no more than a first mate's role.

The playwright should feel perfectly free to express himself to the director. He should be careful, however, to give his reactions privately, never allowing the actors to overhear. If he disagrees with the director's approach to a scene, he should talk it over with him, let him know his point of view. In other words, he should try to work out any differences they may have regarding interpretation. The wise director will listen, though he may not necessarily comply. He may instead offer an explanation for his approach, one that is feasible and perhaps employed to solve a production problem not anticipated by the writer in the preparation of his manuscript. In these conferences subjectivity of writer meets subjectivity of director and often an objectivity of production is obtained.

What does the playwright look for as he watches his play in rehearsal? He watches for needless repetitions in his script and places where action may be more appropriate than dialogue. He checks the consistency of his characters with their actions now that they both can be observed. He watches carefully the development of a character and looks for those places where his actions can be more appropriately motivated. He gauges the total effect and compares it to the impression he had of the play in writing it. In short, he uses the rehearsal period as an opportunity to check everything he conceived on paper as it is translated into live action.

THE PLAYWRIGHT AND THE ACTOR

What should be the attitude of the playwright toward the actor? The answer depends upon whether or not he regards the actor as the living link between his manuscript and the audience. The actor is almost as important as the writer in so far as the success of a play is concerned. Since the playwright cannot address himself directly to his audience, he must rely on the actor to be his spokesman. While the audience is in the theatre it is much more conscious of the actor than of the dramatist. Elmer Rice once said: "There is perhaps not one spectator in a hundred who is able to differentiate a part from a performance."

The playwright, even if he has done his job of character creation well, can and should expect the characterization to be enhanced and enriched by the skillful actor's contribution, since the good actor, like the good playwright, is first of all an artist.

Many writers, upon viewing their plays in rehearsal, invariably discover an actor who appears to be a "thumb" sticking out from "fingers" that blend pretty well together. Although the natural urge is to want the thumb cut off, he should be careful in voicing his objections. If the director is endeavoring to develop a totality of effect with the cast, he may well recognize, as should the writer, that people develop at different speeds. A playwright should have patience with the actors in his play, for they, as artists, must be allowed to develop in their own manner just as the playwright followed his own bent in developing his play from the germ idea to the finished manuscript.

The playwright should initiate a coöperative approach toward the actors. After all, the manuscript is not infallible, regardless of the high opinion the author may hold of it. The skilled actor is a highly developed mechanism with an intuition or an instinct to sense when something is not quite right.

Often an author will hear the actor request, "Couldn't you give me a word or two more in this speech?" or "I can't say this line the way it should be said—can you give me some words that I can handle, that still say the same thing?" The answer, amazingly enough, is often positive to both questions and the playwright soon discovers still another facet of his "art through collaboration."

Oftentimes the writer's service to the actor is in the revising of burdensome lines so that the actor can handle the dialogue with ease and facility. Occasionally the author overwhelms the actor with language, as if he feared the actor could not portray the feeling without it. This is perhaps why so many plays have to be stripped to the bone before they move forward with comparative freedom. The playwright sometimes must adjust the dialogue to fit the actor's individual peculiarities and handicaps, especially if it is necessary to insure the success of the play. Playwrights should look upon this practice as a compromise between the role as he conceived it and the ability of an actor to portray it.

THE AUDIENCE'S ROLE IN REWRITING

Chapter 4 considered the importance of anticipating the needs of an audience in constructing the plot and creating the characters. This anticipation is designed to eliminate many of the revisions that are often found necessary when the play finally meets its audience across the footlights. However, the writer cannot anticipate and plan for every reaction. He can only observe the audience, especially during the tryout period, and make whatever adjustments he can to improve the play.

As the play is tried out on the road, revision conferences are usually held nightly. Why didn't the audience laugh where we hoped it would? Why weren't they overwhelmed with emotion by the seriousness of this scene? Why? Why? Why? ask the producer, the director, and the playwright. They try new dialogue, a shift of emphasis, they cut out complete sections of dialogue or entire scenes trying to adjust the play to the audience.

George S. Kaufman contends that it possible to gauge from certain audience symptoms whether a specific scene is proceeding as planned. "At a key moment in the play the audience remains sublimely disinterested, or else starts coughing its head off," observed Kaufman, "and that's why all those playwrights are locked up in hotel rooms."

It is not necessary to sit among the members of the audience to interpret their reactions. Standing at the side of the stage or at the rear of the house, one can feel the audience's mood. The rustling of programs, shuffling of feet, coughing—all tell their story more plainly than words can express. Each may mean a revision.

The playwrights writing for the other dramatic media—motion pictures, television, and radio—are handicapped by not being able to evaluate their audience's reaction. They can only anticipate and in some way compensate for the absence of an observable audience. Even if the writer could observe the audiences of these media, it would do little good. The play is either on film or being performed for one time only. In neither case can the playwright rewrite his play for another audience. Perhaps this is the reason so many of the successful motion picture and television writers cut their teeth in the legitimate theatre. Having experienced audience reaction, they are more capable of anticipating it than is the purely motion-picture- or television-trained writer.

THE PLAY DOCTOR

It is not at all unusual for a producer to bring in an expert playwright who specializes in rescuing faltering dramas. The "play doctor's" role is akin to the surgeon who grafts on new tissue and injects new blood into his patient. Whatever revision and rewriting he does is usually for a standard fee. Under some circumstances, however, his contribution may be such that he is not only given a share of the royalties but his name is coupled with the original author.

Unfortunately, the play doctor is a last-chance gamble resorted to by producers in a state of panic. The value of the play doctor is greatly overrated. Even those writers who frequently serve as doctors admit they rarely save the patient. However, due to the phenomenal success enjoyed by a few poor-play specialists, it is not unusual for a producer to call in a play doctor when a play in rehearsal is ailing. The miraculous stage cures and the writers who performed them are widely known, not by the general public, but among the men who produce Broadway's annual output of plays. Producers can't be blamed for calling in specialists like George S. Kaufman and Abe Burrows to perform eleventh-hour surgery. Plays are expensive; investors are scarce. The desire to protect an investment often results in a compromise. It is very difficult for one author to capture the style and flavor of another. Whatever changes are made must blend, yet if there is a clash of styles they cannot.

It may be that somewhere there is that rare writer who can plan out each phase of his play so carefully that when he writes "curtain" to the final act the play can stand or fall without a single change or improvement. For the most part, however, writers soon discover the wisdom of Boucicault's adage, "Plays are not written, they are rewritten."

16

Epilogue

AFTER the beginning dramatist has explored the playwriting process and written his first plays, where does he go from there? How does he make the transition from nonprofessional to professional playwright? How does he get his plays produced? What can he expect from those he will come in contact with? What are his chances of financial success?

A young playwright with talent, who wants to make dramatic writing his profession, naturally has questions about getting established. This epilogue endeavors to show some of the devices available to him in making the transition.

THE HIGHLY COMPETITIVE MARKET

The aspiration of every beginning dramatic writer is immediate recognition through a major production on the New York stage, a Hollywood motion picture, or a performance on one of the better network television series. Realistically, however, he should realize that his chances for this immediate recognition are almost impossible. Producers are looking for good scripts, but because of the financial risk involved, they are understandably very hesitant to try the work of an unknown. When they have a choice of plays by authors who have been successfully produced, why take a chance on what appears to be an excellent script by an unknown?

Theatre real estate in New York dwindles each year. Thirty years ago it was comparatively easy for a well-written play to get a hearing, but then there were many theatres and over three hundred new plays introduced each season. As theatres become fewer production costs zoom. Now it takes a small fortune to produce a play and a producer rarely uses his own money—he gets financial backing from investors looking for a return. The risk is high. Less than fifty new plays now appear in New York each year and only a handful succeed, either at the box office or at the hands of the newspaper critics who hold a life and death grip over the professional theatre.

A Broadway production sometimes takes years to attain. Most playwrights never make it. But there are other theatres where skilled but unknown writers can get a hearing. This hearing or production is the important thing to the dramatist. Like the beginning actor, the writer's work must be seen to be appreciated. Once seen he has a better chance of being seen again. As his list of successful productions increases, his chances for a Broadway hearing improve.

Television, being one of the mass media, needs a large quantity of plays to meet its daily needs. The medium is actually a grist mill chewing up the supply as fast as it comes from the playwrights' typewriters. When one considers the number of dramatic scripts necessary to keep a single television station on the air for one day, let alone for an entire year, it is obvious that the beginning playwright has a far better opportunity of being produced on television than he does with any other media. The average daily output of television drama over a single station is seven to ten hours—that is over 3500 hours a year. Considering that there are three major networks and some cities with three to five stations operating simultaneously with different programs, the need for material is fantastic and the possibilities for the talented new writer are fabulous!

Many writers establish their reputations in television and then leave it for the more lucrative motion picture and theatre media. Paddy Chayefsky was considered television's outstanding dramatic writer, but then his play *Marty* became an Academy award-winning motion picture and later his play, *Middle of the Night,* had a successful Broadway run. Chayefsky no longer writes for television; he can't afford it.

ADVANCED TRAINING IN PLAYWRITING

The new playwright exposed only to an undergraduate course in dramatic writing is seldom equipped to make the grade professionally. Naturally, his instincts have been stirred and sharpened, but, after all, a few years work doesn't make him a professional. He needs additional training and most of all an opportunity to see his work produced.

There are several advanced playwriting programs designed to give the playwright a wide range of production opportunities. Several major universities, such as UCLA, Yale, and Texas, offer advanced work to the growing playwright.

The UCLA program is a model more universities could well imitate. In a recent five-year period of presenting one-act plays, 208 originals were produced, reflecting the work of 104 playwrights and 120 directors. With few exceptions these plays came out of the university's playwriting classes. At each performance, members of the audience are asked to fill out evaluation forms covering both the play and the production. Following this, an audience critique is conducted by one of the playwriting teachers. This critique is recorded and made available to all concerned.

New full-length plays are also presented. Many of these are sent in by playwrights throughout the world, evaluated, and the results sent back to the authors. Whenever possible, plays of unusual promise are put in a special new-play library and made available to persons in search of new work. All rights, of course, remain with the playwright.

More and more college and university theatres are offering production opportunities to new playwrights. The program at Tufts has been mentioned. Similar programs may be found at North Carolina, Michigan State, and the University of Wisconsin, to mention but a few. There are also professional theatre schools offering production opportunities. The young dramatist may well select one of these schools offering training through production.

About a decade ago the American Educational Theatre Association recognized the plight of the new dramatist and established a manuscript play project for the purpose of benefiting mutually the college, university, and community theatres wishing to produce new plays, and deserving young playwrights who want to see their plays performed. The Project has the following creed: "Members of the Project, believing that the American Theatre must assume a continuous responsibility for stimulating the writing and production of meritorious plays, are bound together as a coöperative group to find and distribute manuscripts for production."

Anyone interested in the Project or wishing to make use of its services may join. Scripts may be submitted by anyone, but generally they either come from or are recommended by members. When a nonmember's play is chosen for distribution, he is naturally expected to become a member before the play is finally duplicated and mailed. The membership fee, for both an individual and a group, is $15 for one year or $25 for two years.

The Project's scripts are selected by a committee of three regional judges. Once approved, the script is duplicated and a copy sent to every member of the project, who may or may not produce it, as they like. Anyone, anywhere, who is willing to pay the author a fair royalty for the use of his play may produce it. Playwrights and producers may negotiate any agreement they wish. Since the chairmanship and location of the headquarters of the Project changes from time to time, the correct address may be obtained from the office of the Executive Secretary of the American Educational Theatre Association. The quarterly publication of this association, *Educational Theatre Journal,* always lists the address.

THE NEW DRAMATISTS COMMITTEE

An organization which has as its objective the encouragement and development of new playwriting talent is the New Dramatists Committee in New York.

The Committee, in setting forth its aims, asks the following question: "How can talented young writers develop their theatrical craft when opportunities in the commercial theatre are largely limited to mature and experienced writers?" The Committee feels that with the disappearance of local stock companies as a training ground for playwrights and the present concentration of "theatre" on Broadway, there is less and less opportunity for a playwright to develop his talent. It becomes increasingly crucial, therefore, that a means be found to help him. The New Dramatists Committee believes it has a partial solution.

The Committee operates as a chartered nonprofit corporation under the sponsorship of the Dramatists Guild. Their "Plan for Playwrights" consists of five projects, each designed to assist the development of new playwrights.

The first project is theatre admissions, whereby resident members of the group are enabled to see many plays in production. The second is a series of craft discussions whereby members are given an opportunity to discuss their mutual problems with established leaders of the profession, such as Joshua Logan, Howard Lindsay, and John van Druten. The third project arranges for the new dramatist to observe the evolution of a new play from the time it is cast and goes into rehearsal until it opens in New York. The fourth project is the Elinor Morgenthau Workshop. Through a grant from the Elinor Morgenthau Fund playwrights receive an opportunity to learn from their mistakes without involving the tremendous risks of commercial production. This is achieved by two methods: First, the play is read by a "sounding panel" of playwrights who discuss it with the new dramatist; next, it is given a formal reading before a limited audience by a professional cast and rehearsed by a stage director. After the performance, audiences fill out cards which provide the writer with answers to specific questions about his script. Extensive rewriting is the usual result of the rehearsed read‧ing. The fifth and last project sponsored by the Committee is a New Play Circulation plan similar to the Manuscript Play Project. Peri‧odically a bulletin describing new plays is issued, and interested groups may request copies for reading and consideration.

The benefits of the New Dramatists Committee to the playwright are considerable. He may increase his income through royalties; he may have the opportunity to work with directors and theatre groups himself; his reputation can surely be enhanced by the contacts involved. Unfortunately, but understandably, membership is limited to 40 new dramatists a year.

PLAYWRITING COMPETITIONS

The number of playwriting contests and competitions open to young dramatists is on the increase. They are widespread and varied. Some are limited to one-act plays, others to plays for the children's theatre, and still others to specific themes. Many are sponsored by reli‧gious, civic, and educational organizations. For the most part, these competitions are thoroughly legitimate and many, in addition to offer‧ing a prize for the winning play, offer a production and an opportunity for the playwright to be in attendance at rehearsals and performances.

Space does not permit the listing of the many annual playwriting competitions. Notices of them are frequently carried in such profes‧sional journals as *Theatre Arts, Players Magazine,* and the *Educational Theatre Journal.* Every playwriting teacher receives announcements of such competitions and usually posts them.

Some organizations do not conduct open competitions but do en‧courage the submission of new manuscripts. If chosen for production the playwright is subsidized so that he may come to the campus and work with the cast and director in rehearsal. Cornell University oper‧ates such an annual event for the new playwright.

The Samuel French playwriting competitions, open only to writers enrolled in colleges and universities, have done much to stimulate interest in playwriting and otherwise to further the cause of the new dramatist by offering possible publication and the handling of the script for the nonprofessional theatre.

THE NONPROFESSIONAL MARKET

Few people outside of the theatre are aware of the vast number of nonprofessional groups in this country that yearly produce plays. These organizations usually obtain their plays from nonprofessional play companies. Such companies have two types of scripts: (1) plays that have appeared on Broadway and are now available to amateur groups upon payment of a set royalty; (2) plays that have never appeared on the boards professionally. Some of these are directed toward the large high-school market, others toward the one-act play field, and still others toward the community, civic, and stock theatres in various sections of the country.

The playwright is to be cautioned, however, against selling his play outright. He may get immediate payment, but it will be far less than he will ultimately receive on a royalty basis. Arrangements are up to the play publisher and the playwright or his agent. Some offer established writers liberal royalty terms, while giving the new dramatist a fair arrangement. Some companies turn over the royalty in its entirety to the playwright, making their money instead off the sale of individual copies of the play. Others split the royalty with the playwright.

Another word of caution. Make sure you are releasing only the nonprofessional rights to your play. Often professional theatre groups, motion picture companies, or television producers want a specific script. If you control the play, they must deal with you. Some companies—Samuel French and Dramatist Play Service for instance—will also act as an agent for both nonprofessional and professional rights to a play.

THE LITERARY AGENT

Most established professional writers work through an agent in dealing with potential producing units. The practice is so widespread that many producers refuse to deal directly with an author, preferring instead to rely upon the supply furnished by reputable agents. Many production opportunities are denied the dramatist unless he has an agent.

The new dramatist usually has to learn the true value of an agent. Agents are in a position to know the immediate and long-range needs of the various producers. Good agents also can be helpful in suggesting revisions that will make scripts better market material. Since agents work on a percentage basis, they will naturally try to make the best financial arrangements they can for the author. There is an advantage in having the agent handle contract terms. Playwrights are sometimes so anxious to be produced that they will compromise over terms just to get their plays on the boards. The agent is more impersonal. He recognizes a property that is valuable; therefore, he is in a far better position than the writer to barter over the terms of the contract.

Some agents handle a writer's work in all fields, including publishing, motion pictures, radio, and television. Other agents, specializing in literary material only, work in close association with agencies that handle properties for the dramatic media. On no occasion does their combined fee exceed 10 percent.

Since producers in the various dramatic media are usually too busy to read new material, most of them have story editors to read submitted manuscripts. These story editors in turn make specific recommendations to the producer who will then read the plays the editor gives him. Story editors can't read every play sent to them. They don't even try. They prefer to read only plays referred to them by reputable agents. The reason for this is obvious. Since the established agent first screens the plays on his list in terms of the producer's needs, he will send only plays he feels should be considered. Unless you have a personal contact with a producer, it is best to obtain the services of an agent to represent you.

Since selling plays is the agent's business, he makes every effort to protect the playwright's legal rights. In addition, he has contact with all of the purchasing agents of the various dramatic media. It is not at all unusual for a playwright to submit a three-act play to his agent, who, after sending it around to active Broadway producers, finally sells it to the motion pictures.

New writers can secure a list of reputable agents from The Authors Guild of America, 6 East 39th Street, New York. A number of years ago a group of literary agents organized the Society of Authors' Representatives. This is a group of highly reputable agents who subscribe to a rigid code of ethical practices. Since an agent should be chosen as carefully as a doctor or a lawyer, the Society's code is of more than passing interest to the new writer:

1. An agent takes only 10 percent commission on domestic sales and no more than 20 percent on foreign sales.
2. He pays out the author's share of monies as soon as possible after receipt.
3. He charges the author with no expense incurred by the normal operation of his office, such as postage or local phone calls. He does charge the author for such things as copyright fees, manuscript retyping fees incurred at the author's request, and copies of books for submission overseas.
4. He may charge a reading fee for unsolicited material but refunds this in the event of his acceptance of the material.
5. He does not advertise his services.

A list of the members of the Society may be obtained by writing them at 522 Fifth Avenue, New York 36, N.Y.

THE GUILDS

Before the establishment of the Authors Guild of America and its various subsidiary guilds, such as the Dramatists Guild, the Screen Writers Guild, etc., the dramatic writer was pretty much at the mercy of the producers. The Guilds, however, operating much like unions, soon made it difficult for an unscrupulous producer to take advantage of an author. The Dramatists Guild, for instance, has a contract it recommends to producers and writers. This contract spells out the responsibilities of each party and sets forth the terms under which the play is to be produced.

One of the practices of producers that the Guilds have eliminated is the optioning of plays for production to tie them up, thus preventing the competition from getting the script and also denying the writer the right to sell it. The Guild has spelled out the terms under which a dramatic work may be optioned. The longer the producer has the script, the larger the monthly option fee. The option time is usually broken up into six-month periods. The playwright receives a stipulated amount each month. Once the second six-month period begins the option fee goes up. If the producer decides not to produce the play and releases it, the author is under no further obligation to the producer. However, if the play is produced, all option money paid is deductible from the royalty due the playwright.

The Guild contract not only protects the writer but guarantees the producer certain privileges. Usually it gives him a share of motion picture and television rights. It also stipulates the author's duties during rehearsal and tryout periods, such as when he must attend and what his obligations are in changing the play. In turn the writer seldom takes a complete loss, even if the play is a failure. Since his percentage is based on the gross receipts, his royalty check is made out before other production expenses are met. Most Guild contracts give the author between 8 and 10 percent of the gross.

THE ECONOMIC ASPECT OF DRAMATIC WRITING

Despite the publicity given the income of certain established writers, few playwrights are wealthy. Of course there are exceptions. But the income tax and the long years of waiting for a hit tend to cancel out any big money the writer may receive. The sale of plays to motion picture companies is misleading. A script sold for $300,000 will net the author much less. The original Broadway producer gets a large share, the agent who made the sale receives his 10 percent, and the Internal Revenue Department takes most of the balance.

Making a living as a dramatic writer is as hard as any other profession. No one should go into it bedazzled by its lucrative aspects. There are many skilled, highly competent dramatic craftsmen today, who earn no more than $5,000–$6,000 a year.

The transition from beginning dramatist to established playwright takes its toll. The casualty list is much larger than the list of those who make the grade professionally. The writer who thinks in terms of telling a good story well, who can structure this story in a compelling manner and people it with vitally interesting characters, this is the writer who has the best chance of finding a market. There are four dramatic media today—the stage, the motion picture screen, the television picture tube, and the radio loudspeaker—but there remains only one dramatic writer.

Appendix A

Exercises and Projects in Dramatic Writing

EXERCISES and projects in dramatic writing are in no way formulae for writing good plays or becoming skilled playwrights. The value of such exercises is a highly individual matter. Some beginning writers find them very helpful while others discover they are a hindrance to creativity. The exercises in this section are not intended for the experienced writer. They are, for the most part, rudimentary and primarily designed to get the beginning writer started and to introduce him to the peculiar requirements of writing for four dramatic media.

Dramatic writing exercises and projects fall into four categories: (1) those to discipline the writer, (2) those to "free" him, (3) those designed for individual use, and (4) those that can be done only in a playwriting class or by a group of writers working together. Exercises 1 through 53 are for individual use while exercises 54 through 72 are directed toward the teacher of playwriting for use in the classroom.

Many teachers do not use class exercises or projects. There are a number of reasons for this. George Savage of UCLA, for instance, says, "The only process that has worked for me is to find something that the playwright—beginning, advanced, professional—really believes in. If he really wants to write out the idea in dramatic form, he will be forced in actual practice to solve the technical problems of writing and staging." Savage's point of view is shared by others who believe that the only exercise is to write a play—a whole play, no matter how brief it is—and that little pieces of things are of little benefit when it is a sense of wholeness the writer is most in search of. In addition, many colleges and universities offer only a semester or term's work in dramatic writing. Within such a time limitation, it is understandable that the teachers of these courses are often reluctant to take up class time with group exercises. There is nothing, however, to prevent the individual from doing the exercises on his own initiative.

It is a difficult task to nurture the rather fragile beginning talent and at the same time instill a sense of craftsmanship. Substantially, the disciplining exercises are intended to develop that sense in the writer, whereas the freeing exercises are supposed to encourage a sense of permissiveness that will allow his talent to fight its way through the sets of germ ideas, scenari, synopses, etc. Many of these exercises are rather arbitrary and dogmatic in their demands. This is intentional, since it is important that the student of playwriting should not get the idea that every word he writes is sacrosanct and should be immediately shipped off to an agent. Exercises are exercises and should be discarded when they are finished and worked over. The most important thing is that once started the student should continue to write.

INDIVIDUAL EXERCISES AND PROJECTS

1. Write an eassay on *The Nature of Drama* in 500 to 800 words. This is a very difficult, if not impossible, assignment, but an honest attempt *without* reference to "authority" will give the beginning playwright respect for his dramatic inheritance and obligations. If a student, he ought, at the end of one term or after a year's work, to compare his first attempt with a revised and realigned approach to describing this mode of communication. Be succinct and as qualitative as possible. Draw upon your own experiences in recalling the "drama" you have seen in life and the "drama" you have seen in the films, TV, and on the stage.

2. Write an autobiography and keep redoing it, starting back at the farthest event in memory and freely wandering up to the present. This exercise keeps one writing when otherwise stuck, encourages a certain necessary narcissism, and drives the writer back to the experience he knows best to find the material he can't otherwise invent. It often compels him to confront aspects of his experience that are threatening to him, that ultimately provide the most effective and truest dramatic material. (Herbert Blau of San Francisco State says of this exercise: "The students are surprised to find how often, this way, they stumble on events, situations, characters, images, phrases, gestures, intonations,

moods, locales, relationships, that have slipped their memories and that are immediately relevant.")

3. Sit down at the typewriter (or with pen and ink, whichever is easiest for you) and just start writing dialogue without any preparation whatsoever. If necessary just write down "HE" and then put in a line of dialogue; then write "SHE" and another line. The important point is to keep going. The exercise might be well-employed every day as a kind of "loosening up" workout.

4. Collect a number of sensory impressions during a routine day, choosing a place that you frequent regularly such as a dormitory, a commons room, restaurant, drug store, garage, etc. Write down as rapidly as you can—in chart form—the things you see, hear, smell, taste, and touch. Itemize at least 60 sensory impressions. Avoid the generalized image. Describe *accurately* and *vividly* what gives each image its distinction.

5. From the list of sensory impressions organize two separate paragraphs, each one of which catches a *dominant* impression. Select those images that strengthen and give unity to the main idea. Isolate the key word that summarizes the dominant impression. By careful selection and arrangement, organize the images so that there is a resultant *unity of mood* and *unity of idea*. Perhaps here is the germ of a miniature drama.

6. Find a dramatic idea in a person you know, some incident you are familiar with, a newspaper story, a want-ad, local history, a song, a bit of folklore, a title of a book, and an axiom. Jot these down on paper, not worrying as yet how they can be developed.

7. Analyze the "germinal ideas," looking for the potential drama in each, its most appropriate treatment in all literary media, and its most appropriate treatment in length and in the various dramatic media. Use an imaginative "stretch" on the ideas; be freewheeling in your combining of different germinal ideas; arbitrarily change situations, reverse relationships (including sex) to see if this heightens the clash and activates the struggle between a central character and other dramatic entities.

8. From the chart of sensory impressions gathered during a routine day (see exercise 4 above) organize a germinal idea for a "dramatic" attitude towards the material. How do you, the author, feel about it? Next, organize a germinal idea for a "tragic" attitude or handling of material. How do you, the author, feel about it?

9. Analyze the decisions that went into your judgment of your handling

the three basic approaches or attitudes towards the commonplace material. Analyze such matters as desired responses, methods of control, and "tone" in dealing with the three basic approaches or attitudes. Draw tentative conclusions about the basic relationships involved in observing the raw material of life and the author's attitude towards that material. Indicate in your analysis how these relationships are essentially the same even though the technical media of communication may differ.

10. Take any real person and fix him at any given point in time. At this point describe his character as fully as possible. Having characterized him, go into his past and find all of the real reasons why each specific facet of his character is what it is.

11. Take another real person in the same manner. Construct from your imagination logical reasons which will explain why each specific facet of his character is what it is.

12. Construct from your imagination a fictional character in as much detail as possible. Give imaginative reasons why each facet of his character is what it is.

13. Write a first-person speech in which the following characteristics are revealed about the person speaking *without his being conscious of his own possession of those characteristics:* (1) poignancy, (2) horror, (3) disgust, (4) fear, (5) anger, (6) prejudice, (7) love, (8) friendship, (9) admiration.

14. Write several first-person narratives trying in various ones to characterize the speaker *and* the person spoken about.

15. Briefly relate your conversations with people outside your immediate family for a single day.
   a. Develop a story and/or plot from these conversations.
   b. Put one of these conversations into a dialect.
   c. Make an analysis of the individuals spoken to.

16. Write a scene with two people discussing a third person—the protagonist—who will then enter and disprove by his actions and talk what they had said about him.

17. Choose a character—male or female. Describe the character physically, psychologically, intellectually, and also describe background and physical surroundings of character. Repeat this until you have created at least three characters—A, B, and C. It is best if the three characters are apparently unrelated. They will be used in subsequent exercises.

18. Have characters A and B meet. Explain circumstances of meeting.

Write a brief dialogue of the meeting, revealing a short exposition, development, and climax of the meeting. Introduce character C and repeat the exercise.

19. Write a brief narrative description of a situation involving two or three people. This description should be matter-of-fact, indicating simply the situation and the sequence of events. Having written this, write a scene dramatizing the situation and placing the sympathy with each of the characters in turn.

20. Analyze any contemporary play for the following things: the handling of entrances and exits, the sequence of scenes in terms of length (French scenes), number of characters, distribution of speeches among the characters, story telling points made in each scene, character, mood, and locale points made in each scene, and so forth.

21. Use some of the characters already developed in previous exercises and show a plausible reason for the *entrance* of each character in any one or more of the situations above. Trace the "build-up" in speech and action for such an entrance. Note a climactic point in the speech and action on stage which will emphasize the entrance of the character. Use the dialogue and plotting already done wherever possible. This building up of an entrance is most important, and only too frequently neglected by the beginning playwright. Give each character this chance, at least, of a focus—they do not come too often!

22. Use the same characters as before and show a plausible reason for the *exit* of each character in any one or more of the situations developed above. Again trace the "build-up" in speech and action pointing to the possible exit of the character. Note the climactic point and make it strong enough to necessitate the exit of the character. A good exit line helps, but above all, the action must be logical.

23. Analyze any contemporary play for the "tag" indentification of characters, i.e., the identification and characterization of a character by the repetition of a line, costume, device, or piece of business. An example would be "Barkis is willin'" in *David Copperfield*. In drama there are a number of examples. When Saroyan has his Arab in *The Time of Your Life* say, "No foundation, all down the line," we have a tag. The names of characters are often tag-like. (The comic strip, *Dick Tracy*, carries this to the extreme with such tags as "Prune-Face," "Flat-Top," "B. O. Plenty," etc.) The device is particularly noticeable in comedy but it is also used in more serious plays. Odets, for instance, uses it frequently. The advantages of tag identification are that the character

is readily identifiable and can be more or less categorized by the audience; its disadvantages stem from the tendency to use tag identification as a substitute for characterization. Actually, they are phases of the same approach to characterization. People constantly repeat words, phrases, and patterns of thought. We all know people whose next statement we can anticipate without difficulty. Simply stated again: tag identification of character is the repetition of a physical or verbal characteristic to aid in the physical and psychological identification of the character.

24. Prepare a scene about any historical character (Napoleon and Washington are particularly good) in which an attempt is made to treat the person as a human being without slipping into a debunking style.

25. Given: a log, a well-curb, a night scene with a moon, an owl's hoot. Write a plot using these elements.

26. Write a complete but simple play in description of mime action. Be prepared to perform this play.

27. Write a scene introducing the "first complication" of a play. This would be a new element which would change the course of the story. It may be a new character, or new information brought in by an old character, or even a change in the weather; news that the protagonist has just been declared a Communist by a U. S. Senator, or that the Antagonist is being kicked out of school for coming in drunk from a dance, or that she is being run for Campus Queen. In other words: *Invent!*

28. Show *conflict* in short scenes between A and B, A and C, and B and C. Show the source of conflict, its development and climax. The conflict does not need to be great or serious; it can hinge on small events, trifling speeches, or other points. Conflict grows by what it feeds upon, and it is interesting how one can use any one of these exercises to build up into a tragic, full-size conflict. Remember, the War of the Roses started, so it is said, by plucking a red rose and a white rose during a heated argument. Repeat this exercise showing conflict in a scene between all three characters.

29. Show *suspense* in short scenes between characters A and B, A and C, and B and C. Show source of suspense, its development, and climax. Next, show suspense in a scene between all three characters. The suspense in these exercises can arise from events about to happen or that may happen, psychological and physical factors, or an emotional crisis.

30. Show *emotional* reactions between A and B, A and C, and B and C. Attempt to reveal pity of one for the other, then hatred, jealousy, scorn, suspicion, joy or delight, and love. Next, show emotional reactions in a scene between A, B, and C. The emotions may be strong or weak or moderate.

31. Use specific details in constructing a situation in which A wants something and for one reason or another B is opposed to A. In terms of the situation which you have devised, answer the following questions: How many different things can A do to get around B and achieve his goal? In what manner can B obstruct each of these attempts to circumvent him? How many different things can B actively initiate to prevent A from achieving his goal? In what manner can A overcome each of these obstructions?

32. Write a scene in which there is dramatic conflict and in which eating is a functional part of the dramatic action. This scene demands the creation of an environment, usually realistic, and helps the beginning dramatist discover for himself the use of manners and mannerisms as methods of characterization.

33. Try to write a dramatic scene about a playwriting class (without dragging in a murder or a love affair between the professor and a student). Stick closely to the things that do happen in a class and yet make it interesting to someone who is not a playwriting student.

34. Out of many of the above exercises, humor may be developed by twisting the factors into mild or strong ridicule. For instance, the emotion of *suspicion* may be turned into trust by a twist of identity or event. *Suspense* may be turned into a humorous situation by introduction of an unexpected factor such as the suspected burglar turning out to be a belated guest. *Conflict* may be given a humorous turn by interjecting an extraneous query or event; thus, a bitter quarrel can be turned into jest by the entrance of the real antagonist, or by a letter explaining the situation, or any other factor which upsets the balance of the conflict.

35. Write out in detail as many comedy *situations* as you can name that are found in: (1) a new marriage, (2) a G.I. in a foreign land, (3) the Jones family planning a trip.

36. For each of the situations in exercise 35 develop a protagonist, mentioning sex, age, education, background, physical attributes, temperament, etc. Place your protagonist within the situation. What are his reactions? What are his actions? Is there a lesson involved? What is it?

37. Write a short scene of dialogue on almost any topic, serious or comic, just to get the feel of the bounce of dramatic conversation which has to be shared between two people and must never stop in the mouth of one person trying to deliver an oration.

38. Write a scene over several times. One time emphasize the use of verbs to communicate the meaning and play down the nouns and modifiers. The next time emphasize the nouns; finally, emphasize the modifiers.

39. Write the same scene as used in exercise 38 in as simple language as you can, bordering on a primer style. The next time write the scene using an old-fashioned rhetorical style. Try for preciosity. In other words, try to write in a number of different styles.

40. Write a brief scene using as many clichés as you can, then go back through it and eliminate or, rather, alter every line that smacks of cliché or slang.

41. Take an inferior script—a short one—and improve the clarity and expressiveness of the dialogue without violating what you believe to be the author's original intention. Compare the two versions as to unity, compactness, and appropriateness.

42. Write a short scene with a relatively slight plot content in which you attempt to convey a strong sense of mood, place, and time.

43. Write several scenes against the mood that the scene would seem to call for: that is, write a farcical murder scene; a sad scene about children playing; an ugly love scene; a naturalistic scene of fantasy; a fantasy in a naturalistic milieu, etc.

44. A news story tells of the arrest of a quack doctor in a metropolitan city, one of whose patients died as a result of an illegal operation. Also involved, and later arrested, was the girl's mother, a member of a wealthy and socially prominent Jewish family, who had encouraged her to have the operation. The mother, because of racial prejudice, or possessiveness, or some other factor, had forbidden the girl's marriage to a gentile boy, who, by all accounts, was a ne'er-do-well fortune hunter. The mother had succeeded in breaking up the marriage, with a settlement for the boy, and had then tried to erase the incident by taking her daughter to the illicit surgeon. This story is obviously too frank for TV. How would you go about putting the essence of this story into a drama for television, still obeying the broadcasting code?

45. Analyze Strindberg's *The Stronger* and Eugene O'Neill's *Before Breakfast.* Since they are monologues, they are relatively simple plays. De-

velop each into a longer and fuller play with two or more speaking characters instead of the single speaking roles in these pieces.

46. Take a traditional fairy or folk story and write a selected scene from it in a free adaptation, or else stay close to the original development of the scene, or do both.

47. Read and compare the novel *Tess of the D'Urbervilles* by Thomas Hardy with Hardy's own stage version and the more professional, yet Victorian, version by Lorimer Stoddard.

48. Select a short story from the public domain (John Gassner recommends Edgar Allan Poe's *The Cask of Amontillado* as a good choice for the beginning dramatist). Write out a detailed plot scenario as you would utilize the story for your own dramatic purpose. Has the theme been changed significantly? Without writing the dialogue how would you classify your proposed play?

49. Read William March's novel and Maxwell Anderson's play, *The Bad Seed*. Compare carefully the characterizations of Mrs. Penmark and her daughter, Rhoda. How much dialogue of the novel was retained in the play in creating each of these characters? Note the narrative incidents from the novel that were revealed in dialogue in the play. Would you label the play a dramatization, as did Mr. Anderson, or an adaptation?

50. Read Arthur Koestler's novel, *Darkness at Noon,* and Sidney Kingsley's play of the same name. Make a plot outline of each; then compare them. Answer the following questions: (1) How many different scenes in the novel are combined into single scenes in the play? (2) Are there any new scenes or incidents in the play that are not in the novel? (3) Is the climax indentical in each plot outline? (4) Do you agree the play is "based upon" the novel? If so, why; if not, then how would you classify it in terms of the labeling definitions set forth in Chapter 14 on dramatizations and adaptations?

51. Reading Assignment. Read the following plays on which George S. Kaufman collaborated with different writers: *The Royal Family,* written with Edna Ferber, *Beggar on Horseback,* with Marc Connelly, and *You Can't Take It With You,* with Moss Hart. Pay particular attention to the quality of the dialogue, especially those lines calculated to get a laugh. Is there a distinctive style of humor common to all three plays? If so, how is it most often achieved: through situation alone, situation combined with character, or dialogue emerging from character and situation?

52. If you know a foreign language fairly well, translate a scene from any play in that language into good stage English.

53. Select a piece of choreographic music (particularly recommended: "Le Boeuf sur le Toit" by Darius Milhaud; "L'Histoire du Soldat," Stravinsky; "Petrouchka," Stravinsky; "Fancy Free," Leonard Bernstein; "Appalachian Spring," Aaron Copland) and develop a complete description of a mime play to fit the music, working through bar for bar. It is necessary for this exercise, of course, to be able to read music and to have a score.

GROUP EXERCISES

54. A class exercise in automatic writing. The student writes for a short time, putting down everything that comes into his mind, without stopping to organize or to select. Next, the instructor gives a series of words pertaining to one or more of the senses, such as "musty," "acrid," "blinding," "explosive," etc. Each student writes his impressions, again writing very quickly and without taking time to organize. Many times the word will set off a chain reaction in his memory, and he will skip from one childhood experience to another, but all associated in some way with the word. The instructor should call time after two minutes, then give another word.

55. To show what varied directions the human mind can take from a single stimulus, the instructor reads a list of provocative titles of his own creation. The class members then invent plots to fit the titles. These plot outlines are then read in class.

56. Again, to show varied reaction to single stimulus, the instructor describes a character in detail. The class then develops situations that will bring out the character's facets. These situation outlines are then read in class and appraised.

57. Assign the group the project of recording actual conversations, preferably those they can easily eavesdrop on in the "Grill" or the dormitory. Read these in class and then read passages from good prose plays, in order to contrast the conscious composition of our best authors with the aimlessness of most conversation. Point out the *apparent* naturalness and aimlessness of much good dramatic dialogue. Then go back to the recorded conversations to see if there are any "starters" for a play: (1) expression of discontent or desire, (2) expression of strong attitudes toward other people, and (3) foreshadowing of coming events that are pleasurable or painful in prospect, etc.

58. Write the following generalization on a blackboard: "The love between father and son is seldom expressed before it is too late." Have the students write story outlines, clearly indicating protagonist, objective, obstacles, and outcome. Read the outlines in class and establish whether the author and the class would call the story a comedy or a drama. From this exercise the class may discover that theme is not something apart from character and story.

59. Read the class several short summaries based on real-life stories they know well. Have the class members outline the story as follows: (1) Who is the main character? (protagonist). (2) What does he want most of all? (objective). (3) What or who stand in his way? (obstacle). (4) Does he obtain his objective? (climax and resolution).

60. Select a human interest feature story from a daily newspaper. Distribute copies to the class and assign each member to develop a character sketch for the personality involved and a plot outline. Have the outlines read in class. Compare the various approaches and interpretations.

61. Have the students clip little personal news items out of the newspapers and use them as germinal items for plays—asking the students to examine the clues to characters and bits of action, then to let their imaginations run—and putting the results into a one-page outline. (This can be continued beyond the class situation by the individual writer.)

62. Have half the class or group agree to begin on one germinal idea, the other half on a second germinal idea. Each member of the group, from one of the ideas, writes a 200- to 300-word synopsis, proposing alternate lines of development and alternate endings when the main idea is not crystallized.

63. Examine speeches taken from dramatic writing which are left unlabeled and unidentified by the instructor. Try to anaylze the type and tone of drama from which each speech is lifted: period, race, author's attitude towards his material, effect desired in audience; what, technically, do the choice of words, the syntax, the rhythm, the length of phrase, etc., all add up to? This can be an interesting and profitable game if each member of the class hunts up specimens and allows the rest to indulge in a detective hunt as to the speech's derivation.

64. Find the crisis scene of a one-act play or half-hour radio script by an established author—such as Shaw, Barrie, O'Casey, Wilder—and weaken it by insertions of words, alterations of phrases, changes in

sentence structure, etc. Then test it on the members of the class; do not allow them to know whether you are reading the original or your debased version. Analyze collectively the values and virtues of the original version in terms of the playwright's personal style and characteristic flavor.

65. The instructor plays a fairly short musical selection to the class. It is played three times to give the students an opportunity to study the piece as a whole, and perhaps even get a feeling of the structural unity. Then the student is asked to write a scene, or a character analysis, that stems from his own reactions to the piece. Gene McKinney of Baylor University feels that the selection of the music to be played is very important. He recommends the works of contemporary composers offering something fresh and unfamiliar to the ears. He has used Hindemith, Stravinsky, and Bartok. In addition, he has obtained good results from so-called "progressive" jazz exemplified by Dave Brubeck and Chico Hamilton.

66. The instructor brings to class a group of color art reproductions and goes through them holding up one at a time. Each playwright then chooses one painting to study and use as a stimulus. He might use the mood of the painting; or what he thinks the artist is saying; or the composition; or the use of color, mass, or line. McKinney of Baylor, who uses this exercise, feels that the selection of reproductions is very important. Believing that representational or realistic paintings offer little challenge, he restricts his list to modern art—the more stylized and abstract the better. He brings to his classes the work of Picasso, Klee, Kandinsky, Calder (his mobiles), Stuart Davies, Mondrian, and others. These artists challenge the imagination of the student and he usually comes up with a piece of writing that has greater depth and is more of an extension of himself.

67. Select a writing partner of the opposite sex. Each writer should create a character sketch of a member of his or her own sex, supplying characteristic dialogue that will reveal personality traits in several situations. Exchange the sketches, analyze them critically, and then rewrite. Return the sketches to the original author for appraisal and analysis.

68. Select a writing partner who can be worked with in harmony. From idea to dialogue, collaborate on each phase of a one-act play. Work only when both partners can be together. Periodically, by making diary entries after each day's work is completed, attempt to analyze and discover conflicts in resolving individual methods of writing and

style. Strive to develop a "third" style not identifiable with the technique of either writer.

69. Have each playwright in class devise a scenario for a short five- to ten-minute scene showing two characters in conflict. Exchange these scenarios and have them executed into dialogue and action. When this phase is completed return the manuscripts to the scenario author for revision. Analyze all three drafts, the scenario, the initial draft, and the revised scene in order to determine successful execution of original idea and consistency of characterization.

70. Ask members of the class who have some acting experience to improvise a situation that has been dealt with too woodenly in a script. Normally this will work only for realistic plays unless you have actors highly skilled in styles of acting. Though the scene will never develop in the way the playwright wanted it to, the manner of it becomes actable at least.

71. The instructor tape records the audio portion of a "stock" half-hour television drama, then plays it in class. The students write out the action suggested by the dialogue and music on the tape. Next, they combine the dialogue on the tape with their notes suggesting the action, and adapt this play for the stage. (This can be fun, especially if the show is a western.)

72. Utilize the group method of collaboration in writing a play. Through discussion select a topic and devise a story, arrange and amplify it into a plot with a unifying central purpose or theme, and then develop a detailed scenario along with fully conceived character sketches. Next, assign the scenes or acts to be written outside of class; then read and discuss these scenes in class and reassign them for the second draft. Follow this process through at least three or four phases, finally assigning one dramatic writer to coördinate the entire project.

Appendix B

Dramatic Writing Reference Shelf

DRAMATIC writing is an art best learned from personal experience, but much can also be learned from the experiences of others. Since this source is readily available at the nearest library, the following bibliography of books, articles, and essays is offered. The list is only a portion of the many works on writing and the various dramatic media, but it represents many of the experiences and observations of others consulted in the preparation of this volume. Something can be learned from each entry, and since some of them list additional bibliographical sources, there is available to the serious dramatic writer an almost never ending reference shelf.

Plays have been purposefully omitted from the bibliography since many dramas have been specifically cited in the text and others are available in countless anthologies of the world's dramatic literature. Also, each year sees the appearance of additional collections of plays from the various media—stage, screen, radio, and television. Unfortunately, a valuable source of study is denied the beginning playwright since plays that have failed in production are rarely published. However, by attending theatres and motion pictures and by listening to the radio and watching television, the writer can see and hear the good along with the bad.

Many of the works listed below are by or about individual playwrights. There are autobiographies, critical works, appraisals of the various dramatic media, and works related directly and indirectly to the dramatic writing process. Each offers the beginning writer an additional piece of information about his art and profession and should hasten the day when he, too, will write plays that can interest and entertain an audience.

BOOKS

Adcock, A. St. John, *Gods of Modern Grub Street,* Frederick A. Stokes Company, 1923.

Anderson, Maxwell, *The Essence of Tragedy and Other Footnotes and Papers,* Anderson House, 1939.

Anderson, Maxwell, *Off Broadway,* William Sloane Associates, 1947.

Archer, William, *Playmaking: A Manual of Craftsmanship,* Dodd, Mead & Company, Inc., 1937.

Aristotle, *Poetry and Fine Art,* translated by S. H. Butcher, Dover Publications, 1951.

Atkinson, Brooks, *Broadway Scrapbook,* Theatre Arts Books, 1947.

Baker, George Pierce, *Dramatic Technique,* Houghton Mifflin Company, 1919.

Barnouw, Erik, *Handbook of Radio Writing,* D. C. Heath and Company, 1953.

Barrie, J. M., *The Greenwood Hat,* Charles Scribner's Sons, 1938.

Barry, Philip, *The Dramatist and the Amateur Public,* Samuel French, Inc., 1927.

Belasco, David, *The Theatre Through Its Stage Door,* Harper & Brothers, 1919.

Benoit-Levy, Jean, *The Art of the Motion Picture,* Coward-McCann, 1946.

Bentley, Eric, *The Dramatic Event,* Horizon Press, 1955.

Bentley, Eric, *The Playwright As Thinker,* Reynal & Hitchcock, 1946.

Bergler, Edmund, *The Writer and Psychoanalysis,* Doubleday & Company, 1950.

Brown, John Mason, *Upstage,* W. W. Norton & Company, 1930.

Cannon, Fanny, *Writing and Selling a Play,* Henry Holt and Company, 1915.

Clark, Barrett H. (ed.), *European Theories of the Drama,* Crown Publishers, 1947.

Clark, Barrett H., *A Study of the Modern Drama,* D. Appleton-Century Company, Inc., 1938.

Cohan, George M., *Twenty Years on Broadway,* Harper & Brothers, 1925.

Coward, Noel, *Present Indicative,* Garden City Publishing Company, 1939.

Davis, Owen, *I'd Like to Do It Again,* Farrar and Rinehart, 1931.

Davis, Owen, *My First Fifty Years in the Theatre,* Walter H. Baker Co., 1950.

Dickinson, Thomas H., *Playwrights of the New American Theater,* The Macmillan Company, 1925.

Dolman, John, *The Art of Play Production,* Harper & Brothers, 1928.

Egri, Lajos, *The Art of Dramatic Writing,* Simon & Schuster, 1946.

Eisenstein, Sergei, *Film Form,* Harcourt, Brace and Company, 1949.

Ellis-Fermor, Una, *The Frontiers of Drama,* Methuen, 1945.

Ervine, St. John, *How to Write a Play,* The Macmillan Company, 1928.

Felton, Felix, *The Radio Play,* Transatlantic Arts, 1949.

Ferber, Edna, *A Peculiar Treasure,* Garden City Publishing Company, 1940.

Finch, Robert, *How to Write a Play,* Greenberg, 1948.

Flexnor, Eleanor, *American Playwrights 1918–1938,* Simon & Schuster, 1938.

Freytag, Gustav, *The Technique of the Drama,* translated by Elias J. Mac-Ewan, Scott, Foresman & Company, 1904.

Gagey, Edmond M., *Revolution in American Drama,* Columbia University Press, 1947.

Gallaway, Marian, *Constructing a Play,* Prentice-Hall, Inc., 1950.

Galsworthy, John, *A Sheaf,* Charles Scribner's Sons, 1916.

Galsworthy, John, *Another Sheaf,* Charles Scribner's Sons, 1919.

Galsworthy, John, *Candelabra,* Charles Scribner's Sons, 1933.

Galsworthy, John, *Castles in Spain,* Charles Scribner's Sons, 1927.

Galsworthy, John, *The Inn of Tranquility,* Charles Scribner's Sons, 1912.

Garrison, Roger H., *A Creative Approach to Writing,* Henry Holt and Company, 1951.

Gassner, John, *Form and Idea in Modern Theatre,* The Dryden Press, 1956.

Gassner, John, *Masters of the Drama,* Random House, 1940.

Gassner, John, *The Theatre in Our Times,* Crown Publishers, Inc., 1954.

Hamilton, Clayton, *"So You're Writing a Play!",* Little, Brown and Company, 1935.

Herman, Lewis Helmar and Herman, Marguerite Shalett, *Manual of American Dialects for Radio, Stage and Screen,* Ziff-Davis, 1947.

Hopkins, Arthur, *"How's Your Second Act?",* Samuel French, Inc., 1948.

Jeans, Ronald, *Writing for the Theatre,* Edward Arnold & Company, 1949.

Knoblock, Edward, *Round the Room,* Chapman and Hall, Ltd., 1939.

Kozlenko, William, *The One-Act Play Today,* Harcourt, Brace and Company, 1938.

Krows, Arthur Edwin, *Playwriting for Profit,* Longmans, Green & Company, Inc., 1928.

Krutch, Joseph Wood, *The American Drama Since 1918,* Random House, 1939.

Lawrence, Jerome, (ed.), *Off Mike, Radio Writing by the Nation's Top Radio Writers,* Essential Books, 1945.

Lawson, John Howard, *Theory and Technique of Playwriting and Screenwriting,* G. P. Putnam's Sons, 1949.

Macgowan, Kenneth, *A Primer of Playwriting,* Random House, 1951.

Mantle, Burns, *Contemporary American Playwrights,* Dodd, Mead & Co., 1938.

Marrott, H. V., *The Life and Letters of John Galsworthy,* Charles Scribner's Sons, 1936.

Matthews, Brander, *The Development of the Drama,* Charles Scribner's Sons, 1904.

Matthews, Brander, *Playwrights on Playmaking,* Charles Scribners' Sons, 1923.

Matthews, Brander, *Principles of Playmaking,* Scribner's, 1919.

Matthews, Brander, *A Study of the Drama,* Houghton Mifflin Company, 1910.

Maugham, Somerset, *The Summing Up,* Doubleday, Doran & Company, 1939.

Maugham, Somerset, *A Writer's Notebook,* Doubleday and Company, Inc., 1949.

Meynell, Viola, (ed.), *Letters of J. M. Barrie,* Charles Scribner's Sons, 1947.

Middleton, George, *These Things Are Mine,* Macmillan Company, 1947.

Milne, A. A., *Autobiography,* E. P. Dutton & Company, 1939.

Milne, A. A., *By Way of Introduction,* E. P. Dutton & Company, 1929.

Morehouse, Ward, *George M. Cohan, Prince of the American Theatre,* J. B. Lippincott Company, 1943.

Moses, Montrose J., and Gerson, Virginia, *Clyde Fitch and His Letters,* Little, Brown and Company, 1924.

Niggli, Josephine, *Pointers on Playwriting,* The Writer, 1945.

O'Casey, Sean, *I Knock at the Door,* Macmillan, 1939.

Pearson, Hesketh, *G. B. S., A Full Length Portrait,* Harper & Brothers, 1942.

Pollock, Channing, *The Footlights Fore and Aft,* Richard G. Badger, 1911.

Pollock, Channing, *Harvest of My Years,* The Bobbs-Merrill Company, 1943.

Price, William Thompson, *Analysis of Play Construction and Dramatic Principle,* W. T. Price, Publisher, 1908.

Raphaelson, Samson, *The Human Nature of Playwriting,* The Macmillan Company, 1949.

Roberts, Edward Barry, *Television Writing and Selling,* The Writer, Inc., 1954.

Rowe, Kenneth Thorpe, *Write That Play,* Funk & Wagnalls, 1939.

Scheyer, Betty, *So You Want to Be a Playwright,* Exposition Press, 1954.

Selden, Samuel, *An Introduction to Playwriting,* F. S. Crofts & Company, 1946.

Shaw, George Bernard, *Dramatic Opinions and Essays,* Brentano's, 1906.

Shaw, George Bernard, *Our Theatres in the Nineties,* Constable and Company, Ltd., 1932, 3 vols.

Shaw, George Bernard, *Plays Pleasant and Unpleasant,* Constable and Company, Ltd., 1931, 2 vols.

Simonson, Lee, *The Art of Scenic Design,* Harper & Brothers, 1950.

Simonson, Lee, *The Stage Is Set,* Harcourt, Brace and Company, Inc., 1932.

Thomas, Augustus, *The Print of My Remembrance,* Charles Scribner's Sons, 1922.

Thompson, Alan Reynolds, *The Anatomy of Drama,* University of California Press, 1946.

Vale, Eugene, *The Technique of Screenplay Writing,* Crown Publishers, 1944.

van Druten, John, *Playwright at Work,* Harper & Brothers, 1953.

Vardac, A. Nicholas, *Stage to Screen,* Harvard University Press, 1949.

Weaver, Luther, *The Techniques of Radio Writing,* Prentice-Hall, 1948.

Weiss, Margaret R., *The TV Writer's Guide,* Farrar, Straus & Young, Inc., 1952.

Whiting, Frank, *An Introduction to the Theatre,* Harper & Brothers, 1954.

Wilde, Percival, *The Craftsmanship of the One-Act Play,* Little, Brown & Company, 1938.

Wilson, Richard Albert, *The Miraculous Birth of Language,* The Philosophical Library, 1948.

Wylie, Max (ed.), *Radio and Television Writing,* Rinehart & Company, 1950.

Young, Stark, *Immortal Shadows,* Charles Scribner's Sons, 1948.

ARTICLES AND ESSAYS

Abbott, George, "The Broadway Playwright in Hollywood," *Theatre Magazine,* May, 1929, pp. 42 ff.

Anderson, Maxwell, "The Arts as Motive Power," *1938 Essay Annual,* Scott, Foresman and Company, 1938, pp. 38–42.

Barnes, Djuna, "The Tireless Rachel Crothers," *Theatre Guild Magazine,* May, 1931, pp. 17–19.

Beiswanger, George, "Lindsay and Crouse," *Theatre Arts,* February, 1944, pp. 79–84.

Belasco, David, "Dramatizing the Present," *Harper's Weekly,* April 12, 1913, pp. 18–19.

Bird, Carol, "Eugene O'Neill—the Inner Man," *Theatre Magazine,* June, 1924, pp. 9 ff.

Bolton, Guy, "The Art of Adaptation," *Theatre Arts,* June, 1955, pp. 28 ff.

Broadhurst, George, "Plays—the Greatest of All Gambles," *Green Book Magazine,* March, 1916, pp. 530–535.

Broadhurst, George, "Some Others and Myself," *Saturday Evening Post,* November 6, 1926, pp. 28–32.

Busfield, Roger M., Jr., "Journalism As a Training Ground for Playwrights," *The Quill,* May, 1956, p. 14.

Cohan, George M., "The American Play," *Theatre Magazine,* November, 1920, pp. 254 ff.

"Cohan Writes a Play About Cohan," *Literary Digest,* January 25, 1936, p. 18.

Connelly, Marc, "We're Going to Have Better Plays," *Theatre Magazine,* December, 1930, pp. 16 ff.

Crothers, Rachel, "The Construction of a Play," *The Art of Playwriting,* University of Pennsylvania Press, 1928.

Crothers, Rachel, "Four Kinds of Audiences," *The Drama,* May, 1920, pp. 273–275.

Crothers, Rachel, "The Producing Playwright," *Theatre Magazine,* January, 1918, p. 34.

Crothers, Rachel, "Troubles of a Playwright," *Harper's Bazaar,* January, 1911, pp. 14 ff.

Crothers, Rachel, "Why Is Broadway's Approval the Measure of a Play's Success?" *Theatre Magazine,* July, 1926, p. 34.

Dalrymple, Jean, "An Interview with Mr. Shaw," *Theatre Arts,* April, 1948, pp. 34–35.

Davenport, W. A., "Augustus Thomas—From 'Mizzoura,'" *World's Work,* May, 1923, pp. 78–83.

Davis, Owen, "Playwriting," *Saturday Evening Post,* September 27, 1930, pp. 25–28.

D'Estournelles, Paul, "Paul Claudel: The Poet as Playwright," *Theatre Arts,* May, 1946, pp. 301–304.

Downer, Alan S., "Eugene O'Neill as Poet of the Theatre," *Theatre Arts,* February, 1951, pp. 22–23.

Fallon, Gabriel, "Pathway of a Dramatist," *Theatre Arts,* January, 1950, pp. 36–47.

Fitch, Clyde, "The Play and the Public," *Plays by Clyde Fitch, IV,* Little, Brown and Company, 1921.

Galsworthy, John, "The New Spirit in the Drama," *Living Age,* May 3, 1913, pp. 259–266.

Gassner, John, "Our Lost Playwrights," *Theatre Arts,* August, 1954, pp. 19 ff.

Gilder, Rosamund, "The Fabulous Hart," *Theatre Arts,* February, 1944, pp. 89–98.

Gilroy, Harry, "How to Write—By Maugham," *New York Times Magazine,* January 23, 1949, pp. 10 ff.

Hopwood, Avery, "Why I Don't Write More Serious Plays," *Theatre Magazine,* April, 1924, pp. 10 ff.

Horst, Frenz, "Eugene O'Neill in Russia," *Poet Lore,* Autumn, 1943, pp. 241–247.

Hutchens, John K., "Oscar Hammerstein II," *Theatre Arts,* January, 1946, pp. 35–40.

Hyams, Barry, "A Chat with Terence Rattigan," *Theatre Arts,* November, 1956, pp. 20–23.

Inge, William, "The Schizophrenic Wonder," *Theatre Arts,* May, 1950, pp. 22–23.

"Interview with Edna Ferber," *Time Magazine,* February 5, 1945, p. 96.

"Interview with Maugham," *Living Age,* May, 1931, p. 305.

Isaacs, Edith J. R., "Meet Eugene O'Neill," *Theatre Arts,* October, 1946, pp. 576–587.

Kaufman, George S., "A Playwright Tells Almost All," *New York Times Magazine,* September 17, 1944, pp. 20–21.

Klein, Charles, "Critics No Aid to Dramatists," *Theatre Magazine,* January, 1915, p. 12.

Klein, Charles, "The Psychology of the Drama," *The Reader,* March, 1906, pp. 374–377.

Klein, Charles, "Religion, Philosophy and the Drama," *The Arena,* May, 1907, pp. 492–497.

Klein, Charles, "What the Playwright Is Up Against," *Saturday Evening Post*, January 25, 1913, pp. 16–17.

Knoblock, Edward, "Advice to Young Playwrights," *Theatre Arts*, September, 1955, pp. 23 ff.

Koppel, Harwood, "Speedy Sam Shipman," *The Drama*, November, 1919, pp. 58–60.

Krutch, Joseph Wood, "The Case for Courtroom Drama," *Theatre Arts*, July, 1955, pp. 69 ff.

Krutch, Joseph Wood, "The Fundamentals of Farce," *Theatre Arts*, July, 1956, pp. 29 ff.

Krutch, Joseph Wood, "The Playwright Is Still a Poet," *Theatre Arts*, April, 1955, pp. 27 ff.

Kummer, Clare, "The Essence of Drama," *Theatre Magazine*, May, 1921, p. 344.

Kummer, Clare, "The Inspiration of the Play," *The Forum*, March, 1919, pp. 307–316.

Lang, Fritz, "The Freedom of the Screen," *Theatre Arts*, December, 1947, pp. 52–55.

Le Gallienne, Eva, "Sir James Barrie, 'Peter Pan,' and I," *Theatre Magazine*, January, 1929, p. 15.

Lindsay, Howard, "Notes on Playwriting," *Theatre Arts Anthology*, Theatre Arts Books, 1950, pp. 121–127.

Liss, Joseph, "Playwriting Around with Radio," *Theatre Arts*, March, 1947, pp. 61–62.

Mack, Willard, "The New Realism of the Stage," *Theatre Magazine*, April, 1927, p. 21.

Manners, J. Hartley, "The Dilemma of Writing Plays," *Theatre Magazine*, September, 1920, pp. 92 ff.

Maugham, W. Somerset, "A Student of the Drama," *The Golden Book*, April, 1934, pp. 438–440.

Miles, Carlton, "Alan Alexander Milne," *Theatre Magazine*, July, 1923, p. 25.

Milne, A. A., "Dramatic Art and Craft," *The Nation & The Athenaeum*, October 27, 1923, pp. 149–151.

Milne, A. A., "Introduction," *Four Plays*, G. P. Putnam's Sons, 1932.

Nash, N. Richard, "Where Are the New Playwrights?" *New York Times Magazine*, August 18, 1957, pp. 24 ff.

Nathan, George Jean, "Eugene O'Neill after Twelve Years," *American Mercury*, October, 1946, pp. 462–466.

O'Neill, Eugene, "Memoranda on Masks," *The American Spectator,* November, 1932, p. 3.

O'Neill, Eugene, "Second Thoughts," *The American Spectator,* December, 1932, p. 2.

Patterson, Ada, "Harriett Ford—A Successful Woman Dramatist," *Theatre Magazine,* July, 1914, pp. 18 ff.

Patterson, Ada, "Some Theories of Playmaking by a Playmaker," *Theatre Magazine,* June, 1906, pp. 157–160.

"Play Crafting," *Literary Digest,* August 15, 1936, p. 21.

Pollock, Channing, "The Advantages of Illiteracy," *Theatre Magazine,* April, 1917, pp. 199–200.

Pollock, Channing, "Are We Really Like That?" *American Magazine,* July, 1930, pp. 38 ff.

Pollock, Channing, "Wanted: The Theatre's Old Zest," *New York Times Magazine,* November 5, 1944, pp. 18–19.

Popper, H. R., "Collaborators on Broadway," *Theatre Arts,* October, 1946, pp. 598–601.

Rattigan, Terence, "The Characters Make the Play," *Theatre Arts,* April, 1947, pp. 45–46.

Reines, Bernard, "Case History of a Play," *Prologue,* April, 1957, p. 4.

Rice, Elmer, "The Joys of Pessimism," *The Forum,* July, 1931, pp. 33–35.

Rice, Elmer, "New York: Raw Material for the Drama," *Theatre Magazine,* March, 1929, pp. 26 ff.

Rice, Elmer, "Preface," *Two Plays,* Coward-McCann, Inc., 1935.

Rice, Elmer, "Sex in the Modern Theatre," *Harper's Magazine,* May, 1932, pp. 665–673.

Rice, Elmer, "Towards an Adult Theatre," *The Drama,* February, 1931, pp. 5 ff.

Rodgers, Richard, and Hammerstein, Oscar, II, "All the Theatre's a Stage," *Theatre Arts,* September, 1953, pp. 22–23.

Shaw, George Bernard, "The Point of View of the Playwright," Toby Cole and Helen Krich Chinoy (eds.), *Actors on Acting,* Crown Publishers, 1949, pp. 348–352.

Shaw, George Bernard, "Rules for Directors," *Theatre Arts,* August, 1949, pp. 6–11.

Shaw, George Bernard, and Henderson, Archibald, "The Drama, The Theater, and the Films," *Harper's Magazine,* September, 1924, pp. 425–435.

Shaw, George Bernard, and Henderson, Archibald, "Is Shaw a Dramatist?" *Forum,* November, 1926, pp. 256–261.

Sherwood, Robert E., "The Dwelling Place of Wonder," *Theatre Arts,* February, 1941, pp. 120–122.

Sherwood, Robert E., "The Vanishing American Playwright," *Saturday Review of Literature,* February 1, 1941, p. 11.

Shipman, Samuel, "All Life Is Melodrama," *Theatre Magazine,* April, 1919, pp. 198–199.

Smith, Winchell, "How I Write Popular Plays," *Theatre Magazine,* December, 1916, p. 364.

Smith, Winchell, "Take Some Kind of a Plunge," *American Magazine,* December, 1918, pp. 14–15.

Sproehnle, Katharine, and Megrue, Roi Cooper, "The First Three Acts the Hardest," *Saturday Evening Post,* January 16, 1926, pp. 10–12.

Stokes, Sewell, "W. Somerset Maugham," *Theatre Arts,* February, 1945, pp. 94–100.

Sugrue, Thomas, "Mr. Odets Regrets," *American Magazine,* October, 1936, pp. 42 ff.

Thomas, Augustus, "A Playwright's Views," *Review of Reviews,* April, 1927, p. 402.

Thomas, Augustus, "An Inquiry Concerning the Drama," *The Art World,* October, 1916, pp. 52–55.

Thomas, Augustus, "Preface," *In Mizzoura,* Samuel French, 1916.

Tyler, Parker, "The Experimental Film," *Theatre Arts,* July, 1949, pp. 46 ff.

Tyler, Parker, "Supernaturalism in the Movies," *Theatre Arts,* July, 1945, pp. 362–369.

van Druten, John, "Caring for the Theatre," *The Drama,* November, 1927, pp. 37–38.

van Druten, John, "Small Souls and Great Plays," *Theatre Arts,* July, 1927, pp. 493–498.

van Druten, John, " 'Theatre' As I See It," *Theatre Arts,* January, 1928, pp. 62–64.

Vidal, Gore, "Television Drama, Circa 1956," *Theatre Arts,* December, 1956, pp. 65 ff.

Watts, Richard, Jr., "One World: A Challenge to Dramatists," *Theatre Arts,* March, 1946, pp. 142–149.

Williams, Tennessee, "The Timeless World of a Play," *Theatre Arts,* May, 1955, pp. 33 ff.

Wilson, B. F., "A Satirist Turns to Fantasy," *Theatre Magazine,* May, 1926, pp. 30 ff.

"Women Playmakers," *New York Times Magazine,* May 4, 1941, pp. 10 ff.

Woolf, S. J., "Eugene O'Neill Returns After Twelve Years," *New York Times Magazine,* September 15, 1946, p. 11.

Index